SOCIOLOGICAL REVIEW MO

Life and Work History Analyses: Qualitative and Quantitative Developments

The Sociological Review

SOCIOLOGICAL REVIEW MONOGRAPH 37

Life and Work History Analyses: Qualitative and Quantitative Developments

Edited by Shirley Dex

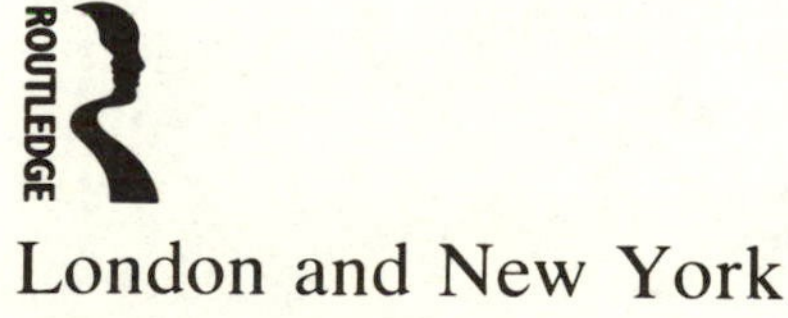

London and New York

First published in 1991 by
Routledge
11 New Fetter Lane, London EC4P 4EE

Set in Times
by Hope Services (Abingdon) Ltd
and printed in Great Britain
by Page Bros. (Norwich) Ltd

British Library Cataloguing in Publication Data

Life and work analyses: qualitative and quantitative developments. – (Sociological Review monograph; 0081-1769, v. 39).
1. Sociology
I. Dex, Shirley 1950– II. Series
301.01

ISBN 0-415-05338-2

Contents

Contributors

David Amigoni is currently Lecturer in English in the School of Humanities at Sunderland Polytechnic. He has studied literature and history at the universities of Cardiff and Keele and taught at Liverpool Polytechnic, where he undertook his research, and University College of Wales, Aberystwyth. He is completing both a Ph.D thesis and a book on an interdisciplinary approach to the cultural study of British biographical writing in the nineteenth century.

Meredith Baker is currently a Research Associate at the Institute for Employment Research, the University of Warwick, and was formerly at the National Institute of Labour Studies, Australia. She has undertaken research in areas including economic aspects of training and education, youth unemployment, the economic impact of shorter working hours, industrial relations issues, the impact of changes in economic protection on the Australian and New Zealand labour markets and the growth in trade union membership.

Paul Bellaby, Senior Lecturer and Head of Sociology, School of Economic and Social Studies, University of East Anglia; previously Lecturer in Sociology and Social Anthropology, University of Keele. Director of the new Centre for Health Policy Research at UEA. Publications in such fields as sickness absence and the social organisation of work; the division of labour in health care; historical sociology; sociology of the school. Current research includes risk-acceptability and road accidents; the impact of closed head injury on the life course perspectives of victims and family carers.

Daniel Bertaux is Directeur de recherche at the French Centre National de la Recherche Scientifique. He was initially trained and worked in the natural sciences (mathematics, physics, aeronautical engineering, artificial intelligence) before changing to sociology. His books include *Destins personnels et structure de classe* (1977); *Biography and Society* (1981); *La mobilité sociale* (1981). He is founder and President of the ISA Research Committee on Biography and Society, and since 1986 a member of the Executive Committee of the ISA where he has been organizing the new project Worldwide Competition for Young Sociologists. His current research interests cover such topics as social mobility, family forms, the processes of production of human energy or 'anthroponomy', social movements, intellectuals.

Peter Coleman is Reader in Social Gerontology at the University of Southampton, a joint appointment between Geriatric Medicine and Social Work Studies. A psychologist by training, he has worked for five years at the Institute of Applied Psychology at Nijmegen in the Netherlands. His research interests are predominantly in the field of adjustment to ageing. His publications include *Ageing and Reminiscence Processes: Social and Clinical Implications* (Wiley, 1986), *Life-Span and Change in a Gerontological Perspective*, (as co-editor, 1985), and *Society and Ageing: An Introduction to Social Gerontology*, (co-editor with John Bond, 1990).

Shirley Dex is a Senior Lecturer in Economics at the University of Keele. Formerly she held posts in sociology and economics at the universities of Exeter and Aston. Her other writings include a number of books on women's employment; *The Sexual Division of Work* (Wheatsheaf, 1985), *British and American Women at Work* (Macmillan, 1986, with Lois B. Shaw), *Women's Occupational Mobility* (Macmillan, 1987) and *Women's Attitudes Towards Work* (Macmillan, 1988).

Peter Elias is a Principal Research Fellow at the Institute for Employment Research. His research interests include the analysis of longitudinal data, particularly that which relates to socio-economic events. The research he has undertaken in this area has covered such topics as women's labour force participation, trade union membership, occupational mobility and migration. He has also conducted a number of important studies of particular labour markets, defined in terms of location, occupation or level of qualification and has been responsible for the development of the *Standard Occupational Classification* for official UK occupational statistics.

Jonathan Gershuny is a Fellow of Nuffield College, Oxford, and Visiting Professor at the School of Social Sciences, Bath University. His books include *After Industrial Society?* (Macmillan, 1977) and *Social Innovation and the Division of Labour* (Oxford University Press, 1983).

Catherine Marsh is a lecturer in Quantitative Methods in the Faculty of Economic and Social Studies at the University of Manchester. Formerly she was a lecturer in methods of social research at the University of Cambridge and Fellow of Newnham College, Cambridge. Her books include *The Survey Method* (Allen and Unwin, 1982) and *Exploring Data* (Polity Press, 1988).

Andrew Miles teaches in the School of History and Archaeology, University of Wales College of Cardiff, and is completing a Ph.D on Nineteenth Century Social and Occupational Mobility.

Leslie Rosenthal, Lecturer in Economics, University of Keele. Previously Lecturer in Economics at the University of Hull. Author of articles on social policy, housing policy, and redundancy and unemployment.

David Vincent is Professor of Social History in the History Department at the University of Keele. His most recent book is *Literacy and Popular Culture. England 1750–1914* (Cambridge University Press, 1989), He is Director of the Keele Life Histories Centre.

Sylvia Walby is a Lecturer in Sociology at the London School of Economics. She was formerly at Lancaster University as a Lecturer in Sociology and Director of the Women's Studies Research Centre. She is the author of *Patriarchy at Work* (Polity, 1986) and *Theorizing Patriarchy* (Blackwell, 1990), editor of *Gender Segregation at Work* (Open University Press, 1988), and joint author of *Localities Class and Gender* (Pion, 1985) and *Restructuring: Place Class and Gender* (Sage, 1990) (with the Lancaster Regionalism Group).

Life and work history analyses

Shirley Dex

Life and work history analyses have been an area of social science where substantial and exciting developments have taken place, particularly over the past two decades. The subject matter of this area has been marked out by two things; a focus on a particular type of data, and integral to that, issues of method which these types of data raise. Life and work histories have in this context usually meant the collection and use of accounts of the lives of men and women, in the form of autobiographies, diaries, oral histories, or structured or unstructured questionnaires. Their essential quality, of course, is that histories span a period of time. The issues of method which such data raise include issues of data collection, data manipulation, theoretical perspectives, interpretation and conceptual, computational and quantitative problems.

Why are life history data important?

First, they are a recognition of a simple but vitally important point; that for many sociological processes, the past, or the lapse of time, is a crucial factor in understanding the present. This relationship may seem obvious, but nevertheless in many areas it had been overlooked. Data about the past often had not been collected, nor was its lack thought to be problematic. This is now much less true, although there is an important recognition that people's pasts do not necessarily determine their current status. Explanations of the earnings of the young in terms of their past employment or unemployment history is an example where researchers debate the effects, as Baker and Elias in this volume illustrate. It seems right and proper to keep an open mind on the precise role of past events, although to ignore it altogether was clearly inappropriate.

Life and work history data are important for other reasons also. They are a recognition of the importance of the overlap in the chronology between individuals' lives and social and institutional structures as well as between related individuals. Both sets of these relationships are important in trying to unravel social life and gain a better understanding of it. It might seem obvious that husbands and wives, for example, influence each other's decisions, but until recently this was rarely studied, particularly in relation to shared past experiences and decisions. Clearly individuals' actions are reflected in their life histories and those of others, but equally, individuals' experiences reflect the structural facts which impinged upon them and moulded or constrained their experiences and actions. Market demand and supply factors (but not solely through labour markets) as well as demographic changes and government policies, legislation and changes in the socio-legal framework are all examples of influences individuals might experience. As well as the recognition of the importance of these factors and their timing in understanding the patterns of individuals' experiences, life and work history analysis can be an avenue to researching other institutional and structural changes. Recently it has been widely recognised that the development and changes of an organisation or group can, in fact, be effectively researched through carefully chosen life histories. Amigoni's paper in this volume illustrates one way in which this can be done. It is thus possible to explore and research social change through life histories. It is also possible both to construct and to test sociological, economic, psychological and historical theories using life histories. It has been said that individuals' lives are the stage on which societal changes are played out. The papers in this volume explore many of these avenues. At the same time they point, as does Walby in this volume, to a danger to be avoided; that of becoming locked into one level of analysis.

Since life and work history data span periods of time, they have raised issues for the methods of research at all levels from design, through collection to analysis and interpretation. Thus issues of method in this field have become integral to it and have been taking up a substantial part of empirical studies. How far can you ask people to recall their past on the basis of memory? What sort of biases will their memory be subject to? Is recollection of the past also affected by current or present experiences and circumstances? What techniques will best reveal the unique over-time elements of these data? These are only a small sample of the questions which have been raised by doing this kind of analysis. Studies are now often specifically designed to focus research attention on such problems. Considerable advances have been and continue to be made on some of these questions.

Recognition of the issues of method raised by life history analysis has occurred in a wide variety of social science disciplines. As well as these common discoveries, the application of life history analysis and methods to a range of subject areas is fascinating and exciting, and it is clearly stimulating to see these new areas of application. For example, the study of the curriculum vitae as a history document and accounts of sickness or absenteeism provide scope for sociologists and psychologists as well as others to apply life/work history analyses. This volume has been partly constructed both to demonstrate the overlaps and to provide stimulus of new kinds from its range of material.

Is this a new area of analysis?

The interest in this area spanning the past two decades undoubtedly has links with earlier research on life histories. Plummer (1983) argues in his handbook on how to carry out life history research using documents that he is reviving the Chicago school's concerns about ethnographic data and methods from the 1920s. It is also possible to find some very early precursors to some of the recent large-scale survey collection of work and life histories and techniques of analysis in this field. For example, a government statistician, William Farr, in 1839 was arguing for the need to collect large-scale life history data,[1] and some of the quantitative techniques which are now being applied in social science were earlier applied in medical and biological research where there has been a longstanding interest in physiological processes of ageing, decay and survival. At the same time, the recent developments clearly are new and different from the past in a number of respects.

There has been new data collection of life and work histories on a large scale. Linked to these exercises, more research has taken place into the reliability of event recall and into the repeat interview or prospective method of large-scale history data collection. Another extremely important development which is taking place is the attempt to integrate qualitative and quantitative research on life and work histories. These two aspects of research are not unique to life history analyses, but in the past there was an association between life history and qualitative analyses, building on the arguments of the Chicago school. It is all the more interesting therefore to see in this field, not just the growth of quantitative studies, but studies which break down what has become a fairly rigid barrier in British sociological research. That we should cultivate this development is definitely a priority for future research in the field.

Recent developments in methods

Developments in research methods have become integral to this subject area, as indicated earlier. Many of the papers in this volume now take these developments for granted, because they are so firmly accepted and established although they are not all equally well known; this makes it worthwhile to draw attention to the range and nature of some of these methods.

At a conceptual level, great strides forward were made in the 1970s by the introduction and elaboration by Hareven (1978) and Elder (1978) of the concept of life course analysis. Many studies now use this framework.[2] It is worth stressing what an innovative concept the life course was and is; how it focuses on the overlaps between individuals' experiences and those coincidental in chronological (or historical) time, be they other individuals, family members, structural changes, policy changes or whatever; how it also focuses on transitions over time between various states and is thus a concept particularly appropriate for longitudinal data. It was designed, of course, with longitudinal data and research in mind. Whilst there is now a general acceptance and use of the life course concept, it is still difficult to do life course analysis on large-scale longitudinal data for a number of reasons. Sometimes longitudinal data are available as a continuous record for some variables, but not for others. If a person's marital and fertility history are complete, for example, but their employment history is only known at certain points then it is difficult to examine the chronological coincidence of these different experiences. The overlap between family members' experiences is conceptually difficult to handle and to describe and researchers are only beginning to tackle these sorts of overlaps in Britain as large-scale data on both spouses' life and work histories has recently become available.[3] These are the developments which future reviewers on the 1990s research into life and work history analyses are likely to be discussing. Other very practical difficulties in doing life course analysis are discussed by Marsh and Gershuny in their paper in this volume; for example, over the choice of software, and how to structure the data. We now have a much deeper appreciation of some of the more specific elements of the methods involved in collecting and using longitudinal data.[4]

Attrition in repeat-interview longitudinal research is a problem which faces small-scale qualitative as well as large-scale quantitative studies. Discussions of attrition can be found in Rhoton (1984), Waterton and Lievesley (1988) and Hsiao (1986). A comparison of individual studies also shows that attrition rates vary at least by the sex, occupation and economic activity of the individuals in the survey.[5] Various methods have been tried to reduce attrition and keep the sample response rate high in subsequent interviews and follow up; these include sending birthday cards as well as change of address cards and monetary incentives. The evidence suggests that the response rate on a second interview is crucial in determining those for any subsequent interviews since individuals are highly likely to remain in a survey if they have stayed in it for two interviews. There is, however, little systematic evidence on how important incentives might be to attrition rates. Researchers involved in some large-scale panel surveys are convinced of the need to offer financial incentives to remain in the survey; however, there is evidence on this topic only from one German government survey which did find that financial incentives improved the response rates.[6] There is the worry that flat-rate incentives can actually introduce additional biases to those already known into response rates. For example, this type of incentive will be more attractive the lower the income of the respondent; more research on this issue is needed. However, there are now methods available for correcting for the biasing effects of attrition when doing multivariate analyses, providing one has some information about non-respondents (see Hsiao, 1986).

The large cost of collecting longitudinal data has always been a serious issue in considerations about whether to embark on such an exercise. Even small-scale research is expensive when there is a plan to follow up individuals or organisations over time; in large-scale surveys the costs can be prohibitive. There also needs to be a commitment of research personnel which is difficult to maintain. It is not surprising therefore that collecting longitudinal data by the recall/memory method has been found attractive. Recall is obviously a cheaper method than repeat interviews and it has other advantages; a systematic record is obtained, coded to one coding frame, unaffected by the biases of attrition or the conditioning which occurs when individuals are interviewed repeatedly. However, memory is obviously subject to biases of its own. There have been some notable advances in researching into the recall method upon which researchers can build in planning to collect history data by recall. Coleman's paper in this collection reviews psychologists' research on this issue and adds his own findings about recall amongst the elderly.

There are some unique issues of quality for recall data. The collection of 'complete' dated work histories in this way will be subject to recall error which will be greater the further back in time the respondent is asked to go. Himmelweit *et al.* (1978) found that the degree of accuracy of recall also varied with the effort of reconstruction required and with the social desirability and association with success of the subject matter. There is evidence, however, that 'key' events (e.g. marriages, childbirth, first full-time job on leaving school etc.) are remembered with a reasonable degree of accuracy (Peters, 1989). Events which are more detailed in nature and shorter in duration (e.g. short periods of unemployment) are subject to a substantial degree of recall error (Moss, 1979; Moss and Goldstein, 1979; Thomas, 1981; Marsh *et al.*, 1981). The recollection of and dating of broad periods of employment was not found to be subject to significant bias with the passing of time by Elias and Main (1982) or Martin and Roberts (1984). However, all researchers in the field rightly remain cautious in their claims about data quality.

The way a questionnaire is structured or the order in which questions are asked has been found to influence recall data quality; certain methods of data collection can improve the accuracy of recall, notably, bounded recall, positive feedback and diaries, as described by Smith (1984). The 1980 Women and Employment Survey found the collection of a life history (fertility and marital) framework first aided recall for the women's work history. The experience of the Social Change and Economic Life Initiative (SCEL) suggests that this approach worked well for women and men. In fact, SCEL researchers go on to make other recommendations on the sequence of data collection; that it worked better to collect the recall history at the beginning of a longer interview; that respondents were not very sensitive to the length of time it took to collect the history, especially at the margin (in fact they loved doing it); that it is preferable to start with the easiest information from memory and work towards the more difficult. In their view the easiest things to remember are geographical histories followed by fertility, marital and household histories ending up with work histories, in a triple-pass interview.[7]

One of the consequences of our improved understanding of the recall method and the techniques of collecting longitudinal data in general is that there has been a growth in the collection of such data. During the 1980s several British sources of large-scale work history data became available[8] and researchers have been mining the wealth of material contained in them. The ESRC gave a number of large grants for collecting work history data, and two of the sources collected are described and used by contributors to this collection, Walby and Marsh and Gershuny. The 1990s seems set to be a decade of very significant data collection in this field in Britain; the 1991 Census will provide a third wave to the census longitudinal survey which began with the 1971 and 1981 linking of census records at the Social Survey Research Unit (City University); the new British Household Panel Study at the ESRC Research Centre on Micro-Social Change (University of Essex) is about to start its ten-year panel in 1991; the National Child Development Study is about to embark upon a fifth wave of this birth cohort from 1958 now that the subjects are in their thirties; and other recall surveys of employment history data are being seriously considered. Panel studies are also well underway in a large number of other European countries so that opportunities for comparative work are also going to increase. There will be no shortage of large-scale data through which developments in life and work history analysis can be advanced, and the 1990s suggest themselves as even more exciting times as far as this field of research is concerned.

We might wonder whether issues of method will be so central to the next decades of analysis in this field as they have been to the past; I expect that they will. There is still a lot to be learnt about how to unravel the past from the present, about different aspects of the reliability of memory, how to minimise attrition, how to handle overlapping household histories and how to conduct causal models in this field. The papers brought together in this volume make a very significant contribution to these issues, but there are still many avenues left to be researched. They were purposely selected to range far and wide in their subject matter, across disciplines, and in the types of data with which they are primarily concerned; qualitative and quantitative data are both used as well as a variety of techniques of analysis. As I have discussed above, the papers have in common a concern about the methods of collection and analysis of longitudinal data. This, as we have seen, is an entirely appropriate concern given the integral development of methods alongside substantive empirical research in the field. They do, however, vary in the extent to which they emphasise this omnipresent discussion of methods. The contributors were all asked to consider a number of issues of method in writing their papers, but at the same time integrate the methods discussion with the substantive empirical concerns of their paper. The issues they were asked to consider were:

—How does the selection of material which constitutes a life history vary with the method of collection or the historical availability, and what are the implications of this selection for our understanding of the processes under consideration? These issues are discussed in the papers by Amigoni, Coleman, Bertaux and Bellaby.

—What is the relationship between the perceptions of the observer/witness, the interaction between the individual and the social structures, and the essentially temporal quality of activity and consciousness? These issues are discussed in the papers by Coleman, Bertaux, Miles and Vincent, Bellaby, and Baker and Elias.

—Are individuals' histories too limiting and should we be focusing on household or family histories, or the interactions between individuals' histories and those of organisations? These issues are discussed in the papers by Bertaux and Walby.

—Are longitudinal data worth the much greater expense of collecting them? Do they provide too much data so that they are difficult to analyse, and do we have the conceptual apparatus and aids to get the most benefit from the data? These issues are discussed in the papers by Rosenthal, Bellaby, Bertaux, Baker and Elias and Marsh and Gershuny.

The inclusion of a wide range of material was decided for a variety of other reasons, both positive and negative. The range is important first to demonstrate the overlapping concerns in different disciplines with life and work history data and analysis. Not only is one struck by the multi-disciplinary representation at conferences which cover life and work history subject matter, but also truly interdisciplinary research is emerging and this is part of its excitement. At a pragmatic level, it is useful to know that researchers in other disciplines are working on the same issues. The potential for cross-fertilisation of ideas is enormous and it is always possible to benefit from new insights developed from within another discipline. Another benefit is the dissemination of techniques for analysis which may be well known in one discipline but unknown in another. For example, many of the quantitative developments which have occurred with respect to life and work history data are not particularly well known amongst British sociologists, even though in some cases they may have been around for some time but applied mainly in other areas. The Cox proportional hazard model as used by Leslie Rosenthal in his paper on re-employment after redundancy is one such example. Knowledge of very new and recent techniques, for example, the SABRE software package for analysing recurrent binary events, can be disseminated in this way, although unfortunately this volume does not contain a specific application since it has only been developed since this volume was conceived.[9]

There are significant consequences from any failure to have techniques and new concepts of this kind widely disseminated. It is not just the lack of benefit from new applications which is missed by a slow rate of dissemination. In the case of some of the techniques which deal with the specific qualities of life and work history data and their over-time nature, it is possible to draw completely erroneous conclusions about the relationships between variables by failing to use the appropriate methods (Davies *et al.*, 1989).

It is too easy to be blinkered in one's research in a way that can be destructive. These papers are dedicated to trying to break down some existing boundaries. Two boundaries in particular have been found to be limiting in this way; they are those of making a distinction between life history analysis and work history analysis, and between qualitative and quantitative methods and techniques. These two distinctions are not unrelated in the history of this research field.

As I have pointed out above, life history analysis was a concept which grew out of the research proposed by the Chicago school of sociology early this century, and it had a distinctly qualitative bias, opposed to the then newer survey methods. Work history analysis, by contrast, is a concept which has grown out of larger-scale and quantitative studies focusing on employment. In fact, as I have argued elsewhere, it has had its formative roots in research on women's employment histories but now extends to both genders. What has become clear through small-scale and more qualitative analyses of life and family histories of the type described and undertaken by Bertaux in his paper, and the large scale and more quantitative analysis of employment of the sort described by Baker and Elias in their paper, is that life, employment and work experiences are all bound tightly up together; also, that it is impossible to understand life without work experiences and vice versa. It is also proving difficult to give priority to one or the other in explanations of attitudes and behaviour of women and men in industrial societies. Whether such unravelling will become possible in future, as we improve in the use of causal modelling and techniques remains to be seen. It is quite possible that these aspects of individuals' and families' experiences are so tightly knit that they are never to be unravelled in this way.

The compartments of qualitative and quantitative social research have had this sort of blinkered and limiting effects on British sociological research for too long. It was, for example, embarrassing to hear a researcher describing the methodological problems of a qualitative longitudinal study at the 1990 British Sociological conference, and saying that the researchers were surprised by attrition when they came to trying to follow up their respondents a year later. Attrition is obviously a serious problem which repeat-interview longitudinal studies need to address from the outset, and about which there is a growing literature. The problem is that the literature and discussion of attrition has taken place in the context of large-scale quantitative studies and data collection which have not been consulted by researchers starting out on qualitative studies. On the other hand it is too easy for those skilled in the use of sophisticated quantitative techniques to be unaware of issues of data collection, selection, reliability and quality. Problems can also arise from this neglect; the tail wagging the dog, as Marsh and Gershuny discuss in this volume. Blalock (1989) has recently argued that far more importance should be given to issues of data quality and that the development of techniques of analysis may have got too far ahead of some of these other vitally important aspects of research. This is not a healthy state of affairs and fortunately inroads are clearly being made to break down these old boundaries.

The papers in this volume seek to contribute to these developments in a number of ways, as described below. What together they are drawing attention to is the need for even development to take place in all aspects of a research field. Also, to a far greater extent than is currently the case, researchers should be prepared to widen their research training to incorporate elements of quantitative or qualitative research methods, to fill in their gaps. It was heartening to hear a paper at a recent conference given by a well-known middle-aged British sociologist prefaced by his thanks to one of this volume's contributors for 'holding his hand' to help him learn some new techniques of analysis which he had previously thought outside his competence. British scholars have still a long way to go in this respect, and there is a bias in the need, especially because there has been an anti-quantitative bias in British undergraduate and post-graduate sociological training whose legacy is now hard to overcome.

These lessons are being learnt with respect to life and work history analysis. Their importance clearly goes beyond this one field of research interest. However, demonstrations of definite progress in one area can be instructive as to how to tackle the same issues in others. This collection holds out the hope that transfers of this kind will be stimulated. In this volume old boundaries between qualitative and quantitative approaches are being broken down by contemporary social research in several ways. Bertaux describes qualitative family histories. The biographical data of Andy Miles and David Vincent and the reminiscence data of Coleman are the traditional source material of qualitative life history analysis. However, in both cases, quantitative generalisations are drawn from the data. Miles and Vincent and Amigoni all analyse selections of life histories in order to construct arguments which relate to structural macro-level theories of society. These are developments which this volume seeks to highlight and of which there are other interesting examples; Abell (1990), for example. Coleman's contribution shows how psychologists have been extending the concepts relevant to life history research beyond those considered by Plummer (1983); in particular through developing the concepts of 'a life review' and 'pseudo memory'; he also reviews how physiological factors and institutionalisation can affect recall in the elderly. Bertaux describes two new concepts for social mobility life history analyses; those of 'anthroponomic distribution' and 'transmission'. Bellaby's paper shows how the common distinction between discrete and continuous variables breaks down when sickness (or health) histories are the subject matter. Bellaby's paper introduces us as well to the methodological problems of having multiple accounts of the same events; this draws attention to the partial nature of any one record of the past. It has considerable implications for the evaluation of epidemiology in general, for attempts to quantify the sudden changes in quality of life, for example, those based on the Bedford Life Events and Difficulties Schedule (LEDS) in Brown and Harris (1989) and for the disputes between epidemiologists and practitioners on the qualitative and quantitative assessment of risk in cardiac disease, (Tudor Hart, 1980).

Many of the papers in this volume wrestle with the partial nature of the data and the selection issues which ensue in terms of the collection and later use of their data. Amigoni takes the issue a step further since he demonstrates how an elite group in the nineteenth century used the selection process and the final published selection of life histories, the *Dictionary of National Biography*, for their own hegemonic ends. In this way Amigoni's paper raises questions for the other contributors to this volume, about the use to which their life histories are being put.

In sum, the volume provides, one hopes, the final landmark in the process of making outdated debates about quantitative versus qualitative life history data and seeks to leave behind the unhelpful and restrictive old distinctions and boundaries between these types of analyses. One of the things which is important to fulfilling this objective is that the papers should be accessible to a range of readers, in ways which cut across the old boundaries. Readers will no doubt judge for themselves whether the volume is successful or not in this respect.

How useful are life and work histories?

How are we to evaluate the past two decades of research on life and work histories? We can see that qualitative and quantitative research on these data are alive and growing. The contributors to this volume would all agree on the value of life history data and approaches for addressing a wide range of issues. However, these contributors are not exactly a random sample of researchers and it is likely that those who work directly with life history data are convinced of its merits. Fortunately, other evidence is available on this issue; for example, there is the response to some of the recent longitudinal data sets, the calls for the need to collect new longitudinal data, and on-going labour market issues which could benefit from the availability of work history data.

It is possible to find a large number of other researchers who are willing to acclaim the value of life and work history data.[10] Specific calls for the collection of more work history data are growing from a wide range of sources; for the investigation of occupational mobility, stratification and social mobility, analyses of class, unemployment, the transition to adulthood, the immobility of labour, ageing and early retirement, the links between education and occupation, further understanding of women's labour force participation and changes in attitudes.[11]

A partial survey of the labour market issues of the 1980s from sociological and economics texts, journals and researchers provides more topics which could benefit from the increase in availability of work history data.[12] For example, areas of research which could utilise work history data include sociologists' interests in the operation and conceptualisation of labour markets, changes in the nature of work, interactions between household organisation, household relationships, and employment behaviour, and the generation of inequalities; also economists' interests in the analysis of earnings differentials and pay discrimination, the consequences of motherhood and fertility decisions, interrelationships between spouses' decisions and employment patterns, occupational choice, life-cycle labour supply, effects of social policies on labour market experiences and behaviour, and the relationship between training and earnings, and labour turnover and mobility. This is far from being an exhaustive list.

Two important labour market changes forecast for the 1990s are first, the demographic decline in school leavers and the associated redistribution of the actual and potential workforce, and secondly, changes which will be brought about by the completion of the full internal common market in 1992 with its concomitant free mobility of labour. These two changes will lead policy makers and researchers to ask a number of questions: for example, how can and will firms' recruitment adapt to the changing demographic structure and shortage of school leavers? How substitutable and (re)trainable are different groups in the workforce? How can the economy cope with serious skill shortages in certain occupations and sectors? How much mobility of labour will be generated after 1992? Policy discussion and formulation on these questions will require employment histories to be well understood. A better understanding of the extent of women's potential for making up deficiencies in the labour force rests in part on modelling their work history patterns. Documenting the effects of the full internal market will necessitate investigations of labour mobility and durations of job tenure in different jobs in and between EC countries. As discussions about policy harmonisation in the EC increase they will need a thorough base in models of labour market work history behaviour, rather than simple simulations, in order to predict likely outcomes. Training and retraining are likely to be high on the policy agenda in Britain, and in other countries, at all ages.

These are only a small selection of issues, all of which would benefit from the availability of men's and women's work histories. In fact, most of these issues could not be examined profitably without detailed and extensive employment histories becoming available.

Conclusions

Certainly the interest in and research on life and work histories is likely to continue and grow over the next decade. The papers in this collection also illustrate that there have been considerable developments in data collection, conceptualisation, analysis and techniques relevant to longitudinal data. The developments in the collection of histories by recall are very important since extensive and large-scale histories can now be collected quite cheaply by recall. If life histories of some kind are the best data for researching a particular topic, the cost is no longer prohibitive in many cases and the value per £ spent is now considerably increased. Another key advance, as has been argued in several places above, has been the breaking down of the rigid and restrictive boundary differentiating qualitative from quantitative studies.

Whilst there have been many advances in the methods of data collection, the papers in this volume illustrate that there are many questions still to be answered which are important; in particular, the ability to interpret correctly some types of recall data. For example, do individuals' perspectives on their past change in systematic ways, over time, over the life cycle, according to specific events or crises, according to their environment or with cultural norms? Similarly does an individual's tendency to have a life review vary according to any of this list of characteristics?

Developments which tackle these methodological issues will benefit considerably our understanding of recall data and our ability to interpret it.

Techniques have also developed considerably, but there is much scope for improvement in the availability and dissemination aspects of longitudinal techniques, certainly within British sociology. A significant step forward in this respect will be when a package like SPSSX contains these techniques as well as specific discussions of ways of handling longitudinal data in general. Whilst it is possible at present to make progress using one's ingenuity, it would increase the circulation and use of longitudinal data if a package like SPSSX advised users of its possibilities in this respect. As we approach the 1990s the number and range of longitudinal data sources which will shortly be available mean that the next decade looks filled with promise, especially for secondary longitudinal analyses.

Notes

1 The advantages of cohort analysis were commented on by William Farr in 1839: 'To determine a question of this sort (Farr was concerned with Tables of Mortality for different sectors of the population) it would be necessary to take a large number of individuals, as 400,000 or 500,000, indiscriminately selected from all ranks and orders of the community, and to trace their lives from the moment of their birth, marking the exact period of the demise of each individual. . .But governments, which alone have the means of framing such tables on an adequate scale, and with the necessary precautions, have been singularly inattentive to their duty in this respect' (W. Farr, *Vital Statistics. A Statistical Account of the British Empire*, vol. 1, p. 413, Charles Knight & Co. 1839). This quote is reported in OPCS (1973) *Cohort Studies: New Developments*. I am grateful to Professor John Fox for drawing it to my attention.

2 See for example, Chandler (1989), Allatt *et al.* (1987), Unruh (1990), Dale (1988), Riley (1988), Blossfeld (1986), Cohen (1987).

3 Data from the recent ESRC Social Change and Economic Life Initiative provides data on both spouses life and work histories.

4 In the case of collecting large-scale survey data discussions of the sampling issues involved in repeat interview or recall data can be found in Kish (1965), Campbell and Stanley (1963), Hyman (1972), Goldstein (1979), Plewis (1985: 11–13) and Glenn (1977); a discussion of how to approach respondents in repeat interview surveys can be found in Goldstein (1979: 8–10). A discussion of the types of questionnaire formats available for collecting recall history data can be found in Elias (1985a and b). Concepts which can be used to describe the results are discussed in Carr-Hill and MacDonald (1973) and Dex (1984a and b); Glenn (1977: 46–57) and Goldstein (1979) have discussions of some of the issues involved in interpreting the results.

5 See for example, Parkhouse and Ellin (1988) and Dex (1988b).

6 The only firm evidence on the effects of incentives on panel attrition has come from a panel survey carried out by the Dutch government, Department of Statistics (1984). They conducted a split ballot to try and get a measure of the effectiveness of respondent incentives, with the following results; in wave one, there was a 14 per cent higher response rate for those who were paid an incentive; in wave two, there was a 93 per cent response rate for those who had been paid an incentive in wave one, and an 84 per cent response rate for those who had not been given any incentive payment in wave one. The new British Household Panel Study about to commence its first wave in 1991 from the ESRC Research Centre on Micro-Social Change at the University of Essex is building in some tests of the value of incentive payments.

7 I am grateful to Peter Elias for providing this information verbally.

8 These included the Department of Employment's Women and Employment Survey, the ESRC Social Change and Economic Life Initiative, the Youth Cohort Study plus the availability of the 4th sweep of the National Child Development Study, and data on another birth cohort from 1946.

9 SABRE was devised as part of an ESRC research project and is described as a GLIM-like software package for modelling recurrent events and sequence effects. It is designed to analyse work or life history data, or any micro-level longitudinal data when the response variable is a sequence of binary outcomes. The package fits a mixture model which allows for residual heterogeneity; see Barry, Francis and Davies (1989). The package is distributed by the authors for a small handling fee plus the cost of the manual: For details contact Centre for Applied Statistics, Lancaster University, Fylde College, Lancaster LA1 4YF.

10 The Women and Employment Survey has been very well received, used and complimented by the academic community. It has been used by sociologists, economists, demographers, actuaries, psychologists and other policy-related bodies. Gallie's review of the recent developments in the study of the sociology of labour markets attributes to WES an important role (1988: 15). It is also instructive that the 5th sweep of the National Child Development Study eventually got some funding largely due to the efforts of some academics who mounted a successful lobby and gained sponsorship for its continuation. The five National Longitudinal Surveys in the USA have also received considerable acclaim.

11 A selection of published requests for the collection of work history data can be found in the following sources: Erikson and Goldthorpe (1988: 50) to research men's and women's social mobility. An EEC Report on women's employment has, as one of its recommendations; 'Promotion of longitudinal studies on the progression of women's careers to reveal further details of the generation effect . . .' (Bouillaguet-Bernard *et al.*, 1985: 27). Peter Moss's review of childcare provision in the EEC states:

'To get a full picture of the part played by parenthood in creating inequality, it is necessary to take a lifetime perspective, which assesses the cumulative consequences over time. The crucial question is – what effect does parenthood have on the employment opportunities and experience of men and women over the full course of their adult lives? To answer this question, it is necessary to collect and analyse the employment histories of individual men and women over their adult lives. The histories of women who have children can then be compared with those of women who remain childless and of men' (Moss, 1988: 26). A paper on young workers in the class structure 'needs a longitudinal approach which takes account of division according to class of origin, access to mobility routes, current occupational class and gender, for a greater understanding of the position of young people in the social structure. Ideally this requires the use of longitudinal data. . .' (Jones, 1987: 506). Lydia Morris's review of the evidence on the effects of male unemployment on domestic labour concludes: 'Definitive conclusions would, however, require longitudinal data on change in individual households. . .' (Morris, 1988: 390). Roberts *et al.* (1985) make some suggestion for the direction for the future research on economic lives and say on the topic of attitudes to careers, training, work commitment and mobility: 'A serious investigation . . . would require a new large-scale longitudinal study that would extend over a substantial period of time' (Roberts *et al.*, 1985: 524). My own review of the evidence on the existence of attitude change makes the same point (Dex, 1988a: 152). Roberts *et al.* (1985: 529) make a similar plea with respect to understanding the experience of unemployment: Economists' reviews of unemployment have made similar points because of the nature and frequency of recurrent unemployment.

12 This list of topics was constructed from surveying the material contained in some sociological reviews of the sociology of work and employment; for example, Gallie (1988), Pahl (1988), Roberts *et al.* (1985). Also considered were the past decade of issues of the following journals; *Sociology*, *British Journal of Sociology*, *British Journal of Industrial Relations*, *Industrial Relations Journal* and *Work Employment and Society*. A small sample of British sociologists and economists known to have used work history data were also asked to say whether there were any contemporary research topics needing the availability of work history data in order to be researched. The list is a subset of their replies.

References

Abell, P., (1990), 'Combining quantitative and qualitative models in a longitudinal context', paper given at BSA Conference, Surrey University, April 1990.

Allatt, P., Keil, T., Bryman, A. and Bytheway, B. (eds), (1987), *Women and the Life Cycle: Transitions and Turning Points*, Macmillan.

Barry, J.T., Francis, B.J. and Davies, R.B., (1989), 'SABRE: Software for the Analysis of Binary Recurrent Events', *Lecture Notes in Statistics*, 57: 56.

Blalock, H.M., (1989), 'The real and unrealized contribution of quantitative sociology', *American Sociological Review*, 54(3): 447–60.

Blossfeld, H., (1986), 'Career opportunities in the Federal Republic of Germany. A Dynamic approach to study life course, cohort and period effects', *European Sociological Review*, 2: 208–25.

Bouillaguet-Bernard, P. *et al.*, (1985), *Changes in Activity and Employment of Women in the European Economic Community*, Report to the Commission of the European Communities v/1252/86-EN.

Brown, G.W. and Harris, T. (eds), (1989), *Life Events and Illness*, London: Unwin Hyman.

Campbell, D.T. and Stanley, J.C., (1963), *Experimental and Quasi-Experimental Designs for Research*, Chicago: Rand McNally.

Carr-Hill, R.A. and MacDonald, K.I., (1973), 'Problems in the analysis of life histories', in P. Halmos (ed.), *Stochastic Processes in Sociology, Sociological Review Monograph* 19: 57–95.

Chandler, J., (1989), 'Marriage and the housing careers of naval wives', *The Sociological Review*, 37(2): 253–76.

Cohen, G. (ed.), (1987), *Social Change and the Life Course*, Routledge.

Dale, A., (1988), 'Stratification over the life-course: gender differences within the household', paper presented to the Stratification Seminar, Cambridge, September, 1988.

Davies, R., Francis, B., Barry, J. and Penn, R., (1989), 'The relationship between a husband's unemployment and his wife's participation in the labour force', paper presented to the Social Statistics Section of the Royal Statistical Society, 16 May 1989, London.

Department of Statistics, (1984), Notes on the planning of the Socio-Economic Panel, Department of Statistics of Income and Consumption, Amsterdam, Holland.

Dex, S., (1984a), *Women's Work Histories: An analysis of the Women and Employment Survey*, London: Department of Employment Research Paper 46.

Dex, S., (1984b), 'Work histories, women and large-scale data', *The Sociological Review*, 32(4): 637–61.

Dex, S., (1988a), *Women's Attitudes Towards Work*, Macmillan.

Dex, S., (1988b), Labour force experience after YTS: Analysis of the YTS Follow-up Survey, Institute for Employment Research University of Warwick, Report to the Manpower Services Commission.

Elder, G., (1978), 'Family history and the life course' in Harevan (1978).

Elias, P., (1985a), 'Work history information and the investigation of social and economic change in Coventry', Institute for Employment Research, University of Warwick.

Elias, P., (1985b), 'The collection of work history data by survey methods', Institute for Employment Research, University of Warwick.

Elias, P. and Main, B., (1982), *Women's Working Lives: Evidence from the National Training Survey*, Coventry: Institute for Employment Research, University of Warwick.

Erikson, R. and Goldthrpe, J.H., (1988), 'Does the class mobility of women differ from that of men? Cross-sex comparisons in cross-national perspective', unpublished paper on CASMIN project, mimeo, Nuffield College, Oxford.

Gallie, D. (ed.), (1988), *Employment in Britain*, Basil Blackwell.

Glenn, N.D., (1977), *Cohort Analysis*, Sage Publications.

Goldstein, H., (1979), *The Design and Analysis of Longitudinal Studies*, Academic Press.

Hareven, T.K. (ed.), (1978), *Transitions: The Family and the Life Course in Historical Perspective*, New York: Academic Press.

Himmelweit, H.T., Biberian, M.J. and Stockdale, J., (1978), 'Memory for past vote: implications of a study of bias in recall', *British Journal of Political Science*, 8: 365–84.

Hsiao, C., (1986), *Analysis of Panel Data*, Cambridge University Press.

Hyman, H.H., (1972), *Secondary Analysis of Sample Surveys*, John Wiley.

Jones, G., (1987), 'Young workers in the class structure', *Work Employment and Society*, 1(4): 487–508.

Kish, L., (1965), *Survey Sampling*, New York: John Wiley.

Marsh, A., Heady, P. and Matheson, J., (1981), *Labour Mobility in the Construction Industry*, Office of Population Censuses and Surveys, Social Survey Division.

Martin, J. and Roberts, C., (1984), *Women and Employment: A Lifetime Perspective*, DE/OPCS Social Survey Report SS1143, HMSO.

Morris, L., (1988), 'Employment, the household and social networks', in Gallie (ed.) (1988).

Moss, L., (1979), 'Overview' in Moss and Goldstein, (1979).

Moss, L. and Goldstein, H. (eds), (1979), *The Recall Method in Social Surveys*, Studies in Education 9, University of London Institute of Education.

Moss, P., (1988), 'Childcare and equality of opportunity', Consolidated Report to the European Commission, v/746/88-EN.

Moss, P., Plewis, I. and Bax, M.C.O., (1979), *The Pre-School Project*, Thomas Coram Research Unit, London University Institute for Education.

Pahl, R. (ed.), (1988), *On Work: Historical, Comparative and Theoretical Approaches*, Basil Blackwell.

Parkhouse, J. and Ellin, D.J., (1988), 'Reasons for doctors' career choice and change of choice', *British Medical Journal*, 296: 1651–3.

Peters, H.E., (1989), 'Retrospective versus panel data in analyzing lifecycle events', *Journal of Human Resources*, XXIII (4). 201–13.

Plewis, I., (1985), *Analysing Change: Measurement and explanation using longitudinal data*, John Wiley and Sons.

Plummer, K., (1983), *Documents of Life: An introduction to the problems and literature of a humanistic method*, George Allen and Unwin.

Rhoton, P., (1984), 'Attrition and the longitudinal surveys of labor force behaviour', *IASSIST Quarterly* (International Surveys for Social Science Information Service and Technology), 8(2): 2–16.

Riley, M.W. (ed.), (1988), *Sociological Lives: Social Change and the Life Course*, vol. 2, Sage Publications.

Rindfus, R.R., Swicegood, C.G. and Rosenfeld, R.A., (1987), 'Disorder in the life course: how common and does it matter?', *American Sociological Review*, 54: 785–801.

Roberts, B., Finnegan, R. and Gallie, D. (eds), (1985), *New Approaches to Economic Life: Economic Restructuring: Unemployment and the Social Division of Labour*, Manchester University Press.

Savage, M., (1988), 'The missing link: the relationship between spatial mobility and social mobility', *British Journal of Sociology*, XXXIX(4): 554–77.

Smith, T.W., (1984), 'Recalling attitudes: an analysis of retrospective questions on the 1982 GSS', in *Public Opinion Quarterly*, 48(3): 639–49.

Thomas, R., (1981), 'Problems in the collection and analysis of individual histories', OPCS mimeo.

Tudor Hart, J., (1980), *Hypertension*, London and New York: Churchill Livingstone, Edinburgh.

Uncles, M.D., (1988), *Longitudinal Data Analysis: Methods and Applications*, Pion/Methuen.

Unruh, D. (ed.), (1990), *Current Perspective on Aging and the Life Cycle*, UCLA Press.

Waterton, J. and Lievesley, D., (1988), 'Attrition, conditioning and attitude change: some findings from the social attitudes panel study', in Uncles (1988).

Histories of sickness: making use of multiple accounts of the same process

Paul Bellaby

'We are safe in saying that personal life-records, as complete as possible, constitute the perfect type of sociological material.' (W.I. Thomas and F. Znaniecki, *The Polish Peasant in Europe and America*, vol. II, p. 1833, New York: Dover, 1927)

Introduction

Life histories have several uses in sociological investigation. None of these can include description of individual cases for their own sake. Cases must be treated as samples of the social: if not probability samples of a defined population drawn to test propositions, then what Glaser and Strauss (1967) call 'theoretical samples', selected to explore the various dimensions of social structure, and to enable theory to be built on evidence (Rose, 1982). The subjectivity of life histories is both a weakness and a strength: a weakness often in creating unreliable records of external facts (Runyan, 1982: chapter 1); a strength in illuminating the encounter between self, life course and society (Pascal, 1960; Plummer, 1983).

The longitudinal form of the external facts which life histories provide allows us to answer questions about continuity and change in social structure (Thompson, Wailey and Lummis, 1983), about regularities in experiences of class (Sennett and Cobb, 1977; Vincent, 1981), about how, why and with what consequences people are socially mobile (Dex, 1987), or about the implications of social change for the typical course of lives (Cohen, 1987).

However, histories or documents of life are not there waiting to be taken. They have to be composed. Like snapshots, they are not panorama but partial views. Consider the typically varied perspectives of such life histories as 'private diaries', 'political memoirs', the 'curriculum vitae', 'medical histories' and a 'staff appraisal form'. Each is constrained by the present purpose for which it is composed. Of the immense range of past events in anyone's life, only some are relevant to each crucial purpose. Life histories may be tendentious; perhaps drawn up as a balance sheet of pros and cons for a proposed course of action by an employer or professional, or simply composed for self-advertisement.

Thus, many accounts may be given of the same life. Triangulation becomes feasible. Moreover, the analyst can focus either on the external facts that multiple accounts refer to or on the internal perspectives from which the accounts view the facts. This paper gives unusual attention to such internal perspectives, but only because they tend to be neglected in the rush to 'tell it as it is' typical of both oral history and sociological ethnography.[1]

Since it is more fruitful to consider implications of this approach for empirical work than to discuss it in the abstract, two case studies will be discussed: the first is from fieldwork already completed (on sickness absence in industry) and reviews several uses of multiple accounts – (1) cross validation, (2) complementarity and (3) uncovering the perspectives from which the accounts are given; while the second deals with fieldwork barely started (on closed head injury and the life course) and concentrates on the third use of multiple accounts. Before analysing these cases, it is necessary, firstly, to expand on 'triangulation', and, secondly, to consider the culturally specific features of the perspective on life which 'life history' itself represents.

Triangulation

Social researchers can ask those individuals whom they interview questions drawn from several perspectives, can use other methods, such as records, observations and the diary, in conjunction with interviews and can collect information from several people. So it is that 'triangulation' occurs, in Cicourel's words (1973), which is to view a process from several angles much as a surveyor views land.

'Triangulation' is a deceptively simple metaphor. There are three distinct reasons for collecting multiple accounts:

1) to seek cross-validation on matters of fact (in which case the accounts cover the same ground);
2) to use different viewpoints on the same reality in order to complete a panorama (where the accounts complement each

other, like a series of aerial reconaissance photographs taken on a grid pattern);
3) to discover a structure beneath the surface of the accounts in spite of apparent contradictions between them (for this there is no simple spatial metaphor).

The differences can be suggested symbolically. Where cross-validation is sought, if account A = account B, then E, the external referent of both accounts, is confirmed. Where a panorama or complementarity of accounts is sought, accounts A + B + C . . .+ N sum to E. Finally, where the latent structure implicit in a series of accounts is sought, I (the internal structure) = f(A,B,C. . .N).

The first and second approaches imply that there is a material reality to which life histories refer. Of course there is, and it relates to humans being embodied and having a life span in historical time and geographical space: when and where the subject was born, reared, educated, employed, unemployed, lived out her last years – all these are facts to which life history accounts usually refer. The third approach focuses on the internal relations within and between accounts, suspending (not dismissing) the question of the truth value of the accounts.

Life history as a cultural form

Life histories are accounts of how individuals independently shaped their destinies or had them shaped in relation to opportunities and constraints. There is space only for a suggestive sketch of the history of the form 'life history'. It is founded upon salvationist religion of the Christian type; reflects the meaning attached to the Life of Christ and the Way of the Cross; evolved from the adoption of pilgrimage – temporary retreat rather than monasticism – as The Way by secular orders and laity in the middle ages; and was brought to fruition with the application of pilgrimage as metaphor to life itself (as in Bunyan's *Pilgrim's Progress*) (Frankenberg, 1987).

Spiritual autobiography, beginning with the isolated instance of St Augustine's *Confessions* (AD 400), but becoming a widespread practice from the seventeenth century (Spengemann, 1980), was the first step in 'life history' proper. There are many extant variations on this relatively modern theme, most of which have only vestiges of the spiritual content of the original. The novel is one (Watt, 1957). Biography and autobiography (including the personal diary and the usually unwritten, often mute 'life review') are others.

Some variations on the life history theme are more typical of the disciplinary post-Enlightenment society (Foucault, 1970 and 1977; Armstrong, 1987) than that which preceded it. They include the curriculum vitae, the employee's personnel record, the criminal record, adoption and fostering files and medical case notes. Each is written in universal not particular terms, and has a specific not a diffuse objective. The professional or bureaucratic variants of lives have accompanied the surveillance of the body in populations that began in the eighteenth century in Europe. They have routinised what originally had a religious impulse.

In modern society, variations on the life history form can be conceptualised in terms of: a) the division of specialised knowledge and the techniques and relations of power associated with each specialism, and b) the division in knowledge and power between people in the public and private spheres (largely men and women respectively). So it is that the police collect criminal records, doctors maintain medical records, educators log their pupil's attainments, politicians write memoirs for eventual publication, and women, especially young women, keep personal diaries to themselves.

This sketch of life history as a cultural form suggests that use of life histories as primary sources on the past must be sensitive to the influence that culture and the division of labour, knowledge and power in society might have on the forms in which such facts are presented.

Case study (1): Sickness and absence from work

In a study of the relation between work organisation and sickness absence in the pottery industry, multiple accounts of events over time in people's working lives, through small spans of time, were used for all three of the reasons outlined above (Bellaby, 1986, 1987, 1989 and 1990).[2]

1) *Cross-validation.* In order to reach a reliable record of when, how often and for how long managers and workers were absent from work (regardless of the reason), management records on

random samples and on work groups in selected departments were cross-validated with two sources: with observations another fieldworker and the author made as participants in the latter departments over six months, and with retrospective reports on interview with the random samples about their absences in the preceding fortnight. Fortunately, there was a large measure of agreement between the management records and our observations for the selected departments.

The retrospective reports of the random samples did not correspond so well to the records. They were probably biased by the failure of some respondents to keep within the fortnight specified. Retrospective reports tend to become even more unreliable when longer time spans are involved. Management records, like our observations, were made on the spot. Obviously, a presence or absence is relatively easily observed, especially among employees who work in one place and who must clock on and off each shift. Moreover, management has an incentive to be accurate because pay is affected by absence. The decision to rely on management rather than employees for reports of absences would have been problematic if managers too depended on memory rather than a daily register checked against clocking-in cards. Cross-validation calls for what may be difficult decisions when multiple accounts do not tally.

2) *Complementary accounts*. When 'sickness' was added to the picture provided by presence/absence, quite different issues arose. Documentary evidence on sickness was of two types: a) medical certificates, usually issued after examination of the subject by a general practitioner, but giving only a brief diagnosis for the employer and employee to see; b) self certificates completed by the absentee to show to the employer and requiring a reason. Not only did any account of sickness as a reason for absence complement records of absence *per se*, but medical and self certificates added different pieces to the jigsaw. From 1 April 1982, medical certificates were required only after a week's absence (instead of three days), and providing self certificates was sufficient for shorter periods. When a short absence ran on and needed a medical opinion, the employee's original report usually bore an intelligible relation to the subsequent doctor's 'diagnosis'. However, the bulk of self certificates were for short absences and, while these were overwhelmingly attributed to personal sickness rather than care for another or other causes, the majority were for

non-serious acute illnesses. The predominant content of medical certificates was more serious acute illnesses and chronic complaints: injuries too usually involved a medical opinion, invariably so if the patient had to visit the casualty department of the district general hospital.

While this does little more than confirm commonsense, it illustrates the extent to which accounts can be used to complement each other, but only so long as there is an independent reason to think they may do so – a sampling frame in other words. Such a frame may have to be constructed in advance of collecting the multiple accounts, for instance by observation of the pathways to care followed by the sick.

3) *Latent structure*. Using this conceptual framework involves two stages. In the first, accounts are treated not as resources but as topics: rather than containing references to the external facts of sickness and absence, they display the ideas, beliefs and values of the account-givers and so require analysis as texts. This shift from 'facts' to 'social construction' need not imply that each history is treated as subjective. On the contrary, accounts are founded (at least partly) on shared language and systems of representation. Moreover, at a second stage, the perspectives from which the accounts are given can be linked to the relative social positions of those who give them, those to whom they apply, and the audience to which they are addressed. Thus the object of the analysis is to relate apparently idiosyncratic features of accounts to a latent structure that is both cultural and social.

This can be illustrated from the sickness absence study, where even unreliable accounts of the external facts of sickness and absence nevertheless make sense when analysed for the latent structure they share. For example, a self certificate might or might not be untruthful but could still present the employee's reason for absence in terms he or she considered the employer would find acceptable: accordingly, 'personal' as a euphemism for menstrual causes was common on self-certificates. There were occasional hints that medical practitioners might write similarly, but use the prestige of specialist language to tell white lies: women in pregnancy could not use pregnancy *per se* as a reason for absence and receive sick pay, but they could claim sick pay if the doctor used some medical term, such as 'hyperemesis' (in this context, morning sickness) on the certificate.

Off the record reports of reasons for absence sometimes brought out the extent to which the content of certificates was conditioned by what the employer would tolerate: they did so by showing how much absence was not due to personal sickness. Off the record reports were given in one of two contexts – either to a fieldworker on the shop floor and often in company, or at a confidential structured interview. In the confidential interview, we were told (largely by young employees, especially men) of numerous absences that were not for sickness, whatever reason was given on the self certificate. However, in the company of other workers, individuals rarely admitted to 'skiving' (taking time off when not sick), because it was not generally acceptable among peers any more than with managers. We were also told (usually by older workers, especially men) of numerous sicknesses that did not lead to absence and would therefore go unrecorded by management.

Again this inconsistent reporting makes sense at another level. The reticence of older men about going sick can be explained by the responsibilities they carry to their households and their knowledge that, with age, manual work becomes less easy to sustain. In spite of their fitness, young men take more time off, partly because they lack such responsibilities, partly because they have licence, indeed are expected to have a good time. It was they who over reported absence in the confidential interview, which reflects their belief that others give them licence, much as it does where reporting of sexual conquests occurs.

In short, these multiple accounts were frequently inconsistent with each other in matters of fact, and yet, when related to the ideas, beliefs and values of those involved, to the specialist knowledge and power of each party and to the situations in which the accounts were given, they fell into place. There was a structure to the accounts taken together, not merely a welter of subjective viewpoints. But it was a latent structure, not one that was transparent from the accounts themselves.

Moreover, when the same evidence is viewed from the standpoint of agency rather than from that of structure, it is clear that individuals' 'competence' as social actors is not absolute but relative, and continually learned. Sickness or injury is a drama that punctuates the routines of life. There are no script and stage directions for this drama. People learn them in the course of interactions which define them for all parties. For instance, in a heated incident involving several women on a production line, a young woman, newly married, who took time off with a medical certificate for depression, was told by an older woman going through the change of life that she should bear her depression stoically and not allow it to interfere with her work, and, moreover, that a young, newly married woman, unlike one undergoing the menopause, had no cause to be depressed. Such stereotypes of age and gender were perhaps always implicit, but they were only defined openly in dramas such as this one involving sickness. Then observers, such as the author, discovered what they were, and 'incompetent' participants, like the young woman, learned how they should conduct themselves in future.

The first case study has illustrated the principles for combining multiple accounts. These accounts covered events over a small span of time, but not a life time. The second case study builds upon the latent structure strategy in particular, considering multiple accounts of lives.[3]

Case study (2): Closed head injury

The second case study concerns: first the perspectives on closed head injury (CHI) and its relation to the patient's life course that victims, family carers, employers, work colleagues, neurosurgeons, nurses, paramedical staff and psychiatrists might have; secondly how these viewpoints might relate to each other internally, and thirdly what implications their interrelation might have for the recovery and social adjustment of patients.

CHI has attracted little attention from sociology or social anthropology. Even in the extensive neuropsychology literature, recovery from CHI has been relatively neglected (but see Finger and Stein, 1982; Miller, 1984; Levin *et al.*, 1984). Here, with rare exceptions (Brooks, 1984), the possibility that adjustment and even recovery might be linked with social relations has been left untouched. There is recognition of the need for and difficulties of professional prognosis and provision for the long term rehabilitation of the brain damaged (Roberts, 1979), but not of the impact that converging/conflicting professional and lay perspectives upon CHI might have on the victim's progress.

Features of closed head injury

CHI is brain damage without externally visible lesions. It is commonly the outcome of the rapid acceleration of the soft tissue of the brain within the hard shell of the cranium, as in a car or bike accident. The consequent brain damage may lead to death or to varying degrees of impairment, some transitory.

The aftermath of CHI is frequently chronic illness. However, it differs, subjectively and socially, from most chronic illnesses and disabilities (Blaxter, 1976; Anderson and Bury, 1988) in a number of ways:

1) It is sudden in onset. In the great majority of cases, there is recovery in course of time, though in the severer cases, it is almost never complete. Estimates based on acute hospital admissions suggest that the average District Health Authority in England and Wales (of 250,000 population) will encounter some 750 minor, 45 moderately severe and 20 severe head injuries per annum (Evans, 1987).

2) CHI, like missile injuries to the brain, falls disproportionately upon young males.[4] A study in Olmsted County, Minnesota, based on an extensive medical records system, showed an incidence per 100,000 head injuries with 'presumed brain involvement' of 274 for males and 116 for females, with a steep rise for males (to almost 700 per 100,000) in the 16–24 age group (Annegers *et al.*, 1980). Thus, the social incidence of CHI differs from other chronic illnesses. Its impact on the life course is radical, because it commonly strikes close to the first entry to the labour market, to the establishment of an independent household; to marriage and to the first child.

3) CHI not only typically disrupts the victim's expectations in life, it also presents family carers, medical, nursing and paramedical staff and employers with the problem of how to relate the victim's past potential to his/her present performance and both to future prospects. There is ample scope for conflict between the assessments each party makes.

4) While other illnesses are commonly seen as either physical or mental, or the product of the mind at work on the body, CHI is hidden in the head, yet manifest to all in behaviour that is both physical and mental.

Some of the victims of closed head injury die. Some do not recover consciousness. Death or coma after recovery occur sometimes as a result of secondary brain damage (caused by undetected haematomas or infections). In this context I am concerned with those who survive.

The aftermath of CHI as a status passage

The imminence of death at a young age places the victims of severe CHI in a quite different relation to modern society than the routinely expected and handled death of the aged. Only in wartime does death when young even approach the routine. This is illustrated by the extravagant attention given to the young deaths of James Dean, Che Guevara, Marilyn Monroe and John Lennon. In severe CHI, even when the threat of biological death recedes, the victim faces the possibility of premature social death, becoming 'senile' before his/her time, and, at worst, 'vegetative'.

Severe closed head injury abruptly separates individuals from their prior statuses and places them 'on the danger list'. Frequently they are comatose for hours or days: indeed severity is measured in periods of unconsciouness. For days or weeks beyond recovery of consciousness, they do not commit anything to memory, and so have no direct knowledge of the circumstances of the injury or its sequel. Recovery of memory is similarly followed by several weeks or months in which cognitive faculties return, but often incompletely and at a retarding rate beyond the first six months to a year after the injury. Victims appear to those who knew them before the injury to undergo a change of character. They tend to lose inhibitions and to become labile, libidinous and aggressive. They are also in a highly dependent condition, though of course to a diminishing degree as they recover.

Clearly these conditions have a neurological infrastructure: Luria referred to the 'shattered world' of one with brain damage in his famous case study (1975). Nevertheless they have social and cultural features that cannot be simply reduced to brain damage. Together these features resemble the 'antistructure' that Turner (1982) associates with the state of 'liminality'. For a period after their separation from their prior status, victims of CHI are in a liminal state in which their world is upside down, and they await passage to a new status, which may be one of recovery or of a certain degree of impairment of function.

The concept of 'liminality' was derived from studies of tribal societies: van Gennep synthesised pre-existing ethnography, while Turner did first-hand research among the Ndembu of what is now Malawi. Van Gennep (1960) assimilates numerous rituals with which changes of individual status or states of collective activity are marked, to a three stage model: separation (from the initial state), transition (between the initial and an improved state) and incorporation (into the new state). The same three stages are plainly seen in the passage from fitness, through severe CHI to recovery or adjustment to impairment. However, there are crucial differences from the tribal model. These must be understood if we are not to misapply 'liminality' to CHI and its aftermath, and yet we are to use it constructively.

The rites of passage in a tribal context are obligatory. Initiation into manhood and womanhood, for example, is normally required of all who attain that approximate age, regardless of physical maturity, and is neither elective, nor (as in the case of the head-injured) occasioned by accident. The passage is to an improved status. Ideally in the case of CHI, victims should return to their former status, as is the case in all healing processes in Western societies. Even ideally they do not pass to an improved status, except by comparison with how they were directly after the injury. In practice, a decline of status is the norm.

Surgeons, nurses and rehabilitators have sometimes been compared to ritual specialists in rites of passage, and their procedures, such as scrubbing up, waking patients for sleeping pills, and basket-making have been likened to rituals. The implication is that health workers have not 'advanced' beyond tribal conduct: but this is of course a mischievous use of comparative method, as derogatory to tribal societies as it is to our contemporaries. Surgery and the rest are routinised technical interventions in the patient's illness, formally void of charismatic or moral content. They are not ritualised. On the other hand, health workers who do seek to effect a status passage for the victims of CHI that is not merely a matter of surviving or even being restored to bodily fitness. The status passage is a matter of 'healing' or being removed from sickness and restored to normal social rights and obligations.

In view of the balance of similarities and contrasts between status passage involving CHI and rites of passage in tribal societies, the aftermath of CHI is best characterised as liminal-like, or 'liminoid'. The approximate equivalent to liminality, according to Turner (1982) is found in societies not based principally on kinship and affinity as are tribal societies, but based on class relations of production and distribution as is modern capitalist/industrial society, or 'class-divided' as was medieval Christendom (Giddens 1973).

The aftermath of CHI and the perspectives of specialists

Surviving victims are usually treated and cared for by a succession of specialists and thereafter, sometimes permanently, by partners and/or family. Each of these parties, including the victim, is likely to have a different perspective on the injury and its aftermath. In Figure 1 below is depicted the passage of victims into and (in most cases) out of the liminoid state. The figure shows how at different stages various specialists are in control, while victim and family carers are present throughout. They are considered to have typically different time-perspectives on the head injury, consisting of a point of entry (*) in the past and a 'horizon' in the future which is indicated by a dotted curve.

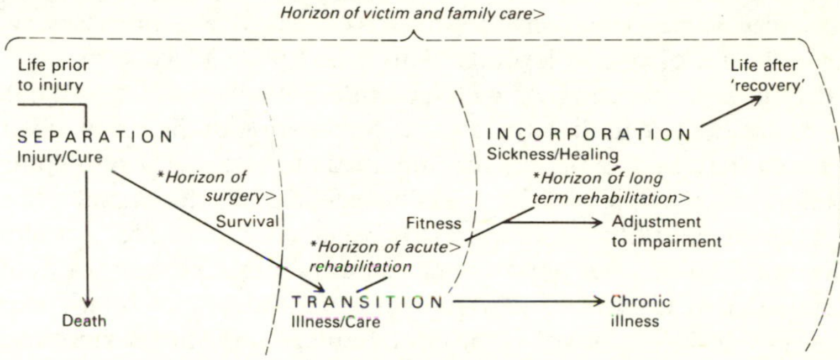

Figure 1

The trajectory of closed head injury: the horizons of victim, therapists and carers

1) *Separation*. At the point of 'separation', the victim enters surgery. Of all medical specialisms, surgery is most inclined to view the presenting problem as exclusively biomedical, especially with hot (or emergency) as opposed to cold (or elective) operations, where little if anything is learned of the patient as a person and his/her experience of the condition before intervention. The neurosurgeon who admits the victim and operates is largely restricted in practice to securing his survival. Thus the couple: 'injury' (of the victim) and 'cure' (of the presenting condition), sets the horizon.

This is not to say that neurosurgeons do not take an interest in the rehabilitation of their patients. Indeed many have been active in attempts to ensure that rehabilitation is organised for patients not only while they remain inpatients but also for long after discharge.[5] However, they do not have direct control beyond the post-operative ward. It could be argued that the fact that they seek indirect control of rehabilitation indicates the importance to them of authority gained from the 'healing' or incorporation moment of the status passage (Fox, 1989).

2) *Transition*. Assuming that the victim survives, there follows a period of transition in which he becomes a 'novice' under the tuition of nurses, occupational therapists, physiotherapists and others, much like the initiate in a puberty ritual such as Chisungu (Richards, 1982), and attempts are made to restore as many as possible of the functions lost due to injury. Recovery of consciousness and memory may be the first steps; followed at an interval by recovery, in part or wholly, of any loss of use of limbs or senses, of speech, and of cognitive skills. This phase takes place within the hospital as a rule and is known as 'acute rehabilitation', though it does not often lead directly to the incorporation of the person into normal life. In this phase, the implications of the injury for the person as a whole – his 'illness' – become the focus, and the specialists, with the supervised involvement of family or partner, become 'carers' (as opposed to 'curers'). The horizon of this process is the discharge of the patient from the hospital as 'fit'. The concept of 'fitness' involves more than mere survival (Fox, 1989). In practice, the victims may be discharged to prolonged periods of chronic illness and impairment.

The staff in acute rehabilitation departments are far more likely than the surgeon and his/her team, to learn about the person with the injury – at least through family or partner. They will form a concept of how well that person is likely to adjust to life once incorporated into it, and how much support family or partner are likely to be. They may glimpse, though this is less likely, what kind of person the victim was and what personal relations he had before the injury. On the whole, however, the entry point of acute rehabilitation is set to the left (in Figure 1) by receiving a survivor from surgery, and its horizon to the right by sending that person out fit or chronically ill.

Specialists here have little control over patients' rehabilitation once discharged to the community. Nor, of course, do they have any control in the surgeon's domain. Cases may thus be handed on from stage to stage with little more coordination than case notes allow. The patient's 'life' becomes his medical record for practical purposes. This cannot be true for the victim or his family or partner, but – while he is still an inpatient – non-medical perspectives are likely to be dominated by medical. Nursing staff are best situated to mediate between the long-term perspectives of victim and family carers and the specialised and short-term perspectives of surgeons and other rehabilitation staff. Their success or otherwise is a test of the power relations of the hospital. It may also have implications for the long-term recovery of the victim.

3) *Incorporation*. 'Incorporation' (or re-aggregation) is the term by which van Gennep understood the restoration of normal life in a status passage. Since tribal societies mark definite changes, usually upward steps in status, by communal ritual, incorporation after closed head injury fits the van Gennep type imperfectly. There is no ritual. The discharge to the community is individual and often routine (marked only by the signing of papers and the departure of an ambulance). Incorporation is not accomplished in a single step, but is a matter of prolonged 'adjustment' to a status that is unlikely to be the same as that prior to injury, far less an improvement. Following Parsons (1979), incorporation normally involves exit from 'sickness' (or the sick role) and the concomitant process of 'healing' usually at the hands of a specialist, which enables the community to accept the patient as a normal citizen. Many victims of severe and moderately severe closed head injury may never leave the sick role or be healed.

It follows that the horizon of long-term rehabilitation is much the most difficult to draw. Victims emerge from acute rehabilitation with a variety of prognoses: from chronic illness through partial recovery to total recovery. There have been attempts to delimit statistically the period of time after injury beyond which further recovery is unlikely or becomes progressively smaller. Such exercises still leave much room for uncertainty in individual cases. Of course, they do not take account of the differences of perspective that surgeons, acute rehabilitators, victims, family carers and psychiatrists might have, and what the effects of such differences among members of the victim's role-set might be on his actual recovery. For outside the hospital context or 'in the community', there is a less clear cut hierarchical division of labour and much that can be readily supervised in a closed space becomes inaccessible to specialist staff. One perspective, such as that of the neurosurgeon is much less likely to dominate outside than it did within the hospital. On a day to day basis, it is the perspectives of family carers and victim that may carry most weight.

Time perspectives of family carers and victims of CHI

Every life history account contains a 'perspective' on time – past, present and future. In this case study, we are concerned with time perspectives on the life course of the victim of severe CHI that are held by himself and by the various members of his role set. Such time perspectives are constrained by the point of entry that the observer made in the victim's life (for example before or after the injury) and by the horizon the observer has for practical purposes.

1) *The family carer's perspective*. A follow up study of war veterans with closed head injury revealed that family carers might have widely different views of the person they knew before injury and of his state in the aftermath of injury (Rosenbaum and Najenson, 1976). In particular, spouses rejected the dependence their husbands now showed, while mothers welcomed the same in their sons. Both were distressed by apparent changes in personality, but these weighed more heavily on wives, because their husbands had become aggressive, sexually demanding and often impotent, as well as prone to low moods. Since wives resented their husbands' new physical and emotional dependence, faults of personality seemed unendurable. Marriages often broke up.

Family carers normally knew the victim before injury and faced the prospect of caring for him long after discharge from hospital. Since victims who are young men (as most are) are passing through the protracted and ambiguous change from dependence on family of origin to establishing a family of procreation and gaining independence as a full adult, injury frequently cuts off the possible achievement of adulthood but makes feasible a regression to dependence. So far from 'healing', medical practitioners often sanction continued, chronic occupancy of the sick role, or at best living with impairment. So it is that victims may find themselves between the Scylla of long-term sickness and the Charybdis of rejection and isolation, unable to find the passage between them.

2) *The victim's perspective*. The victim's view in all this is coloured by a peculiarity of closed head injury that remains to be examined. CHI fractures the boundary that our culture maintains, especially

for men, between self and body and feelings. On the other hand, the boundary between self and society, which the culture also maintains, impairs victims' capacity to bring the condition under control.

As the result of a history of manners (Elias, 1978) that parallels those of life-as-pilgrimage and the surveillance of populations and disciplinary practices referred to above, modern Westerners experience their selves as separate from, not coextensive with, their bodies and emotions (cf. Ohnuki-Tierney on contemporary Japan (1984) and Kleinman on Taiwan (1980)). Ideally, the self, conceived as wilful intellect, masters the body, restraining its 'animal' functions in public, containing emotions and drives of sex and hunger, showing stoicism in the face of pain and discomfort. The ideal is essentially masculine (Seidler, 1987). Women are subjected to it, but also acquire a sense of being under the control of their bodies – in menstruation, pregnancy and the menopause, which a masculinist culture requires them to regard as a source of inferiority (Martin, 1989).

Closed head injury is, of all illnesses, the most difficult to reconcile with the model of intellect in control of the body and emotions. First, it is an invisible injury inside the head which affects what is conventionally attributed both to the intellect and to the body and emotions: cognitive and language abilities on the one hand; the senses, coordination and emotional stability on the other. Second, it usually involves periods of loss of consciousness and of memory, in neither of which is the will apparently in control.

Western culture not only separates self and body, but also self and society. As a result, the probable response of victims to their closed head injury may be that they individually should master both body and social situation. An autobiographical account of closed head injury by a young woman illustrates three aspects of this argument (Kiers, 1986). First, she sought her friends' accounts of what was happening to her while she was unconscious, and while (after consciousness) she continued to suffer post-operative amnesia. This was literally in order to complete an interrupted biography. Their account, having become hers, restored her sense of continuous control. This is an awesome illustration of the deep cultural significance of the life history form: like other cultural forms (faith in God, the confessional and so forth) it is frequently therapeutic. Secondly and conversely, as a dancer of distinction, and a woman, she was unusually open to the body's rhythm controlling her. Through dance, where freedom of movement is realised by an interplay of discipline and 'natural' rhythm, she recovered a large measure of the functions lost to her by severe injury. Thirdly, Keirs offered her account to the self-help group *Headway* which published it. She thus demonstrates, by being typical, the compunction of Westerners to cope single-handed and to bring body and situation under the will, and, by being exceptional, what can be gained by bringing the body into partnership with the wilful intellect, and by bringing the self into active partnership with others who have similar problems to solve.

On the argument that I have advanced, men should be yet more concerned than women by experiences which characterise CHI: slowness in movement and thought, tendencies to involuntary outbursts of emotion, imperfect memory and inarticulateness in speech. Men will tend to become frustrated by the gap between what they wish to become and what they are, and at worst discouraged by the gap between what they believe they were, and what they have now become. For from neither point of view does the self appear to be in adequate control of the body and of feelings.

3) *Perspectives on the past*. What family carers and victims usually have (or think they have) and specialists in the treatment of closed head injury seldom pretend to have, is knowledge of what the victim was like before injury. It is here, perhaps, more than in any other aspect of this case study, that the difference between the third, latent structure approach to life history and the first and second approaches stands out. In this context, 'the past' is not what was the case in fact, but what construction different parties presently place upon it. As for the future – prognoses or constructions are the best anyone can offer.

The fact that closed head injury occurs most frequently (during peacetime) in road accidents, often involving young men, invites the use of social stereotypes to make sense of the past in individual cases. What are at first experienced by family carers as changes of personality: aggression, lack of inhibition, even clumsiness, may come to seem in retrospect as continuous with the past, and the original causes of the injury: he was always a young tearaway.

4) *The interplay of time perspectives and its effect on the victim of CHI*. As we have seen, there is sociological value in using life history methods to discover the various perspectives that members of the CHI victim's role-set have on his past, present and future,

and how far they accord with the victim's own. There may also be therapeutic value. Their time-perspectives presumably have a bearing on how they act; though how and to what degree must be treated as problematic. In turn they may contribute positively or negatively to the victim's recovery or adjustment to impairment. Figure 2 outlines possible relations between recovery and adjustment, and how combinations of active/passive therapy and present/absent social support may influence the victim's progress.

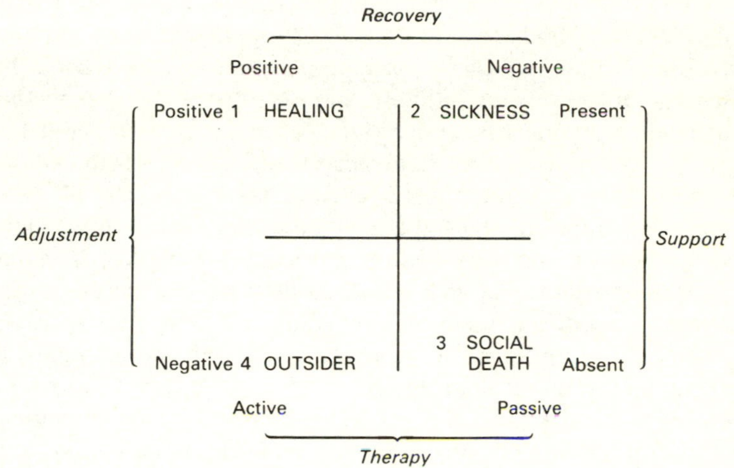

Figure 2
Recovery from and social adjustment to CHI

The model implied in Figure 2 treats as independent variables, a) recovery of functions lost by brain damage and b) adjustment to a new status. Their separation allows for three possibilities apart from 1) the 'incorporation' through healing depicted in Figure 1. These are: 2) adjustment while still impaired (or embrace of the sick role); 3) failure both to adjust and to recover (or a tendency to relapse into social death); 4) and recovery without social adjustment (or becoming a truculent outsider). Figure 2 also associates therapy with attempts to promote the recovery of lost functions, and social support with progress towards social adjustment. The therapy the CHI victim receives from the surgeon, and to a large degree that which he gets in acute rehabilitation, is instrumental. Expressive support is left largely to family carers if anyone. We have seen that this support may be problematic. The victim may alienate his partner for instance, or return to a state of dependence on a mother.

Figure 1 suggests that the various members of the victim's role-set – surgeon, rehabilitators, family carer and so on – are likely to have entered the process of his separation-transition-incorporation at different points and to have different horizons when looking into the future. For example, the neurosurgeon enters after the accident that causes CHI, and his horizon is confined to the survival of the victim. He may well have a longer time-perspective on CHI, but in practice can only exercise remote control over progress after discharge from the post-operative ward. Neurosurgeons often give a careful prognosis to family carers upon the discharge of the severely injured, and warn them about expecting too much after the first few months of what may be rapid but partial recovery. However, family carers are largely left to find out for themselves what these words mean. Their actions are likely to have considerably greater impact on the victim's social adjustment and perhaps his recovery of function too than the words of the neurosurgeon, however well-informed they are clinically.

Western medicine takes an individualised and 'internalising' (Young, 1986) approach to therapy which seeks adjustments of body and mind rather than changes in social relations. Clinics lend themselves to treating the victim rather than his immediate household, and even community psychiatric nurses who visit households must find a patient's relations with kin, with peers, with the employer and in the market and the political arena relatively inaccessible. Nevertheless, conflict of time perspectives on CHI and its aftermath among the victim, carers, employers, peers and professionals, may be expected to have an impact on the victim's social adjustment and possibly the rate and final extent of his recovery.

Frequent comments from therapists about the 'lack of insight' among head injury patients point to the conflict between a professional's and the patient's own interpretation of the same situation. Severe head injury frequently gives rise to an existential crisis for its victims. Symptoms of such a crisis would include extremes of apathy and depression on the one hand and aggressive and impulsive behaviour on the other. The first extreme is approached when the individual plays safe in a situation where he cannot recognise what is expected of him or her or he is capable of (cf. entering a room in which only a foreign language is spoken). The other extreme occurs when, instead of playing safe, the individual tries too hard to respond to what he mistakenly takes to be high expectations, or imagines he has infinite capacities (cf. acting under the influence of drink or drugs in a crowd). This complex has been found to be absent in severely physically disabled patients (Rosenbaum and Najenson, 1976), which suggests that frustration at loss of conscious control of one's situation is probably at its root.

Reflection on the existential crisis of the CHI victim returns us to the point of departure for the examination in this paper of a latent structure approach to the analysis of multiple accounts of lives: that is, the reflections on life history as a cultural form, which at once offers an account of life and is lived. The aftermath of CHI as experienced by the victim and acted upon by others in his role set is 'antistructure'. It turns upside down much that ordinary Western people take for granted about who they are, and so can provide both them and the sociologist or social anthropologist with a unique opportunity for learning.

Conclusion

Life histories have been used where found as diaries, biographies and the like, or where sought in interview, to document lives. There is every reason to continue with this practice, whether in oral history or in sociological ethnography. However, it can be refined by attending to how multiple accounts, even if from different types of source, can be combined, either to cross-validate each other or to complement each other in forming a larger picture than any one account makes possible.

A qualitatively distinct use can be made of life history material. This focuses not on the content of accounts or their references to the external world, but on their form and who uses that form and how. In short it treats life histories not as sources of fact but as social constructions. In this paper, I have illustrated this procedure in two contexts: uncovering the latent structure of 'going sick' at work, and the social dynamics of closed head injury and its aftermath.

The three strategies come together on the argument that life history is itself a cultural form, bounded in place and time, with variants that conform to the specialised knowledge and techniques of control associated with different professions and bureaucracies. An understanding of the production of the accounts that one might use as primary sources is important if they are to be used to the limits of their reliability. For, as the worked examples in this paper show, the latent structure approach and 'subjectivity' must not be confused. To demonstrate that accounts are socially constructed is not to render them inaccessible to rational empirical enquiry.

Notes

I thank Shirley Dex and Martin Hollis, who kindly read an earlier version of this paper from the rather different viewpoints of sociologist and philosopher, for valuable comments.

1 Often oral history and sociological ethnography alike come close to 'empiricism', in ignoring the extent to which findings are produced by both questions (or theory) and ways of gathering and processing evidence (methods). Research reports do not always pay proper attention to fieldwork relations or to how the data was analysed (Rose, 1982).

2 The study was supported by grants F1225 0001 and F0925 0036 from ESRC. Judith Sidaway and Sheila Cleverly shared fieldwork with me. I am grateful to directors and employees of Staffordshire Potteries Limited for access.

3 I am grateful to Ken Barrett, the neuropsychiatrist, for introducing me to this field, to Ronnie Frankenberg for encouraging me to use Victor Turner's work as I have done here, and to Nick Fox, Ruth Pinder and Alan Prout for helpful comments on earlier versions of the argument about closed head injury.

4 Because of its male incidence, I shall conventionally refer to each victim of CHI as 'he'.

5 Jennett and Teasdale (1981), for instance, have devised measures of long term rehabilitation and advocate control of community rehabilitation by a paramedical key worker.

References

Anderson, R. and Bury, M. (eds), (1988), *Chronic Illness*, Unwin Hyman.

Annegers, J.F., Grabow, J.D., Kurland, L.T. and Laws, E.R., (1980), 'The incidence, causes, and secular trends of head trauma in Olmsted County, Minnesota', *Neurology*, 30: 912–19.

Armstrong, D., (1987), 'Bodies of knowledge: Foucault and the problem of human anatomy', in G. Scambler, (ed.), *Sociological Theory and Medical Sociology*, London: Tavistock.

Bellaby, P., (1986), 'A sociological alternative to stress and coping discourse in explaining sickness absence from work', *International Journal of Sociology and Social Policy*, 6(4): 52–68.

Bellaby, P., (1987), 'The perpetuation of a folk model of the life cycle and kinship in a pottery factory', in A. Bryman, B. Bytheway, P. Allatt, and T. Keil (eds), *Rethinking the Life Cycle*, London: Macmillan.

Bellaby, P., (1989a), 'The social meanings of time off work', *Annals of Occupational Hygiene*, 33: 423–38.

Bellaby, P., (1990), 'What is a genuine sickness?' *Sociology of Health and Illness*, 12: 47–68.

Blaxter, M., (1976), *The Meaning of Disability*, London: Heinemann.

Brooks, N., (1984), 'Head injury and the family', in N. Brooks (ed.), *Closed Head Injury: Psychological, Social and Family Consequences*, Oxford: Oxford University Press.
Cicourel, A.V., (1973), *Cognitive Sociology*, Harmondsworth: Penguin.
Cohen, G., (1987), (ed.), *Social Change and the Life Course*, London: Tavistock.
Dex, S., (1987), *Women's Occupational Mobility: a Lifetime Perspective*, London: Macmillan.
Elias, N., (1978), *The Civilizing Process, vol. I, The History of Manners*, translated from the German by E. Jephcott, Oxford: Blackwell.
Evans, C., (1987), *Headway* Conference, Sheffield, 5–6 November.
Finger, S. and Stein, D.G. (eds), (1982), *Brain Damage and Recovery*, London: Academic Press.
Foucault, M., (1970), *The Order of Things*, translated from the French by A. Sheridan, London: Tavistock.
Foucault, M., (1977), *Discipline and Punish*, translated from the French by A. Sheridan, London: Allen Lane.
Fox, N.J., (1989), 'Surgical Healing: Power and Social Structure', Coventry: University of Warwick, unpublished PhD thesis.
Frankenberg, R.J., (1987), 'Life cycle, trajectory or pilgrimage?' in A. Bryman, B. Bytheway, P. Allatt and T. Keil (eds), *Rethinking the Life Cycle*, London: Macmillan.
Giddens, A., (1973), *The Class Structure of the Advanced Societies*, London: Hutchinson.
Glaser, B. and Strauss, A., (1967), *The Discovery of Grounded Theory*, New York: Aldine Press.
Jennett, B. and Teasdale, G., (1981), *Management of Head Injuries*, Philadelphia: F.A. Davis.
Keirs, J., (1986), *A Change of Rhythm*, Nottingham: Headway.
Kleinman, A., (1980), *Patients and Healers in the Context of Culture*, Berkeley: University of California Press.
Levin, H.S., Ewing-Cobbs, L. and Benton, A.L., (1984), 'Age and recovery from brain damage: a review of clinical studies', in S.W. Scheff (ed.), *Ageing and Recovery of Function in the Central Nervous System*, London: Plenum Press.
Luria, A.R., (1975), *The Man with a Shattered World*, Harmondsworth: Penguin.
Martin, E., (1989), *The Woman in the Body*, Milton Keynes: Open University Press (first published by Beacon Press 1987).
Miller, E., (1984), *Recovery and Management of Neuropsychological Impairments*, Chichester: John Wiley.
Ohnuki-Tierney, E., (1984), *Illness and Culture in Contemporary Japan*, Cambridge: Cambridge University Press.
Parsons, T., (1979), 'Definitions of health and illness in the light of American values and social structure', in E. Jaco and E. Gartley (eds), *Patients, Physicians and Illness*, 3rd edn, London: Collier Macmillan.
Pascal, R., (1960), *Design and Truth in Autobiography*, London: Routledge and Kegan Paul.
Plummer, K., (1983), *Documents of Life*, London: Allen and Unwin.
Richards, A., (1982), *Chisungu: a girls' initiation ceremony among the Bemba of Zambia*, 2nd edn, with an introduction by J. la Fontaine.
Roberts, A.H., (1979), *Severe Accidental Head Injury*, London: Macmillan.
Rose, G., (1982), *Deciphering Sociological Research*, London: Macmillan.
Rosenbaum, M. and Najenson, T., (1976), 'Changes in life patterns and symptoms of low mood as reported by wives of severely brain injured soldiers', *Journal of Consulting Clinical Psychology*, 44: 881–8.
Runyan, W.M., (1982), *Life Histories and Psychobiography*, Oxford: Oxford University Press.

Seidler, V.J., (1987), 'Reason, desire and male sexuality', in P. Caplan (ed.), *The Cultural Construction of Sexuality*, London: Tavistock Publications.
Sennett, R. and Cobb, J., (1977), *The Hidden Injuries of Class*, Cambridge: Cambridge University Press.
Spengemann, W.C., (1980), *The Forms of Autobiography*, London: Yale University Press.
Thompson, P., Wailey, T. and Lummis, T., (1983), *Living the Fishing*, London: Routledge and Kegan Paul.
Turner, V., (1982), *From Ritual to Theatre*, New York City: Performing Arts Journal Publications.
Van Gennep, A., (1960), *The Rites of Passage*, translated by M.B. Vizedom and G.L. Caffee, London: Routledge and Kegan Paul.
Vincent, D., (1981), *Bread, Knowledge and Freedom*, London: Europa.
Watt, I., (1957), *The Rise of the Novel*, London: Chatto and Windus.
Young, A., (1986), 'Internalising and externalising medical belief systems: an Ethiopian example', in A. Currer and M. Stacey (eds), *Concept of Health, Illness and Disease*, Leamington Spa: Berg.

A land of 'boundless opportunity'?: mobility and stability in nineteenth-century England

Andrew Miles and David Vincent

Introduction

Hailed as 'an issue at the centre of contemporary sociological discussion'[1] and supported by an ever-increasing body of research, social mobility has emerged as a major element in the post-war analysis of 'stratification systems'. Central to this interest has been a concern which stretches back at least as far as Plato;[2] namely that of the relationship between the extent and direction of movement and the stability of the social structures within which it takes place.[3]

Historical research in the field began in earnest in the United States in the 1960s, and more recently there has been a resurgence of work in continental Europe. In Britain, the technical and methodological difficulties involved in generating substantial and appropriate data have hindered the development of historical perspectives on social mobility. Nevertheless, the shortage of hard evidence has not discouraged historians from speculating about the nature and significance of patterns of mobility in nineteenth-century Britain.

The post-war paradigm defines two types of mobility: intergenerational and intragenerational – movement between father and son, or over the course of an individual career. In practice, intergenerational mobility has received much the most attention. A further conceptual distinction is made between *absolute*, observed rates of movement and *relative* measures of mobility. Absolute rates of movement provide a perspective on the implications of mobility for class 'formation' in the basic demographic sense of 'formations of aggregates of individuals or families that are identifiable through the continuity of their class locations over time'.[5] Relative rates are measures which take account of the structural influences on observed mobility flows and can therefore indicate how far changes in absolute rates are reflective of a genuine redistribution of mobility chances between classes or categories, rather than a mere concomitant of wider economic development.

This paper begins the long overdue task of plotting the terrain of occupational and social mobility in a country once presented by Samuel Smiles as a land of boundless opportunity. A product of the first project to attempt a systematic and detailed study of the dimensions and dynamics of movement in Victorian and Edwardian society,[6] it seeks, in the limited space available here, to establish the basic features of intergenerational movement between and within classes[7] and, in the process, to cast clearer light on the nature of working-class sectionalism during the course of the nineteenth century. Empirically-speaking, therefore, it follows that absolute rates will receive the bulk of our attention here.

The foundations of social mobility research

The foundations of the sociological study of mobility were not laid until the early decades of this century. In his review of the various 'social interests' which have shaped the development of the twentieth-century enterprise Goldthorpe follows the earlier commentary of Van Heek in arguing that an intellectual and ideological basis for mobility research only emerged at the end of the nineteenth century.[8]

Underpinning classical liberalism was the conviction that within nineteenth-century society there existed every opportunity for the individual citizen to attain a position commensurate with his capacities, whilst 'orthodox' Marxism condemned the notion of social mobility as an illusionary diversion. Nevertheless, as Goldthorpe shows, Marx himself clearly acknowledged the significance of mobility as a stabilising phenomenon, potentially antagonistic to the process of class formation.[9] Furthermore, in his discussion of the 'intermediate strata' existing in between the two great classes in capitalist society Marx recognised not only the small independents destined to contract and decline, but other *dritte Personen* – managers, office workers, public servants – clearly expanding in the wake of capitalist development.[10] It was revisionist concern with the implications – which Marx failed to confront – of such developments, that provided the stimulus for closer examination of the extent and significance of the mobility permitted by economic growth.

Developing from this base, and punctuated in particular by the work of Pitrim Sorokin,[11] twentieth-century research has been marked by a liberal interest in mobility as a value to be preserved. Thus the principal concern underpinning the post-war research of Lipset and of Blau and Duncan in America was the amount and direction of mobility conducive to the health of liberal-democratic society.[12] Yet, in sharp contrast to the American line of development, it was a positive socialist interest in mobility that underpinned the first major mobility enquiry on this side of the Atlantic – David Glass's LSE study in the late 1940s.[13] Glass's approach was firmly grounded in an indigenous ethical socialist tradition formed in opposition to the canons of classical British liberalism. Its critique concentrated on highlighting the contradiction between the claims of liberal ideology and the reality of everyday life, thus leading to the conviction that effective equality of opportunity was a virtue to be pursued.

Historical perspectives on mobility

The spate of post-war research activity in the United States took place against a background of a long-running debate about whether American society, once seen by Marx as notably fluid, was beginning to ossify along 'traditional' European lines.[14] Here the interest of the sociologists did eventually prompt an historical response, most notably in the work of Stephan Thernstrom whose researches have offered only qualified support for the original premiss on which the whole debate rested – the 'national obsession' that 'the United States has long been "the land of opportunity" for the common man'.[15] However, in Britain the effect of Glass's authoritative enquiry was, first, to discourage further empirical essays, and then to stimulate not a historical rejoinder but rather a more extensive and technically complex study of contemporary mobility patterns by the Oxford Social Mobility Group in the early 1970s.[16]

Hence, what we know about the nature, extent and direction of mobility in nineteenth-century England is still extremely limited.[17] Liberalism's refusal to .consider mobility as a problem was legitimated by the 'literature of success' – a series of tracts, pamphlets and books promulgating a 'gospel of advancement' organised around the figure of the self-made man and the doctrine of self-help.[18] The doyen of this enterprise was Samuel Smiles whose *Self-Help* of 1859 marked the development of the genre into a full blown mobility ideology. Potted biography, outlining the inspirational rise of great men from humble origins demonstrated that, 'What some men are, all without difficulty might be. Employ the same means and the same results will follow'.[19]

As to the substance of such a claim, Harold Perkin has written in *Origins of Modern English Society* that ' "What some men are, all without difficulty might be" was an argument which overwhelmed statistics and made the self-made man of the nineteenth century what the football pools winner is to the twentieth'.[20] However in Perkin's own work, such statistics are nowhere to be found. His assertion that 'There is of course no doubt that there was a considerable amount of upward mobility in mid-Victorian England as in all periods of English history'[21] rests only on the application of 'Petty's Law' – the tendency within economic development for movement from low to higher paid occupations as agricultural employment gives way first to manufacture and mining and then to trade, transport and particularly services.[22] He cites the decline of patronage and of free grammar school education for the poor as evidence that mobility was no higher than in the eighteenth century, and refers to Charlotte Erickson's findings on the small and declining number of steel and hosiery manufacturers recruited from humble origins[23] as indicating that 'upward mobility for the working class was probably at its nadir'.[24]

The one direct attempt to transcend this approach was Michael Sanderson's 'Literacy and Social Mobility in the Industrial Revolution in England'.[25] Rather than elite recruitment, Sanderson analysed the rate of upward mobility achieved by two samples of workers' sons – one taken from the Lancaster Charity School Register in the late eighteenth and early nineteenth centuries and one from a collection of marriage registers in the late 1830s. Being the first and only study to rest on quantitative foundations, his conclusions that the factory system closed off important channels of elevation for workers' sons, and that therefore industrialisation drastically reduced upward social mobility, have carried great weight amongst social historians. Yet, for all its novelty, the research, as Sanderson recognised, was extremely limited. It was confined to the early industrial revolution in Lancashire, and the samples were small, unrepresentative and lacking in comparability.

Elsewhere, data on social mobility has been generated as a by-product of the influential debate about the nineteenth century 'labour aristocracy'.[26] As they sought to explain the absence of revolution in the world's first industrial economy, Engels[27] and Lenin[28] drew attention to the role of an elite of skilled, unionised workers, whose militancy, they argued, was bought off with the proceeds of Britain's exploitation of less developed economies. Eric Hobsbawm revived interest in the concept in a pioneering article[29] in which he listed the distinguishing characteristics of this section of the workforce. These included not only pay and conditions, but also, 'relations with the social strata above and below' and 'prospects of future advancement for themselves and their children'.[30] He argued that, 'socially speaking the best paid stratum of the working-class merged with what may loosely be called the lower middle class', but 'if the boundaries of the labour aristocracy were fluid on one side of its territory they were precise on the other'.[31] However, Hobsbawm's only evidence was some very limited material on the social background of pupil teachers and the attitude of nineteenth-century trade unions. Also, in suggesting that the relationship between the labour aristocracy and 'higher strata' worsened at the end of the nineteenth century he was willing to concede that, 'Here we are on badly surveyed territory, for little is known about such subjects as the prospects of promotion of "rising out of the working class" and about similar subjects'.[32] It was not until his thesis was tested in a number of local studies that some statistics were collected on the scale of movement into and out of this sector.

In his work on early and mid-Victorian Kentish London, Crossick provided a limited amount of evidence of occupational and marital mobility which highlighted the degree of continuity at the top and bottom of the working class and appeared to substantiate the claim that labour aristocrats' contacts upwards were more fluid than those with sectors below them. His figures also suggested slightly more association with higher strata and increasing social distance between skilled and unskilled families over time.[33] Further confirmation was supplied by Gray's study of inter-marriage in Edinburgh,[34] but he also showed that the internal barriers to social interaction in the third quarter of the century subsequently began to weaken significantly, and at the same time the rate of labour aristocrat marriage into the lower middle class started to fall.[35] As the British economy came under pressure from overseas competition, employers and the state sought to challenge the privileged work and market positions of the skilled working class. Further prised apart from his master and downgraded in status by the rapid expansion of a hostile white collar stratum, the artisan is seen becoming increasingly 'pressed into a common and apparently inescapable working-class universe';[36] and for Hobsbawm, Gray and others, the broadening class organisation on both the industrial and political fronts in this period is a more or less natural corollary of these structural developments.[37]

Data sources and organisation

Sociological research generates its evidence for both inter- and intragenerational mobility mostly through the sample survey conducted by means of a taped interview or a questionnaire. Historians, however, cannot interrogate their witnesses in such a manner, and must turn instead to sets of data often collected for quite different purposes. In this study we have made use of the requirement of the 1836 Registration of Births, Deaths and Marriages Act that marriage registers should record the occupations of the partners and their parents. Each wedding thus provided a snapshot of occupational movement between the generations, as well as associated information on residence, age and literacy. The nature of these data introduce methodological issues which are common to this sort of analysis.[38] A sample of 10,000 entries was taken from ten Registration Districts in England between 1839 and 1914.[39]

The concept of 'mobility' presupposes the existence of categories between which movement can take place, and in this case our raw material consists of occupations of the groom, his father and his father-in-law (the occupation of the bride was rarely recorded). Yet the monitoring of transitions between the thousands of job titles thrown up by the registers can only have limited meaning without some grouping of occupational information which takes account of broader characteristics of the economy and society under consideration. If we accept Sorokin's assertion that 'Any organised social group is always a stratified social body',[40] it follows that notions about the structure of 'social space'[41] are crucial to the study of occupational and social mobility. How and where we decide to divide up social space according to occupational group will not only determine what is meant by 'mobility' but also how 'much' of it there can be.

Sociological studies of mobility display a variety of solutions to the classification of occupations along vertical and hierarchical scales. For the most part it is possible to locate their approaches either in the liberal tradition, where society is seen as a continuum justifying ranking systems based on 'status' or 'prestige', or in a *marxisant* framework within which occupations are grouped into discrete categories based on their 'class position'. Attempts have been made, however, to conflate one type of categorisation with an analytical framework more appropriate to the other. Thus, in his formidable study of structure and mobility in nineteenth-century Marseilles, William Sewell Jr constructs an elaborate occupational status scale by 'scoring' different occupations on the basis of the relative levels of literacy displayed by men in different jobs, together with the 'prestige' of the witnesses they attracted to their weddings and the employment status of their wives. He then discusses mobility in terms of movement between the peasantry, the urban working class and the bourgeoisie; that is, in terms of class mobility.[42]

For nineteenth-century English society it seems desirable to adopt a system of categorisation which reflects the widespread use of the language of class.[43] However such an approach is fraught with difficulty. In using occupation as an indicator of class[44] rather than of prestige or socio-economic status, Goldthorpe and his associates in the 1970s adopted a sevenfold scheme of class positions adapted from a thirty-six category version of the Hope-Goldthorpe occupational scale.[45] This was designed to provide a high degree of differentiation in terms of both occupational function and employment status, 'which. . .we take as the two major components of class position'.[46] The system is attractive, but impractical for occupational descriptions as laconic as those entered in the marriage registers. Whilst the number of different occupations cited runs into thousands, they rarely identify the precise market positions of a given worker. The description of a cabinet maker on the register could be a small master, a foreman or a journeyman, all of which would affect the man's class position.

As no general scheme of classification sensitive to the bewildering array of nineteenth-century occupations exists, we were therefore faced with the choice of constructing our own occupational hierarchy or searching further beyond the refined frameworks of modern investigations for alternative, simplified twentieth-century schema which we can adapt for our purposes. The first option is only acceptable when dealing with a local economy with a limited range of employment. With more than 30,000 entries from all over the country it was found that the most satisfactory solution was the Registrar-General's occupational and social classification scheme for the 1951 census.[47] Here many thousands of job titles are organised into 981 occupational groups which are further divided up into twenty-eight occupational orders. Most importantly, each occupational group is additionally coded for one of five broad-based 'classes', or as we prefer to call them, class sectors, which divide the non-manual middle class between professional/higher occupations and 'intermediate' or petit bourgeois occupations – sectors I and II – and the manual working class into skilled, semi-skilled or unskilled occupations – sectors III, IV and V.[48] Here, the criteria by which occupational 'unit groups' are allocated to classes are much less sharply defined than in Goldthorpe's scheme, but in practice it would appear that the same principal conditions apply.[49] The fit between the 1951 and nineteenth-century occupational worlds was not perfect, but there were surprisingly few anomalies, and the task of making minor adjustments to the coding paled into insignificance in the face of the advantage of a ready-made, comprehensive, and machine readable system. The Keele data were categorised and coded accordingly, placed on file at the University of Manchester Regional Computer Centre and analysed using the SPSS and SPSSX statistical packages.[50]

Intergenerational outflow mobility

We begin by mapping the extent and direction of mobility between the generations, in broad class sector terms, across the entire sample. Table 1 is an *outflow* matrix describing the *distribution* of grooms from different sector backgrounds. The clustering of figures along the diagonal, which shows the percentage of men who follow in their father's footsteps, highlights the essential structural stability of English society in this period. Throughout the sample population six out of every ten men experienced no change in terms of their immediate social background, with those from the skilled and unskilled sectors of the working class particularly unlikely to move away from their respective class sector origins. Yet if the impression is one of relative constancy, the table also shows that this society was far from stagnant. Whilst less than three in ten men from skilled working-class backgrounds could expect mobility in class or class sector terms, at least half of

Table 1

Class distribution of grooms by class of father, 1839–1914

		Son's class sector (percentage by row)						
		I	*II*	*III*	*IV*	*V*	%	*N*
	I	42.8	33.2	15.9	4.3	3.8	(2.0)	202
Father's	II	2.7	50.1	25.9	12.2	9.1	(17.3)	1767
class	III	0.3	6.7	72.9	10.2	9.9	(42.0)	4288
sector	IV	0.4	7.3	33.2	45.6	13.4	(11.6)	1188
	V	0.0	2.8	21.2	14.1	61.8	(27.0)	2758
	n	156	1407	4596	1595	2455		10209
	%	(1.5)	(13.8)	(45.0)	(15.6)	(24.0)		

those from the semi-skilled manual sector or from either of the two non-manual sectors could do so.

Turning to more specific relationships, the figures reveal that for those born below it, the line running between the manual working class and non-manual middle class represented a fundamental cleavage in nineteenth-century society. The extent of upward movement across this line was universally restricted, regardless of sector of origin. Moreover, if an individual with working-class credentials was lucky enough to be amongst the one in twenty of his generation crossing this social barrier, the overwhelming likelihood (twenty to one on if he were a betting man) was that his achievement would extend no further than the corner shop or the clerk's stool. Here we have some confirmation of Perkin's 'football pools winner' analogy. The myth of the self-made man, dragging himself up from rags to riches, was just that. Less than one in a thousand sons of the labouring poor made the transition from class sector V to class sector I, and we have to remember that our sector I is not a classic elite, but a much broader-based category with its foundations in the entrepreneurial and professional middle class.

Yet if the sons of working men were united in their class prospects, within their class they were deeply divided. This was no homogeneous proletarian mass; working-class individuals were not equally likely to have their origin in any class sector. Internally, as indicated by the father–son continuity in sectors III and V, the class was sharply differentiated about the axis of skill. Only the semi-skilled showed signs of 'homogeneity' having origins in a wide range of class sectors. At either end of the working-class spectrum, men's horizons were overwhelmingly those of the sector into which they were born.

That said, such division did not mean isolation. The amount of internal movement, that is between skill sectors, was far more extensive than journeys out of the class as a whole. Only five in a hundred labouring men escaped from their class but one in three was mobile elswhere within it. Downward mobility from the skilled sector was unlikely, but it was hardly rare, and the one in five who made such a drop were as likely to fall right down into unskilled company as they were to end up in class sector IV. Lower in the class spectrum, opportunities for advancement were not inconsiderable. One in three with semi-skilled backgrounds had climbed up into skilled occupations by the time they came to take a bride, and they outnumbered those unable, at least, to maintain their position by almost three to one. Similarly, thirteen times as many men born into class V (35.3 per cent) were upwardly mobile within the working class as made it out of the class altogether, and nearly two-thirds of these were mobile as far as the skilled sector.

For opposite reasons, the view from the other side of the manual/non-manual division was almost equally unpropitious, certainly for those close up against the fence. This was a semi-permeable membrane. In both non-manual sectors, more were mobile than not, which led to a surprising degree of downward class mobility however, although one in four skidded right across the class divide, men born into the occupational elite were far less likely than their lower middle-class contemporaries to make the big drop. More than half falling from class sector I found places in class sector II, so that 'elite' sons as a whole were just over 75 per cent class static in the wider non-manual sense. Moreover, of those who were sent crashing into the working class, a large majority had their fall broken in class sector III, where they at least retained the relative respectability of a skilled position. By comparison, the lower-middle class was strongly associated with the world of manual labour. Whilst only three in a hundred men born into class sector II were ascendant within the non-manual grades, nearly one in two had become downwardly mobile into the working class by the time of their marriage; and even if skilled occupations were again by far the most likely destinations, more than one in five of the sector as a whole, 40 per cent of all those making the drop, ended up in semi- and unskilled work. A man born into the lower-middle class was as exposed to the descent into the lower reaches of manual labour as his skilled working-class counterpart. The dearth of movement in the other direction, from II into I, indicates a multiple barrier effect where upward mobility is concerned. Even were the son of a worker to make it across the manual/non-manual line into a low-grade 'white collar' or petty bourgeois occupation, the chances of his son, in turn, maintaining that upward momentum and securing a position within class sector I remained almost negligible.

Intergenerational inflow mobility

How this pattern of movement away from one generation worked itself out in the composition of the next can be seen in Table 2, an 'inflow' matrix, which describes how each class sector was

Table 2
Class composition of grooms by class of father, 1839–1914

		Son's class sector (percentage by column)						
		I	*II*	*III*	*IV*	*V*	%	*n*
	I	57.1	4.9	0.7	0.6	0.3	(2.0)	208
Father's	II	30.8	62.9	10.0	13.5	6.5	(17.3)	1767
class	III	8.3	20.5	68.0	27.5	17.2	(42.0)	4288
sector	IV	3.2	6.2	8.6	34.0	6.5	(11.6)	1188
	V	0.6	5.5	12.8	24.4	69.5	(27.0)	2758
	n	156	1407	4596	1595	2455		10209
	%	(1.5)	(13.8)	(45.0)	(15.6)	(24.0)		

recruited on the basis of its members' origins. Both class sectors I and II show strong tendencies to recruit from amongst their own. With well over half the grooms in either case being second generation men, they were clearly social formations of considerable structural cohesion. In terms of contact with 'outsiders' there was, as in Table 1, a basic divergence. The external component of the elite was overwhelmingly non-manual, whilst the bulk of new entrants in the lower-middle class were workers' sons. The relative sizes of the sectors was central to the structuring of this recruitment. Both the non-manual sectors recruited more heavily from the much larger manual community than the very low rates of upward outflow amongst workers' sons would seem to allow. Of the 8,234 sons of working-class fathers, just nineteen made it up into class sector I, but they took up as many as one in eight of all available elite positions. Within the lower-middle class, such recruitment made a yet larger impression, with roughly a third of all class sector II positions occupied by the sons of workers. Although marginally less 'able' to break the bonds of their manual upbringing than their semi-skilled peers, the sheer volume of skilled sector sons ensured that they were twice as common inside the middle class as those of class sectors IV and V combined. The greater weight of the petit bourgeois inside the non-manual community meant that only one in twenty of their members were sons of elite fathers. At the same time, the more limited outward movement in the opposite direction translated into a much higher rate of recruitment. Class sector I drew nearly 90 per cent of its total complement and 70 per cent of its external recruits from the non-manual world, the equivalent proportions in class sector II being two thirds and just 13 per cent.

Below the line of manual/non-manual division, the very high rates of inheritance in sectors III and V translated into equally high rates of self-recruitment in each generation. Sons followed fathers, and worked predominantly alongside men with the same class sector background, strengthening the divide between the skilled and the unskilled. However, what still bound all the sons of manual fathers together was the common unlikelihood of encountering the offspring of white-collar fathers. Even the anomalously cosmopolitan semi-skilled sector, which drew in twice as many of its personnel from without as from within, a rate double that of class sectors III and V, took in four out of every five of its outsiders from elsewhere within the working class, rendering it over 85 per cent manual in origin. Right across the working class, inflow from the elite remained minimal, ranging from a recruitment rate of 0.7 per cent to the skilled sector to 0.3 per cent to the unskilled. Again, differentials in class size counteracted the substantial outflow from the top end of society into the manual sector and particularly the skilled grades. Even the substantial volume of downward mobility from the lower-middle class appears to have made little impression on the manual cohesion of the three working-class sectors. Only in the case of class sector IV was recruitment from class sector II greater than one in ten.

Taking the working class as a whole, three out of every four men drawn in from outside individual sectors came from elsewhere within the class. Even the relatively exclusive skilled sector drew in over a fifth of its men from below. Despite the much stronger rate of semi-skilled outflow up to class sector III, it was men with labouring backgrounds who predominated within this contingent of upgraded men, taking up one in eight of all available skilled positions in the filial generation. The disparity in sector sizes also influenced the composition of the semi-skilled which served as a staging post between the cohesive occupational cultures of the skilled and unskilled. Neither class sector III nor sector V sent more than 15 per cent of its sons into sector IV, yet in the sons' generation men from immediately above and below each occupy a quarter or more of the semi-skilled positions. As might be expected, the unskilled sector contained fewest entrants from outside the working class, recruiting no less than 93 per cent of its total complement from a manual background of some kind. Again, sector size differentials meant that although sons of semi-skilled workers showed a greater rate of decline, there were three times as many sons of skilled workers within class sector V.

The pattern of sector interchange between generations displayed by Tables 1 and 2 indicates that the degree of working-class integration with the non-manual world was at best slight, and with its upper echelons, virtually non-existent. The barrier between the classes was high, and below it was to be found a body of men whose perspectives and origins were largely confined to the sphere of manual labour. The impression of working-class homogeneity is qualified, however, by the complex system of cohesion and movement which characterised its internal relations. At this level, fathers could still entertain real hopes and serious fears for their sons, whose workmates would not always have shared their degree of good or bad fortune. Whilst the working class was sharply divided by 'skill', there was a sufficient degree of movement between the sectors to influence the perceived career horizons. Thus a skilled man's son could grow up in the knowledge that he was fairly safe from demotion, but if he did follow in his father's footsteps he would see one in five of his contemporaries lose their status as skilled men, nearly three times as many as were heard of moving up to the next class. Likewise a labourer's son could certainly expect to follow his father into unskilled work but would see from the amount of movement around him that it was not inevitable, and even that 'respectability' in the occupational sense was far from unobtainable. In between, for men born into the semi-skilled sector, to move was more normal than to stay put. The degree of intergenerational redistribution meant that those who did follow in their fathers' footsteps experienced more than occasional 'contact' with 'outsiders' from elsewhere within the class. This was spectacularly so in the case of the semi-skilled sector but even the overwhelmingly second generation skilled and unskilled sectors witnessed significant incursions of first generation men, enough to dispel the image of the skilled sector as a closed shop, or of the unskilled sector as a self-perpetuating proletarian rump.

Patterns of movement over time

The tensions between mobility and stability are further revealed by Table 3, which provides a simplified measure of the changing pattern across the period. This time series re-emphasises the

Table 3

Total mobility rate by marriage cohort[51]

	Date of marriage					
	1839, 1844 1849, 1854	*1859, 1864 1869, 1874*	*1879, 1884 1889, 1894*	*1899, 1904 1909, 1914*	*all*	*n.*
Percentage of all grooms in:						
(a) same class sector as father	67.8	65.2	60.8	54.0	62.2	6345
(b) different class sector from father	32.2	34.8	39.2	46.0	37.8	3864
(upwardly mobile)	15.0	17.7	19.6	22.2	18.5	1890
(downwardly mobile)	17.2	17.1	19.6	3.8	19.3	1974
n.	2848	2846	2352	2523		10209

residual stability of English society in the nineteenth and early twentieth centuries; at no point do the mobile outnumber the static. Nevertheless, there is a clear and increasing tendency for society to become more mobile. One third of the earliest cohort of grooms experienced some degree of class sector mobility, and by the turn of the century the ratio of movement to stasis had increased to nearly one in two. In the context of Perkin's speculations, upward mobility in this general sense, with no precise indication of where sons were coming from or going to, does seem to be high but so too does the volume of downward mobility.

The gain to the sons of workers from the loosening up of society must be kept in perspective. Table 4 shows that although there was a tendency for upward class mobility to increase quite extensively in proportional terms,[52] right up to the early 1900s the absolute rate of movement out of the working class remained little more than a trickle. On the eve of the First World War, the great majority of the sons of working-class fathers were destined to become working-class fathers themselves. Much more significant was the reduction in barriers between skill sectors within the class. Even before mid-century, intra-class movement was far from insignificant and throughout the period over 80 per cent of all inter-sector transitions involving working-class sons took place amongst the manual grades. By 1900, whilst most workers' sons still experienced no change in skill status, the rate of internal movement had risen to substantially more than one in three. Here there was a considerable excess of upward over downward moves, the size of the differential holding up right through to the 1890s, after which there was a significant acceleration in the volume of intra-class demotion.

Whilst we cannot deal directly with Perkin's assertion that the amount of working-class upward mobility was less in the mid-Victorian period than at the end of the eighteenth century, it is evident that the 1860s and 1870s did not represent a low point in a process of decline. Whether we choose to consider sector mobility or class mobility more generally, the clear tendency is for such movement to expand throughout. Accepting a rather broader time span for the process of industrialisation than allowed by Sanderson, it is apparent that in the longer term the developing capitalist economy began to provide *more* rather than less chances for working-class advancement. Nevertheless as the chances of rising within the class, and even of leaving behind the world of manual

Table 4

Working class outflow/inflow mobility by marriage cohort

	1839, 1844 1849, 1854		*1859, 1864 1869, 1874*		*1879, 1884 1889, 1894*		*1899, 1904 1909, 1914*		*All years* %		*All years* *n.*	
	out	*in*	*out*	*in*	*out*	*in*	*out*	*in*	*out*	*in*	*out*	*in*
(a) Class mobility												
I	0.1	0.5	0.2	0.3	0.2	0.8	0.5	0.7	0.2	0.6	19	50
II	4.1	10.2	4.9	8.4	6.2	10.1	7.1	9.7	5.5	9.6	453	834
Static	95.8	89.3	94.9	91.3	93.6	89.1	92.4	89.6	94.3	89.8	7762	7762
(b) Internal mobility												
Static	73.4	68.4	67.9	65.3	63.4	60.3	55.0	53.3	65.2	62.1	5371	5371
Mobile	22.4	20.9	27.0	25.9	30.2	28.8	37.5	36.3	29.0	27.7	2391	2391
(c) Direction of internal movement												
Above	13.8	12.9	15.8	15.2	17.9	17.0	19.5	18.9	16.6	15.8	1370	1370
Below	8.6	8.0	11.1	10.7	12.3	11.8	18.0	17.4	12.4	11.9	1021	1021

Key:

Class mobility	out:	movement from working-class to middle-class sectors
	in:	entrants into working-class from middle-class sectors
Internal mobility	out:	movement between working-class sectors
	in:	entrants from other working-class sectors
Direction of Internal movt.	out:	direction of movement between working-class sectors
	in:	origin of entrants from other working-class sectors.

labour altogether, increased, so did the likelihood of status degradation, particularly towards the end of the period.

Viewed in terms of inflow, Table 4 provides a simplified indication of the changing composition of the working class. It shows the manual sector retaining a high degree of coherence throughout the period. In contrast to the slow rise in upward mobility, dilution from above shows little change. There was no tendency towards greater class heterogeneity. Given that the absolute extent of upward outflow, though expanding, never exceeded 7.6 per cent, the identity of the Victorian and Edwardian working class as a manual formation remained largely undisturbed. Internally, by contrast, the decline in sector bonding suggested by the outflow columns is confirmed. Those making no move in each generation worked with an increasingly cosmopolitan peer group. For the working class as a whole, the near doubling of in-migrant populations in the space of seventy-five years suggests a substantial process of homogenisation.

A more detailed perspective on working-class sectionalism across the period can be gained from Table 5. Men from all three sectors become more likely to cross the manual/non-manual divide as time goes on. The most rapid increase in such movement amongst the sons of the skilled was the first half of the period, coinciding with the mid-Victorian expansion of the shopocracy and an apparently quite novel tendency to move into white collar employment. Overall the sons of semi-skilled men were most likely to take this latter route, whilst those few making the long trek up from class sector V were, until the end of the period, confined to more traditional pathways. All sectors benefited from the rapid expansion of white-collar work at the end of the century, which probably accounts for the overall increases in upward movement amongst semi- and unskilled men's sons in cohorts three and four respectively. However, it was from within the skilled sector that the strongest and most consistent pattern of movement into white-collar work across the period took place.

Within the class there was an increase in long range movement in both directions, but particularly from the bottom up; the proportion of class sector III men becoming unskilled increased by a fifth, whilst the numbers making the reverse journey rose by 60 per cent. However the most substantial change involved 'half-way' movement into semi-skilled employment which in both cases accelerated throughout and as much as trebled across the period as a whole. From within the semi-skilled sector there was a significant

Table 5

Working-class sector outflow/inflow mobility by marriage cohort

	1839, 1844 1849, 1854		*1859, 1864 1869, 1874*		*1879, 1884 1889, 1894*		*1899, 1904 1909, 1914*		*(all periods) n.*	
	out	*in*	*out*	*in*	*out*	*in*	*out*	*in*	*out*	*in*
Skilled										
I	0.1	0.7	0.4	0.3	0.2	1.1	0.5	0.8	13	33
II	4.9	11.1	6.4	8.5	7.5	10.4	8.2	9.7	289	458
III	80.7	69.9	75.3	70.0	72.0	66.9	63.6	64.6	3124	3124
IV	5.2	5.8	8.1	8.1	11.0	9.1	16.5	11.9	439	395
V	9.1	12.6	9.8	12.9	9.3	12.5	11.1	13.0	423	586
n.	1135	1311	1036	1112	975	1049	1142	1124	4288	4596
Semi-skilled										
I	0.4	1.0	0.4	0.6	0.7	0.7	0.3	0.2	5	9
II	6.4	17.0	5.1	12.5	8.6	14.8	8.5	11.2	87	216
III	30.5	19.0	33.1	24.4	33.9	26.4	34.6	35.3	395	439
IV	47.8	38.3	46.7	36.9	45.4	31.4	43.7	31.6	542	542
V	14.9	24.8	14.7	25.6	11.4	26.7	12.9	21.7	159	389
n.	249	311	272	344	280	405	387	535	1188	1595
Unskilled										
I	0.0	0.0	0.0	0.3	0.0	0.2	0.2	1.1	1	8
II	2.4	6.5	2.6	6.1	3.0	5.9	3.6	7.9	77	160
III	18.0	12.1	19.9	15.5	21.5	17.9	28.9	28.8	586	423
IV	8.4	4.4	12.1	6.1	17.7	6.3	23.0	11.3	389	159
V	71.2	77.0	65.4	72.0	57.9	69.6	44.4	50.8	1705	1705
n.	918	849	725	658	610	507	505	441	2758	2455

increase in movement up into skilled work but no expansion in downward mobility.

By the end of the period inter-generational continuity amongst the skilled had declined from four-fifths to two-thirds and the proportions heading downwards had risen from one in seven to one in four. Yet this still has to be considered a very stable and coherent culture. The son of a skilled man had a far better than even chance of following in his father's footsteps and there had been no fundamental shift in the composition of his workmates. Dilution from below had increased, but only from almost one in five to one in four, and this was accounted for by the upwardly mobile sons of semi-skilled men. The unskilled sector was shrinking as it sent increasing percentages upward, and so the proportion of men with unskilled origins within the skilled sector remained constant.

The effects of the homogenisation process were more sharply felt towards the bottom of the social scale. The semi-skilled sector, relatively fluid and cosmopolitan throughout, maintained its contact with the lower reaches of the class and continued to cultivate its association with the stratum above. But the greatest transformation was to the identity and integrity of the labouring sector which had been 70 per cent inter-generationally static and over three-quarters self-recruiting before mid-century. By the end of the period there were more sons leaving for enhanced manual futures alone than staying put, and, in terms of recruitment, the sector now took in virtually half of its membership from above and nearly one in three from the top end of the manual grades, compared to initial rates of a quarter and one in eight.

A labour aristocracy?

Thus far, the evidence gives qualified support to the existence and proposed 'chronological trajectory' of a labour aristocracy.[53] There was throughout the second half of the nineteenth century a distinct skilled culture within the working class. However, the limited extent of upward movement and the restricted dilution from above hardly suggests a merging with the lower-middle class.[54] The chances of crossing the class boundary were one in five and the presence, within the filial generation of skilled men, of a similar proportion of upwardly mobile outsiders indicates that the

Table 6

Skilled working-class outflow/inflow by marriage cohort (decades)

	1840s		*1850s*		*1860s*		*1870s*		*1880s*		*1890s*		*1900s*	
	out	*in*	*out*	*in*	*out*	*in*	*out*	*in*	*out*	*in*	*out*	*in*	*out*	*in*
I	0.2	0.8	0.3	0.3	0.4	0.4	0.0	0.9	0.4	0.8	0.4	1.2	0.7	0.9
II	5.5	11.6	5.8	9.4	7.5	8.7	6.3	8.4	7.6	10.5	7.8	10.3	7.8	11.8
III	81.0	69.4	79.1	73.7	71.2	70.1	77.2	68.7	72.3	67.4	67.3	66.1	62.8	63.5
IV	4.2	7.3	6.3	6.0	9.0	6.8	8.2	8.6	10.5	8.8	14.4	10.3	18.4	10.4
V	9.1	10.9	8.6	10.6	11.9	14.0	8.2	13.3	9.2	12.6	10.1	12.1	10.3	13.4
n	548	640	573	615	521	529	474	533	488	524	562	572	565	559

boundaries beneath the sector were neither as fixed nor precise as Hobsbawm originally suggested.[55]

Although it shows a tendency towards increasing internal recruitment through to the end of the 1850s, the more detailed decade analysis of skilled sector mobility patterns in Table 6 confirms that working-class sectionalism did not suddenly develop out of a more homogenous formation in the manner suggested by Foster.[56] Instead of growing 'exclusivity' the consistently high rates of father–son continuity were at their peak around mid-century. There was a sharp increase in upward mobility generally into the mid-Victorian period, but thereafter such movement was never closed off. A break in the pattern occurred in the 1870s but was not followed by the expected contraction. Rather, the last two decades of the nineteenth century witnessed the recovery of a slowly expanding upward trend. In terms of inflow, contact with the non-manual world was actually at its lowest in the classical period of the labour aristocracy. The 1880s and 1890s certainly look to have been the key decades in the acceleration of downward movement from the skilled sector, but for those successfully following in their fathers' footsteps there was only a marginal increase in the volume of incursion from below after the 1860s, with dilution from the very bottom of the social scale remaining virtually constant across the last quarter of the nineteenth century.

But the skilled sector defined by the census classification is, of course, much broader than the privileged grouping to which the concept of the labour aristocracy usually refers. Without a great deal of additional information on wage rates, conditions of work and cultural affiliations for each of the 4,000 or so class III men in the sample it is impossible to identify accurately the size and composition of this elite. Nevertheless, the Registrar General's more finely graded occupational classification enables us to examine the mobility of sons born to fathers in a number of specific trades usually included within the skilled elite.

Table 7 shows the combined mobility profile of several trades included in Hobsbawm's 'super aristocracy' between the 1840s and the First World War.[57] Those born into this group of elite occupations were over 50 per cent more upwardly mobile than all skilled workers' sons, and left the class at double the rate of working-class sons as a whole.[58] There was less downward mobility generally from these trades and, in particular, less movement down into the unskilled grades. In terms of composition the pattern is confirmed of greater, but still by no means extensive,

Table 7
Labour aristocrat outflow/inflow by marriage cohort

	1839, 1844 1849, 1854		*1859, 1864 1869, 1874*		*1879, 1884 1889, 1894*		*1899, 1904 1909, 1914*		*All years*	
	out	*in*	*out*	*in*	*out*	*in*	*out*	*in*	*N*	%
I/II	7.4	19.7	10.7	13.6	6.6	14.0	17.3	16.7	36/55	11.1/15.8
III	83.8	71.8	68.0	63.6	69.7	62.4	63.5	66.7	227/229	70.3/65.8
IV	2.9	5.6	13.3	12.5	15.8	11.8	12.5	8.3	37/34	11.5/ 9.8
V	5.9	2.8	8.0	10.2	7.9	11.8	6.7	8.3	23/30	7.1/ 8.6
n	68	71	75	88	76	93	104	96	323/348	

integration with the non-manual world, and rather less association with those of more lowly origin.

Again the very strong degree of skilled sector stability at the beginning of the period suggests that an elite existed within the working class well before the heyday of British industrial capitalism. The significant increase in upward mobility into the mid-Victorian period does lend some support to the idea of increasing advantage and differentiation, but the other side of the equation is lacking; in the same cohort the proportion of men becoming downwardly mobile, mostly into semi-skilled positions, trebled. There is evidence of the other dimension of the proposed homogenisation process in the third cohort when the rate of upward mobility dropped back, but whilst the total volume of downward movement continued to expand, there was no further increase in the rate of descent into the labouring sector. As we move into the early twentieth century the argument appears to break down completely. The proportion falling into the lower ranks of the working class began to decline and the chances of becoming class mobile increased sharply from one in fifteen to one in six.

Although the pattern of recruitment from above is divergent over the first three cohorts there are, once more, strong similarities between the outflow and inflow profiles over time. Just as there was a tendency for the sons of men in these elite groups to become more downwardly mobile over the latter part of the nineteenth century, but for this trend to cease after the turn of the century, so the rate of incursion from below rises substantially and then falls in the final cohort. Moreover, inflow from above also increases in the 1899–1914 period, mirroring the rise in upward outflow.

Conclusions

In volume IX of *Life and Labour of People in London*, Charles Booth wrote:

> When we endeavour to trace the road by which each individual has travelled or is travelling the dynamic forces at work are impressed upon us. Together with the permanence of the industrial type, we become conscious of the incessant change that is taking place in the conditions of a large proportion of the individual lives. Restlessness, ambition, ability, folly, hesitancy,

indifference or dullness, carry men along, up and down, and down and up again, in the industrial as in other roads of life.[59]

This paper has examined only one dimension of this road, the journey undertaken by sons away from their fathers. It has established that whilst Booth was right to draw attention to the incidence of mobility, it was neither as extensive nor as unstructured as his observation implied. Within the working class, the horizons of most families were confined to their own sectors, and beyond it the greener pastures of the middle class could only be reached through a high mountain pass. An equivalent structuring of recruitment consolidated the manual identity of the working class but also reinforced its internal polarities. Over the period as a whole, an increasing number of journeys were undertaken, and as a result the distinctions between the manual grades began to blur. Nevertheless, with the skilled sector retaining much of its earlier coherence, and only marginal changes occurring in the relationship between classes, the basic features of a divided, hierarchical society remained in place.

All that may be said for Smiles's land of boundless opportunity was that industrial capitalism was moving towards rather than away from his vision. Whether it was doing so by breaking down the structure of advantage and disadvantage between men of differing social backgrounds or by redistributing jobs across sectors is a complicated question to which a comprehensive answer is attempted elsewhere.[60] Structural shifts have undoubtedly contributed to the absolute rates of mobility we have observed in our sample. As the secondary and in particular the tertiary industries began to grow at the expense of the primary there was a 30 per cent increase in the relative size of the lower-middle class, and a 95 per cent growth in the semi-skilled working class.

A simple impression of the influence of structure on trends in particular relationships can be gained from disparity ratios between outflow percentages which indicate 'whether or not changes in the structure of objective mobility opportunities over time are being equally reflected in the mobility experience of individuals of all origins alike'.[61]

In the case of access to the expanding lower-middle class, Table 8 shows a clear decline in the relative advantage of grooms who are born into class sector II over men from working-class backgrounds, which suggests that the increasing amounts of observed upward class mobility were not purely a function of the changing shape of

Table 8

Disparity ratios showing the chances of the sons of working-class men being found in the lower-middle class relative to those of grooms born into class sector II (chances of working-class men set at 1 in each case)

	Date of marriage			
	1839, 1844 1849, 1854	*1859, 1864 1869, 1874*	*1879, 1884 1889, 1894*	*1899, 1904 1909, 1914*
Sons of II v	9.2	8.3	6.9	6.3
Sons of III	1	1	1	1
Sons of II v	7.0	10.3	6.0	6.0
Sons of IV	1	1	1	1
Sons of II v	18.8	22.0	17.2	14.3
Sons of V	1	1	1	1

the first industrial nation. Nevertheless, if these figures reveal a growth in 'openness' between class sector II and the manual grades beneath it, the continuing size of the disparities in favour of the former indicates that, even for rewards substantially inferior to those obtained by the Smilesian heroes of *Self Help*, the competition remained a profoundly unequal one.

Notes

1 See the Series Editor's introduction to A. Heath, *Social Mobility* (London: Fontana, 1981).
2 Plato, *The Republic*, translated, with an introduction, by Desmond Lee (Harmondsworth: Penguin, 1974).
3 For an important criticism of the theoretical concentration on stratification and social order in mobility research, to the neglect of the occupational processes upon which studies of 'social' mobility are usually based, see, Geoff Payne, *Mobility and Change in Modern Society* (Basingstoke: Macmillan, 1987).
4 For a summary of work carried out in America and Europe see Hartmut Kaelble, *Social Mobility in Nineteenth and Twentieth Centuries. Europe and America in Comparative Perspective* (Leamington: Berg, 1985). More recent research is surveyed in Andrew Miles and David Vincent (eds.), *Building European Society* (Manchester University Press: Manchester, 1991).
5 John H. Goldthorpe (in collaboration with Catriona Llewellyn and Clive Payne), *Social Mobility and Class Structure in Modern Britain* (Oxford: Clarendon Press, 1980) p. 253.
6 Andrew Miles, 'Social Mobility in Victorian and Edwardian Britain', Doctoral Dissertation, University of Keele, forthcoming.
7 For Geoff Payne, this still has to be done satisfactorily for twentieth-century Britain. See his critique of the Glass study, Payne, *op. cit.*, chapter 6.
8 Goldthorpe *et al.*, *op. cit.*, chapter 1, on which the remainder of this section is

based; F. van Heek, 'Some Introductory Remarks on Social Mobility and Class Structure', in *Transactions of the Third World Congress of Sociology*, vol. iii (London: International Sociological Association, 1956), pp. 130–1.

9 See his comments on the fluid nature of American society where, in contrast to more venerable European social formations, he argues that classes *in* themselves had not yet become structures settled enough to generate consciousness of shared interest and the necessity for political action, or classes *for* themselves, thus accounting for the under-developed state of the American labour movement. Karl Marx, 'The Eighteenth Brumaire of Louis Bonaparte' in Karl Marx and Friedrich Engels, *Selected Works*, vol. 1 (Moscow: Foreign Languages Publishing House, 1962) p. 255; 'Wages, Prices and Profit', *Selected Works*, p. 444; his letter to Joseph Weydemeyer, 5 March 1852, in Karl Marx and Friedrich Engels, *Collected Works*, vol. 39 (London: Lawrence and Wishart, 1963) pp. 60–6.

10 *Capital*, vol. III, p. 293.

11 Pitrim Sorokin, *Social Mobility* (New York: Harper, 1927) and see, for example, S.M. Lipset and R. Bendix, *Social Mobility in Industrial Society* (London: Heinemann, 1959).

12 P.M. Blau and O.D. Duncan, *The American Occupational Structure* (New York: Wiley, 1967).

13 D.V. Glass (ed.), *Social Mobility*, (London: Routledge and Kegan Paul, 1954).

14 See, William Peterson, 'Is America still the Land of Opportunity?', *Commentary*, vol. 16, (1953). Cited in Goldthorpe *et al.*, *op. cit.*, p. 13, note 49.

15 S. Thernstrom, *Poverty and Progress: Social Mobility in a Nineteenth-Century City* (Cambridge, Mass.: Harvard University Press, 1964), p. 1. In this first study of the small New England community of Newburyport, Thernstrom's findings led him to refute the 'blocked mobility' hypothesis . . . 'it is difficult to resist the conclusion that chances to rise from the very bottom of the social ladder in the United States have not declined visibly since the nineteenth century; they seem, in fact, to have increased moderately in recent decades. To say this is not to say that opportunities are boundless in present-day America . . . the climb from the bottom rungs of the social ladder is not often rapid or easy, but it *never was* . . .' (pp. 222–3). His more extensive follow up study of Boston caused him to reappraise these conclusions, 'The American class system, in short, allowed substantial privilege for the privileged and extensive opportunity for the underprivileged to coexist simultaneously', and to speculate that whilst the 'open' new world/'closed' old world dichotomy could not be sustained . . . 'future research will on the whole support the contention that the American social order has been distinctly more fluid than that of most European countries, and that the availability of superior opportunities for individual self-advancement in the United States did significantly impede the formation of class-based protest movement that sought fundamental alterations in the economic system.' See, *The Other Bostonians. Poverty and Progress in the American Metropolis 1880–1970*, (Cambridge, Mass.: Harvard University Press, 1973) pp. 258–9. Although there are obvious problems with comparability, when placed against his figures for absolute rates of intergenerational movement in Chapter 5, the results of the Keele study would certainly seem to bear him out.

16 For the major findings of this study see Goldthorpe *et al.*, *op cit*.

17 See, Hartmut Kaelble, *Historical Research on Social Mobility. Western Europe and the U.S.A. in the Nineteenth and Twentieth Centuries* (London: Croom Helm, 1981), pp. 41–4.

18 See, for a fuller discussion, J.F.C. Harrison, 'The Victorian Gospel of Success', *Victorian Studies*, vol. 1 (December, 1957).

19 Samuel Smiles, *Self Help* (London: Murray, 1859) p. 234.

20 Harold Perkin, *Origins of Modern English Society* (London: Ark Edition, 1985) p. 225.
21 Ibid., p. 424.
22 Ibid., pp. 124–33, p. 424.
23 Charlotte Erickson, *British Industrialists: Steel and Hosiery, 1850–1950* (Cambridge: Cambridge University Press, 1959).
24 Perkin, p. 427.
25 Michael Sanderson, 'Literacy and Social Mobility in the Industrial Revolution in England', *Past Present*, 56 (1972). See also Thomas Laqueur's review and Sanderson's rejoinder in *Past and Present*, 64 (1974).
26 Apart from this, and numerous narrow studies of 'elite' recruitment, limited, localised or incidental data on social mobility have been presented in a range of work. See, for example, S.J. Chapman and W. Abbot, 'The Tendency of Children to Enter Their Fathers' Trades', *Journal of the Royal Statistical Society*, 76, (1913); Michael Anderson, *Family Structure in Nineteenth Century Lancashire* (Cambridge: Cambridge University Press, 1971); Brian Preston, 'Occupations of Father and Son in Mid-Victorian England', Reading University, Department of Geography, *Geographical Papers*, (1977); P.E. Razzell, 'Statistics and English Historical Sociology' in R.M. Hartwell (ed.) *The Industrial Revolution* (Oxford: Blackwell, 1970); G. Crossick, 'The Emergence of the Lower Middle Class in Britain: a Discussion', in Crossick (ed.), *The Lower Middle Class in Britain, 1870–1914* (London: Croom Helm, 1977).
27 F. Engels, 'England in 1845 and 1885', incorporated into the Preface of the 1892 English edition of, *The Condition of the Working Class in England*, reprinted in Karl Marx and Friedrich Engels, *On Britain* (Moscow: Foreign Languages Publishing House, 1953), pp. 28–33.
28 V.I. Lenin, 'Imperialism: The Highest Stage of Capitalism' in *Selected Works* (Peking: Foreign Languages Press, 1975), pp. 128–31.
29 E.J. Hobsbawm, 'The Labour Aristocracy in Nineteenth-Century Britain' in his, *Labouring Men* (London: Weidenfeld and Nicolson, 1964).
30 Ibid., p. 273.
31 Ibid., p. 275. 'An artisan or craftsman was not under any circumstances to be confused with a labourer.' He suggested, however, that between these two poles there existed an intermediate group who 'belonged to neither' but 'shaded into each'. More recently Hobsbawm has accepted that there may have been rather more interaction between skilled and unskilled, at least from the bottom up, than indicated in his original study. E.J. Hobsbawm, 'Artisans and Labour Aristocrats?' in his, *Worlds of Labour: Further Studies in the History of Labour* (London: Weidenfeld and Nicolson, 1984) p. 265.
32 Hobsbawm, *op. cit.*, 1964, p. 295. The problem is not just one of evidence. If, as Hobsbawm argues, the 'aristocrats' had merged with, or even gained a higher status than sections of the lower middle class (pp. 273–4), it becomes very difficult to employ terms such as 'rising out of the working class' or 'promotion'.
33 Geoffrey Crossick, *An Artisan Elite in Victorian Society* (London: Croom Helm, 1978), chapter 6. It is the figures for intermarriage which suggest this trend. Although there is no clear overall pattern, the figures for intergenerational *occupational* change show several trades suffering increasing incursion from below combined with declining recruitment from above.
34 R.Q. Gray, *The Labour Aristocracy* (Oxford: Clarendon Press, 1976), chapter 5.
35 Ibid., p. 120. 'Analysis of intermarriage confirms the impression of a weakening of social segregation and cultural distinctions within the working class. Whereas the earlier part of the period (based on data for 1865–69) saw the emergence of a distinctive upper artisan stratum, its second half (based on data for 1895–97) saw a blurring – albeit on a limited scale – of the distinctions between working-class strata.' Our brackets. The developmental perspective originally offered by

Hobsbawm suggests that the more fundamental changes occurred on the stratum's upper boundaries, 'by the end of the Edwardian era the gap above the labour aristocracy had widened, though that below it had not yet significantly narrowed.' Hobsbawm, *op. cit.*, 1964, p. 297.

36 E.J. Hobsbawm, 'The Aristocracy of Labour Reconsidered', in Hobsbawm, *op. cit,.*, 1984, p. 251.

37 Hobsbawm, *op. cit.*, 1964, although in his later articles he seems to have shifted to a rather less mechanistic position. As well as 'The Aristocracy of Labour reconsidered', see, 'Debating the Labour Aristocracy' in Hobsbawm, *op. cit.*, 1984, pp. 221–6; Gray, *op. cit.*, chapter 9; for a classic example, see, Standish Meacham, 'English Working-Class Unrest before the First World War', *American Historical Review*, LXXVII, 1972). For a recent reappraisal of the relationship between social structure, culture and working-class politics, see, Michael Savage, *The Dynamics of Working Class Politics. The Labour Movement in Preston, 1880–1940* (Cambridge: Cambridge University Press, 1987). See note 53 below.

38 The main objection to the use of marriage registers for this exercise is that they are biased towards youth; that in most cases there would be scope, at least, for further movement over the remaining part of the grooms' lives. This, in turn, begs the whole thorny question of what constitutes 'origin' and 'destination' in these terms. But it remains the case that marriage register entries are the only long-run quantifiable evidence of intergenerational mobility available to historians which can provide samples of adequate size. Census-tracking, a favoured method in the United States, is time-consuming and suffers from the disappearance of individuals between censuses. Nor does it overcome the snapshot problem as such. The fact that the registers carry information about age is not as helpful as it would, at first, appear. Quite apart from the problem of small and ever-decreasing sub-samples associated with looking at older age groups, the practice of entering one's age in the register was neither consistent over time nor across social categories. The wider study from which this paper comes is using a sample of working-class autobiographies to investigate the question of intragenerational, or 'career', mobility. See, John Burnett, David Vincent and David Mayall (eds), *The Autobiography of the Working Class. An Annotated, Critical Bibliography. Volume I: 1790–1900* (Brighton: The Harvester Press, 1984).

39 For a full description of the procedures involved in collecting these data see, David Vincent, *Literacy and Popular Culture. England 1750–1914* (Cambridge: Cambridge University Press, 1989) Appendix B.

40 Sorokin, *op. cit.*, p. 12.

41 Ibid., p. 3.

42 William H. Sewell, Jr, *Structure and Mobility. The Men and Women of Marseille 1820–1870* (Cambridge: Cambridge University Press, 1985).

43 See, Asa Briggs, 'The Language of Class in Early Nineteenth-Century England', in Asa Briggs and John Saville (eds), *Essays in Labour History* (London: Macmillan, 1967).

44 For a justification, see G. Payne, *op. cit.*, chapter 2. Citing Gosta Carlsson, *Social Mobility and Class Structure* (Lund, Sweden, 1958), Thernstrom writes, 'The historical study of mobility requires the use of an objective criteria of social status. The most convenient of these is occupation. Occupation may be only one variable in a comprehensive theory of class, but it is the variable which includes more, which sets more limits on the other variables than any other criterion of status', Thernstrom, *op. cit.*, 1964, p. 84.

45 See John H. Goldthorpe and Keith Hope, *The Social Grading of Occupations: a New Approach and Scale* (Oxford: Clarendon Press, 1974).

46 Goldthorpe, *et al.*, *op. cit.*, 1980, p. 39.

47 Census 1951, *Classification of Occupations* (HMSO, 1955). See, W.A.

Armstrong, 'The Use of Information about Occupation', in E.A. Wrigley (ed.), *Nineteenth Century Society* (Cambridge: Cambridge University Press, 1972) for further discussion of the suitability of this classification.

48 Nobody entered themselves in the registers as 'unemployed'. For the vast majority of workers in the nineteenth century periods of intermittent or short-term unemployment were the norm. It would seem that the 'institutionalisation' of unemployment is a twentieth-century phenomenon.

49 *Census* 1951, p. vii; Armstrong, ibid., pp. 202–3.

50 *Statistical Package for the Social Sciences* and *Statistical Package for the Social Sciences Extended*.

51 In each district samples were taken at five year intervals between 1839 and 1914, hence the division of the time series into four groups of four sampling years.

52 Large proportional increases are obviously 'easier' when starting from such a low base.

53 See, Roger Penn, *Skilled Workers in the Class Structure* (Cambridge: Cambridge University Press, 1985), pp. 31–2, 159–60, who generates a 'composite theory' of the labour aristocracy from the available evidence which he then tests using evidence of marital mobility in Rochdale for the periods 1856–65, 1875–84, 1900–9, 1920–9 and 1955–64. His findings lead him to reject the theory and, along with it, any simplistic causal relationship between the political and non-political spheres. See note 37 above.

54 See note 58.

55 See note 31.

56 John Foster, *Class Struggle and the Industrial Revolution* (London: Weidenfeld and Nicolson, 1974). Foster argues that the development of 'revolutionary class consciousness' in 1830s and 1840s Oldham was reflected in the social solidarity of the Oldham working class, and uses evidence of marital mobility to substantiate his argument. For a criticism of his approach and conclusions, see Penn, *op. cit*.

57 Engineers, masons, furniture makers, printers, and cotton spinners. See Hobsbawm, *op. cit.*, 1964, pp. 276–90.

58 Somewhat at odds with the earlier impression of what was meant by a 'merging' with the lower-middle class the later Hobsbawm has stressed the comparative unattractiveness of white-collar work to tradesmens' sons . . . 'the right to a trade was not only a right of the duly qualified tradesman, but also a family heritage'. Tradesman fathers 'wanted nothing better for their sons . . . a trade was at least as desirable or better than anything else effectively on offer.' By way of substantiation he offers a biographical sample taken from Bellamy and Saville's *The Dictionary of Labour Biography* which shows non-tradesmens' sons as considerably more likely to make such a move. Hobsbawm, 'Artisans and Labour Aristocrats?' in Hobsbawm, *op. cit.*, pp. 264–5. On the face of it the higher rate of class mobility from the semi-skilled sector in the Keele sample would seem to support this argument. However, the relatively poor performance of the skilled sector as a whole in this regard was, in fact, more a function of the extreme occupational stability of other groups, such as miners and potters. Whilst adherence to 'the trade' may well have had an inhibitory effect on the overall extent of upward mobility, closer investigation of the trades highlighted by Hobsbawm above, and indeed of those in the 'super-aristocracy', reveals, for the most part, greater rates of movement into white-collar employment than from non-trades.

59 Charles Booth (ed.), *Life and Labour of the People of London*, Vol. IX, (London: Macmillan, 1897), p. 393.

60 Andrew Miles, 'How "Open" was Victorian and Edwardian Society?: Structure, Mobility and Fluidity in the First Industrial Nation', forthcoming.

61 Goldthorpe *et al.*, *op. cit.*, 1980, p. 74.

From methodological monopoly to pluralism in the sociology of social mobility

Daniel Bertaux

Introduction

The sociology of social mobility has until now been constructed entirely around a quantitative paradigm. The paper recalls some of the inherent limits in this approach and emphasises the need to develop other quantitative and qualitative approaches. In particular, it outlines the potentialities of life histories and family histories. The issues at stake are not only methodological; the adoption of new methods will bring about a transformation of sociological thought – the question it asks about 'social mobility', the processes it tries to elucidate and concepts devised to delineate these processes.

The choice of a technique of sociological investigation can have implications reaching far beyond the technical considerations involved. Nowhere is this more strikingly illustrated than in research into social mobility. From the beginning this has almost invariably been conducted by means of sample surveys. Perfected in the United States during the 1940s, these became the chief means of empirical sociological enquiry, proving their worth in the study of elections and in market research. Their most notable advantage was that, on the basis of responses by two thousand people, it was possible to reach conclusions about the lives, attitudes and behaviour of millions of individuals. It is readily understandable why first American, and later European, sociologists were fascinated by this approach.

Apart, perhaps, from electoral sociology, nowhere was the technique more widely used than in the sociology of social mobility where its contribution to statistical knowledge was considerable, mainly in illuminating the correlation between social origins and adult status. In France these investigations were carried out by *statisticians* of the National Institute of Statistics, the INSEE. As statisticians they did a superb job, collecting high quality data on large samples (n = 20,000 for the first, 1964, survey; then n = 60,000 for the 1970, 1977 and 1986 surveys). They analysed the data as experts on social statistics, showing the influence of some variables on some others, testing some of the sociological hypotheses; for example, about structural mobility. They also gave the precise intervals of confidence of their figures; ironically, these figures showed that any modelling of the patterns of social mobility would not be that accurate (Thélot, 1980, 1982). They did not try to make sociological sense of the data, since it was *not* their job.

But the same compliments cannot be paid to those American or European *sociologists* who adopted the technique of survey research (or were adopted by it) without asking themselves whether it was suitable to their particular sociological analyses. The result has been that, rather than defining 'social mobility' through a process of genuine sociological thought, and then deciding how best to examine it empirically, they took for granted the definition of social mobility which is implicit in the *technique* of the survey itself. As a result, many sociologists write and teach that the study of social mobility is mostly a matter of empirically observing and discussing statistical relationships derived from a random sample of the (working) population, linking such variables as 'social origin', 'occupation' and a range of intermediate variables like education. This is a social-statistical conception of social mobility, not a sociological one at all; but it is often mistaken, not only for a sociological conception of social mobility, but for the only possible one. . .

The three sociological ways of examining collective processes

If the study of social mobility is to be tackled in a sociological manner the starting point must surely be not individuals or families but the collective processes a 'society' is made of. A 'society' functions only if people can be found to undertake the various types of task created by its history of relations of production and the division of labour stemming therefrom; these could be midwives or undertakers, slaughterhouse workers or experts on gastronomy, coalface workers or airline pilots, sewermen or perfumers. Note, incidentally, that language has only *one* set of terms to cover both *jobs*, and the *people* who hold them. This dual usage masks the problem, namely that all jobs must be filled.

If job slots are all filled, including those nobody wants, this is because there is some overall process, some constraining societal process, by which the members of a society, whether they like it or not, are directed, sorted, distributed and assigned to different jobs as they are defined by a socially constructed state of the division of labour. The moment we accept the idea of such a process (which I shall call the process of *anthroponomic distribution*),[1] we have an acceptable definition of the sociological phenomenon so unsatisfactorily described by the expression 'social mobility'.

Once this way of presenting the problem is accepted the road lies open for sociological thought. Unfortunately that road is practically deserted. A handful of theorists of social structure have from time to time tried to explore its broad outlines. Thus we find in Marx and Engels some of the elements of a theory of class structure, and a rather sketchy outline of the concept of 'production of men themselves' which might well have led to the idea of anthroponomic distribution had not Marxism been so eager to forget it. Marx considers relations to the means of production to be the central phenomenon, so logically those must be studied first. This would lead one to ask the following research questions: How does one become a capitalist entrepreneur? By inheritance, by co-optation, by marriage, by the managerial route? What are the obstacles to entrepreneurial status, ensuring that the vast majority of the population remain wage-earners – that is, in Marxist terms, proletarians? Can the educational system be analysed as a process of recruitment to the bourgeois class, and thus a cleavage mechanism? Can state employment or the emergence of the new middle strata of salaried managers and supervisory staff be analysed in terms of the dichotomy capital/labour or must we add another basic principle relating to the phenomenon of the development of bureaucracies?

It was Weber who set the notion of 'market' at the centre of thought. Contrary to what is often thought his view does not deny the crucial importance of the relationship (ownership/non-ownership) to the means of production, but treats it as a specific example of a more general determinant, namely market position. Today his detailed classification of 'market positions' may seem unconvincing. Yet the idea of a market, in the sense of competition between individuals, has been embraced enthusiastically in the United States, where it corresponds perhaps more closely to the reality of social relationships.

There is a paradox here. When he discusses class, Marx, that most profound of analysts of the capitalist mode of production, draws on the sociopolitical realities of the Britain and France of his day. Yet these two societies were still riddled with survivals from the 'feudal' period. His vision of classes as antagonistic human groups presupposes implicitly that social position is something that clings to one for life like a skin, indeed that it is inherited from earlier generations: a typical feature of feudalism, not of capitalism. His analysis of the structural contradiction between the characteristic interests of capital and labour as empty positions remains thoroughly valid; but it can only be applied to the *individuals* occupying these positions if and to the extent that it is impossible for them to change class.

Weber on the other hand thinks in terms of individual actors rather than positions, which precisely corresponds to the ideology of a 'free market' society. Interpretations of Weber have, by passing over some parts of his thought and distorting others, too easily resulted in the notion of a completely fluid society in which everyone has an opportunity for advancement. There is of course some degree of sociological truth in this optimistic view; it is not difficult to see why American sociologists found it so plausible. North American society was forged amid a struggle for national independence, which entailed the rejection of aristocratic structures and which set the democratic ideal at the heart of the Constitution. North America was also able to develop in the vast, rich 'virgin' spaces of a continent that had previously been emptied of its indigenous peoples, so offering immigrants from every corner of the world undreamt of opportunities to retain the fruits of their labour for themselves and even to become wealthy. Thanks to highly sophisticated and worldwide politico-financial mechanisms, the USA is still able to pre-empt for its own benefit a sizeable share of the world product. This is why the ideology of *generalised fluidity* suits it.

Two North American sociologists, K. Davis and W. Moore, imagined a theory of social structure (and, implicitly, of social mobility) which seems to push the idea of the market to its extreme limits. In their view, if there is a social structure, i.e. 'inequalities', in income and working conditions between various occupations, this is simply because some jobs are more important than others. If someone performs work badly the consequences are more serious if that person is a surgeon or senior manager than if he or she is a street-sweeper (or a sociologist for that matter, D.B.). The reason why surgeons are so highly paid, according to

Davis and Moore, is simply that 'society' is concerned to ensure that the most able and skilful in their generation become surgeons (Davis and Moore, 1945).

The Davis–Moore hypothesis is *not* Weberian at all; it is thoroughly functionalist. It derives from a mode of thinking which looks at social processes from the point of view of 'the whole society'; Durkheim has been its main exponent. This is squarely at odds with the 'theoretical individualist' position (also called methodological individualism) which claims to draw its inspiration from the first chapter of Weber's *Economy and Society*. Marx embodies a third point of view, as he mostly thinks in terms of classes and interest groups. Societies, classes, individuals: these are *three levels* of social life, of social action, and it is no coincidence that our discipline has chosen Durkheim, Marx, and Weber as its leading founding fathers: for this 'infernal trio' covers the whole range of 'pure' sociological perspectives.[2]

This being understood, three questions arise:

1. Is unity of sociology possible, or is it condemned forever to mix 'explanations' drawn from logics which are both nominally and perhaps really distinct?
2. What kind of a research programme on 'social mobility' or rather anthroponomic distribution can be derived from such a broad vision? What does it mean to think about flows of social trajectories in terms of societal processes, of class interests and conflicts, of social competition between individuals (and families)?
3. Where does the survey-research form fit into the picture? What is the sociological meaning of survey data on social trajectories?

We will not deal here with the first issue, which concerns the whole of our discipline, but only with the second and the third.

First sketches of a research programme

If the study of anthroponomic distribution is to be worked through successfully, we need to take *all three levels* into account simultaneously: society, classes, individuals. Each level requires its own mode of theorising and of observation, for the working of institutions cannot be studied in the same way as power relationships between classes or generalized competition between individuals. In order to achieve a fit between the '*problématique*' and the technique of observation, we need some methodology. But methodology's genuine goal is not the goal so often assigned to it, namely the perfecting of techniques of observation and analysis; it is rather the 'right choice' of technology, the choice of techniques of enquiry which are adequate to the observational tasks required for the successful construction of sociological interpretations. In the absence of a '*problématique*' (a set of ideas of hypotheses, and concepts) both empirical research *and*, eventually, sociological theory too let themselves be determined by whatever techniques happen to be available. The sociology of social mobility is, alas, the outstanding example.

It is only by focusing upon the process of anthroponomic distribution that one can outline a programme of empirical observation of this process. The first step in this process would be to study the anthroponomic differentiation (the construction of differences between individuals) which occurs by means of differences in family socialisation, which in turn reflect (among other things) differences in the ways of life of families and ultimately class differences. Another stage is to examine the process of selection within the educational system, at the end of which differences between individuals are formalised in the differential distribution of credentials. Labour markets must also be included – complex, shifting mosaics of loci of competition (neither pure nor perfect) by means of which individuals' educational or other 'qualifications' and talents are converted more or less efficiently into jobs and career paths. Matrimonial 'markets' are also parts of the overall process of anthroponomic distribution. These, too, are far removed from pure and perfect competition; through them individuals pair off under the influence of desire – but also of social pressure, to constitute units of reproduction. One sees also the need for a whole series of more detailed studies of official norms (and real practices) relating to recruitment of staff by institutions like the civil service, nationalised industries, big companies and small business, and of what 'society' does with those it considers cannot be assimilated to its norms, and who are relegated to marginality, drug addiction, exile, confinement or suicide.

Survey data and their in-built limits

It must be said candidly that much of the sociology of social mobility has never even tried to design a research programme based on prior sociological thinking. Although the articles, reports and books devoted to methodology would fill a library, their apparent diversity masks a unity of viewpoint: they invariably rest on questionnaires administered to random samples. The technique existed; therefore it was used. Nobody asked whether it was capable of achieving the desired end.

Such statistical investigations have, of course, considerably advanced our knowledge. Thanks to them we now have a detailed knowledge of the relationship between social origin, educational qualifications and occupational status.[3] We can also map the pattern of 'human' (anthroponomic) flows by which one generation of males replaces another in the social structure, and we have quite sophisticated statistical studies demonstrating the effects of a range of variables like mother's education or grandfather's occupation on current status.

It would be absurd to dismiss survey research as mere empiricism or number-crunching. What must be challenged, though, is the *monopoly of scientific legitimacy* this approach enjoys within, especially, North American sociology – which, like it or not, influences sociology all over the world. For a long while this monopoly of legitimacy prevented the development of other approaches, even though these are absolutely essential for a complete grasp of the processes concerned.

Surveys have the defects of their virtues. The problem is not one of questionnaire construction, since they are usually well enough drafted, but of *the observational limits inherent in the technique itself*. The main ones are as follows:

1. For the sample to be representative, individuals must be taken *at random*, and thus *out of context*. This means never including more than one person from the same family, the same street or the same place of employment. This (latent) principle of statistical representativity is by definition decontextualising.
2. If the questionnaires are to be dealt with identically, then they must in turn be identical, whether administered to men or women, workers or managers, public employees or farmers. *Standardised tools* inevitably standardise the pictures given of

the widely different processes by which social trajectories take shape.

3. An adult male's occupation is usually sufficient to place him in the social structure, and most men have an occupation. But this is not the case for all women at all stages of their adult life. To situate them socially without knowing their context is more difficult (though not impossible). Recoiling at the difficulties involved, most statistical investigations of social mobility carried out in a number of countries are based on entirely *male samples*.

4. Finally, the whole undertaking rests on observations relating to *individuals*. Structural levels of analysis, such as the family level, professional or occupational groups, social milieux or major institutions lie outside the field of observation.

Even more serious are the consequences *on theoretical thinking* of using only survey data. By its very nature the questionnaire forces theoretical discussion into what Lazarsfeld calls the language of variables – a language that is statistical rather than sociological.

To demonstrate the problem, let us take the following example. If one wants to know to what extent the social destiny of individuals depends on their social origin, a good idea should be to begin by comparing the social trajectories of brothers or sisters born to the same parents. If it appears that in many cases these trajectories are very similar, that is an indication that social origin has a powerful influence. But if they are not, this immediately indicates that one should also look for other factors than social origin. Yet, surprisingly, surveys of social mobility shed no light whatever on this fundamental point, simply because the number of brothers or sisters varies between individuals; consequently it is not easy, for technical reasons, to frame questions or to code the answers in advance. As a result there exists no statistical knowledge of career differentiation among siblings; and, even worse, the very processes through which siblings' social trajectories take up different shapes have not been studied at all. This illustrates how apparently technical considerations can dictate the substantive content of investigations.

The same is of course true of the various logics shaping the trajectories of women: for a very long while they remained outside the scope of theoreticians, because 'data were not available for technical reasons'. If only one had given second thought to these 'technical reasons' one would have perhaps perceived the sexist bias which is actually in-built in occupational mobility surveys; and the validity of using *only* surveys would have been questioned instead of mechanically repeating that the survey is the only valid 'method'.

Given the sociological conception of 'social mobility' proposed earlier, it is clear that we cannot be content to study it only by means of a method which is incapable of revealing several of its main features. It should be clear by now that surveys have built-in limits. They cannot be used to study institutions (the Durkheimian perspective) or class conflicts (the Marxian perspective). It is not even sure they are adequate to study competition between individuals (the Weberian or rather, neo-Weberian perspective), since what is at work *between* competitors, that is the hidden rules of the social game, lies forever beyond a standardised questionnaire's reach.

Can one imagine a study of a country's economy being conducted solely on the basis of statistics relating to the distribution of goods, taking no account of the strategies of the main industrial corporations, the banks and the State, and failing to examine the various sectors of industry, investment decisions or financial markets? Yet that is the sort of basis on which much of the sociology of social mobility has been built up. Accordingly, it was inevitable that, sooner or later, sociologists would attempt to find an alternative.

Towards an alternative

In reaction to the quantitative nature of the data arising from questionnaires, scholars looking for an alternative first turned towards the 'qualitative'. But, first, the term has little meaning, being merely a synonym for 'non-quantitative'; and, above all, the problem with surveys is not that they produce quantitative data. On the contrary, that is their most valuable aspect (L. Bertaux 1981).

Rather than being only one, there are several 'alternatives'. One approach consists of a qualitative development of the quantitative approach itself. The transverse (or synchronic) character of questionnaires is manifestly ill-suited to revealing the character of inherently diachronic processes (Bertaux, 1974). But the first attempts at longitudinal enquiries, in the seventies, were inconclusive; the sociologists concerned were overwhelmed by the volume of data and were forced to admit their inability to tackle its profoundly diachronic character. More recent surveys, such as the 'triple biography' project conceived and conducted at the INED by Courgeau (Courgeau, 1985, 1987), may hopefully provide us with major advances in statistical knowledge of patterns of social mobility and migration, family cycles and the interactions between them.

But one should also develop other, *more flexible* techniques of observation, since the phenomena to be observed vary in kind. For example, there is not one labour market but several, resting on quite different logics. The official rules and real norms relating to recruitment and promotion in government employment are not the same as those operating in the private services, in large long-established private corporations, in medium-sized firms, or small business. In the larger institutions the internal markets (of administrations or companies) are all that counts, because most people, once taken on, stay until retirement. In France one person out of three has a career lying entirely within a single institution; the proportion is still higher for the people with qualifications. By contrast, in smaller companies, the construction industry, and personal services like hairdressing and restaurants, the prevailing pattern is one of mobility between employers. An internal market on a national scale which is highly structured by binding rules on promotions and in which institutions are characteristically permanent, cannot be studied in the same way, and certainly not by the same questionnaire, as a market dependent on local or contingent factors where recruitment may rest on quite different dictates.

A recognition of the heterogeneity of labour markets also gets one away from the obsession with 'national' representativity, since it is clear that sectoral effects are crucially important: not only do norms governing recruitment and internal competition for promotion vary between the Post Office, an automobile company, the newspaper industry, or the building trades, but movement *between* sectors is by no means easy when the 'human capital' of professional experience accumulated in one sector of the economy has value only within that sector. Finally, some sectors of the economy are expanding while others are in decline, and the opportunities thereby created can help or hinder professional advance, thus creating an effect on collective mobility.

Thus if we are to succeed in identifying the processes determining careers in internal markets it will be by combining investigations based on statistics (like in France Alain Darbel's and Dominique Schnapper's (1972) or de Singly and Thélot's (1988) studies of civil servants), or analysis of career records (as Catherine Paradeise and Françoise Vourch (1982) have done for the merchant navy) with the accumulated knowledge of personnel departments as collected through interviewing, and perhaps with some professional life stories tapping the subjective logics of the actors. In short, a plurality of approaches will allow an investigation to reach beyond the social-statistical level, on which social processes leave merely a recorded trace, up to the genuine sociological level.

Flexibility of the techniques of observation is all-important. Take for instance the issue of the processes mediating the links between social origin and professional achievement. Surveys give priority to education. This is indeed a factor determining access (or lack of it) to specific segments of the labour market. Yet the possession of educational credentials does not in itself 'explain' subsequent career. Why then is it the *sole* mediating variable used in so many surveys? Simply because it allows for standardisation: *every* adult can be classified according to educational level. Other characteristics, such as membership of an ethnic group, a trade union, party, or powerful association, or other specific personal qualities (such as entrepreneurship) may also have a significant effect on career patterns; but since they lead to small samples and cell sizes in survey analysis there is resistance to including them in a questionnaire. Here again one can see how an initially technical consideration leads to the upgrading of one 'variable' and the omission of other ones, thus distorting the sociological theorisation itself.

The standardisation of questionnaires in national surveys also means that processes specific to a sub-population will pass unobserved. The transition from wage-earning to independent (self) employment is a case in point. In all the vast literature on social mobility it is barely mentioned, although it is obvious that it represents a bid for upward mobility by the individuals concerned. One excellent way of getting to grips with this is the life history approach. This conclusion was reached from the study of small bakers I undertook jointly with Isabelle Bertaux-Wiame. This method proved entirely satisfactory in demonstrating the process by which a substantial proportion of bakery workers manage to set up on their own account. Moreover, the small-scale (and therefore relatively simple) organisation of the industry means that only a few dozen life histories need to be collected and compared before one reaches 'saturation' (Bertaux and Bertaux-Wiame 1981a, 1981b and 1988). The saturation of a sociological understanding of a given social process, shows that, contrary to the widely held belief, qualitative studies do lend themselves to generalisation. In the same way Danielle Gerritsen has shown by her work on small firms in the canal transport industry, and later on on taxi drivers, how well suited life histories can be in identifying the nature of a 'trade', the relations which organise its forms and determine the career patterns of the people engaged in it (Gerritsen, 1989). Bernard Zarca has shown how a social typology of artisans can be given flesh and detail through a reasoned use of case histories (Zarca, 1988).

Among other processes of social mobility which are specific to sub-populations let us consider the process by which adolescents become delinquent, or rather engage in the form of delinquency most powerfully stigmatised in our society; that of theft with violence. The norm in the studies of juvenile delinquency is that sociologists conduct statistical investigations while psychologists concentrate on case studies. The outcome is endless argument between the two disciplines, each accusing the other of taking only one aspect of reality into account. The use of life histories by Christian Leomant and Nicole Sotteau-Leomant (1987) now enables us to leave such debates behind. It has been said often enough that the delinquents (or at least those who are caught) come from deprived backgrounds, invariably from the areas of high population density where such families are housed. But not every child from such a background becomes delinquent! The Leomants took seriously this powerful argument that the psychologists level at social statisticians. The life histories they gathered make it possible to show why some young people fall into illegal activities, while others escape the vicious circle of poverty-delinquency-prison-poverty-delinquency. What they found were not so much psychological processes as lacerations in the relational tissue in the one group, or regeneration of that tissue in the other; what they describe are a set of micro-social phenomena, not in themselves psychological, but with important consequences for the psyche and therefore for behaviour. Such insights do not challenge wider sociological explanations, such as the effects of unemployment or class stigmatisation on delinquency; but they do allow their effects to be specified.

Generally speaking it may be argued that the concept of 'social trajectory' is a more adequate and more sociological one than the concept of social mobility (Cachon Rodriguez, 1989). It captures an essential feature that is left out by the mainstream approach, i.e. the time dimension of mobility processes. They are all processes of becoming, which unravel within a larger space; and the 'trajectory' concept expresses it nicely. The meaning of 'trajectory' need not be restricted to individual trajectories; families, professional groups, whole segments of societies also may have social trajectories. An 'historical' approach, that is one which follows the development of a process is required here. If the unit of observation is the individual, history is the correct instrument.

Family histories

Life histories lead inevitably to family histories. Here is a sociological technique by which we can set out concretely how the trajectories of women are constructed, how the destinies of children of the same couple become differentiated, and how the real line of descent in a family can be a feminine one, the female lineage being the pivot of a family's history over several generations (Bertaux-Wiame, 1986; Thompson, 1990). In France a growing number of researchers are adopting this approach; their key concept is the concept of *transmission* (i.e. what gets transmitted from one generation to the next); see Anne Muxel and Annick Percheron (1988), Gotman (1988), and Bertaux and Bertaux-Wiame (1988). In the latter paper the processes of transmission between generations are studied in a family over four generations, and the concept of differential *transmissibility* of various forms of capital is proposed.

The study of family histories is not new; it is as old as the oral tradition itself; the notion of life history is certainly much more modern. However, the sociology of social mobility has so far shown little interest in family histories, just as it has shown little interest in the life history as a way of describing both a social trajectory and the means by which it is progressively shaped. The day will surely come when this omission will be thought remarkable, because the histories of individuals, and even more family histories, are such extraordinarily rich sources of hard information directly relating to the construction of social trajectories. This failure will be blamed on the obsession with statistical representativeness and the fetish for statistics which is characteristic of a certain period in sociology, from which we are only now and with difficulty emerging.

As with any form of history, even when it is in the hands of historians, there are of course many ways of relating family histories. The investigator's point of view, while not in this case creating what is studied, shapes the way it is presented; and there are as many points of view as there are histories. This is readily confirmed by having several members of the same family tell its history. What holds true of the history of any subject with a precise empirical identity, such as an institution or a nation, is even more the case with something like the family, for which there is no precise definition. There are almost no limits to the way it can be extended to cover earlier generations or first, second or Nth cousins.

Does the difficulty in defining a family lead us to conclude that a family does not exist? Certainly not. And does the multiplicity of forms a family history may take force us to conclude that the method is unscientific? Surely not: that would simply reflect a naive belief in the possibility of totally objective accounts, which would be akin to confusing the map with the territory it represents. There is no single way of drawing, painting or photographing a bridge like the Pont des Arts in Paris; there are an infinite number of ways of doing so. Yet the Pont des Arts remains the Pont des Arts and will never be the the Pont Mirabeau.[4]

Actions affecting an individual constitute the warp and woof of that individual's existence, whether he or she is the subject or the object of those actions. As far as the family is concerned I suggest that its core is constituted by its social genealogy. A social genealogy is a genealogy adapted to the needs of sociological research, extending less towards earlier generations and more towards collateral descendants, above all tracing the social trajectory of each member of the genealogy. Even so simple a diagram will bring out a number of phenomena; for example, the differentiation of siblings' trajectories or the transmission of trades (métiers) between generations. But social genealogy, far from providing a complete representation of a family's history, is no more than a starting point.

Family histories need to be gathered with a desire to understand the processes contributing to the construction of social trajectories of their members. There is no point in undertaking case studies if they are simply going to be reduced to a few variables. Each family history must therefore be examined in some depth. There must be an awareness that what one has under one's eyes is not a 'family' but an interweaving of lines of descent, each bringing a specific history with it (father's line, mother's line). 'The family' or, rather, *le groupe familial*, dissolves and reconstitutes itself with each generation.

How can family histories advance sociological understanding of anthroponomic distribution? The answer is that they provide illumination not just about individual trajectories but about the relationships between them. Family histories are not made up of abstract 'relations' between statistical variables like 'father's occupation' and 'son's occupation', but of the accounts of real relationships between real people. The concept which summarises the many ways in which earlier generations bear on the present one is *transmission*.

The two generations interact over a long period. The story of that interaction will, for the most part, remain unknown not only to us but to the actors themselves, if only because parent-child relationships are forged mainly at sub-conscious or unconscious levels. It is a history shaped by a host of totally unremarkable day to day occurrences. Even so, it is enough to read a family history, however superficial, to realise how much one can learn from it.

The literature on the family might be expected to provide a rich source of material for our discussion of anthroponomic distribution. This has not been the case in practice, however. The dynamic processes of anthroponomy operate over time, sometimes over a considerable period, whereas studies of the sociology of the family have tended generally to relate to a particular point in time. Even work on the family life cycle has not enabled us to identify the internal dynamics of real families. Questions remain unanswered: What has happened between members of a given family in the long run? What attractions, conflicts, dramas are subsumed by that simple black line indicating marriage on a genealogy? What dynamic does its quiet simplicity conceal? And what of those apparently crystal clear lines linking the couple and their children; who can say what hopes, disappointments, affections, projections, identifications, rejections, breakdowns and reconciliations have made them point by point? And what, in the end, has been transmitted by means of this largely unconscious drama?

The need to shift attention from individuals to the relations between them also applies at a *family* level of study. Another sociological level remains to be explored *in the 'blank spaces' between families*. Inter-family relationships represent the never-ending interplay of social competition. We become aware of it when we group families from the same social milieu who, though belonging to the same social class, stand for that very reason objectively in a relation of competition to each other. Comparing the destinies of such families over several generations allows us to uncover the process of differentiation through competition.

Finally, by comparing the social trajectories of children from different social backgrounds we can read, in the blank spaces separating these family flows, the effects of class relations. These are what generate not only handicaps or advantages, but distortions to the (collective) rules of competition; distortions such that, notwithstanding the democratic ideals in which our societies take such pride, open competition usually results in the transmission of social statuses, high to high and low to low. And here we touch the heart of the phenomenon.

Such, then, is the paradox of the life history or family history approach: the sociological is to be found in the 'blank' spaces separating individuals, or families, or classes. Is this because the method is illogical or defective in approach – or does it reflect the fact that the social, being invisible, cannot be grasped directly? Criticism that the approach is too indirect should first be levelled at studies using questionnaires, which characteristically never rise above the individual level at which they began. Nor is there with a questionnaire a prospect of reaching any different level by increasing the sample, for the change required would be qualitative. A family is more than a juxtaposition of its members, and so is a social group – unless the founding fathers of sociology were all totally mistaken.

Bringing women back in . . .

The family history approach restores women to the centre of attention. But why did sociologists working on social mobility 'forget' them for so long? Why was their attention focused entirely on men?

Feminists have attributed this attitude to the fact that these sociologists were male. This is an incomplete explanation; when male sociologists study the family they do not exclude women. Indeed to exclude women from studies of the family would be patently absurd. In the case of anthroponomic distribution the absurdity is less obvious. If we combine this with the fact that women have also been overlooked in theories of social class or the social structure, and that theorists as advanced as Marx or Weber took this omission for granted, we move to another explanation for the neglect of women. It is a fact that, at least until recently, the place assigned to women in society was not the same as that assigned to men; and sociologists were merely reflecting the societal divisions in their work. Women were *assigned* to family life as men were to employment, and the fact that most women worked until marriage and that some never married, or that some men were not gainfully employed, in no way altered this social norm, nor even the fact that the textile industry developed by exploiting women with children.

As long as this sexual division of work was the norm, the study of the distribution of individuals in the social structure raised completely different issues for women than for men. So if male sociologists writing on social structure or social mobility should be criticised, it is not so much for omitting women from discussions of a world which was conceived as entirely male, but for failing to raise questions about the sexual division itself; both in terms of women's place in the social structure, and of the specific mode by which they were distributed within that structure.

Even if it were to be shown – which has yet to be the case – that marriage is more decisive for the destination of women than for men, then marriage would still have to be analysed. It is not enough to treat marriage as a mere device for achieving a class destiny which was already there since birth, or alternatively as the site of a whole range of possible futures among which the blind hand of love chooses at random.

Today the 'traditional' system of differential assignment based on gender is changing; the modes of assigning women are becoming more and more similar to those applying to men. This change, marked by the massive entry of women onto the labour market and a great increase in the educational levels women achieve, the two go hand in hand, is now under way. As yet we are far from having grasped all its consequences, not only for the female population but also for the male population and for the ways in which they form couples. This change applies only in the most developed societies, and in 'state socialist' countries also, where it is the most pronounced: there the norm has long been for every woman, married or single, to have a job.

In Western Europe, as in North America, 'housewife' status still exists. The infrastructures which would allow all mothers to enter paid employment are still lacking. These countries are therefore in transition between two systems, and transition is the most complex of empirical situations. We must first understand how each of the two systems functions (call them the traditional system and the unisex system) before we can hope to understand how they are linked. If we try to avoid distinguishing between these two modes of assigning women, we condemn ourselves to remain at the level of social statistics.

Let me risk one last hypothesis. Perhaps it is so that, along with the three 'levels' of analysis identified by Pierre Tripier (1984), that is, society, classes, individuals, a fourth level may be identified: not the level of interaction but the level of *families*. That it has not been perceived so far is entirely consistent with the blindness of the founders of sociology to the female half of the population. Obviously there is a paradox in the fact that this family level is becoming visible, like a reef at low tide, at the very moment when the traditional system of specific assignment of women is on the verge of being dissolved in the most developed societies. But the idea is worth exploring further: between the level of classes and that of isolated individuals lies this reef of familial forms which tend to subsume to their specific interests the wills of the individuals composing them.

Much, therefore, remains to be done. Through this small breach in the hegemony of a method, we have opened out a whole universe of phenomena; forms and relationships may appear which have hitherto lain unnoticed by sociologists of social mobility. Here is indeed material enough for future generations of sociologists to investigate and reflect upon.

Notes

A first version of this paper has been published in *Annales de Vaucresson*, 26 (1987), special issue on Histoires de vies, Histoires de familles, Trajectoires sociales (in French). I am very grateful to Professor Martin Harrison (University of Keele) who translated this first version into English, and to Shirley Dex who gave me the opportunity of revising it.

1 The term *anthroponomy* has been proposed (Bertaux, 1977, 1983) to refer to a whole set of processes and relationships which all contribute to the *process of production, distribution*, and *consumption* of 'labour power' or, better said, *human energy*. Thus the idea of anthroponomy stands in relation to this huge and multifaceted process in the same relation that, say, Adam Smith's idea of political economy stands in relation to the process of production, distribution and consumption of things.

In other words, any social formation (society) produces not one but two kinds of material products: things, and *people themselves*. People are produced; and they also get distributed into the social division of labour. This latter sub-process, to which sociological custom refers by the expression 'social mobility', is therefore part of a larger process; it is its distributional moment. It cannot be sociologically understood in itself, since as a subprocess of distribution it is closely linked to the processes of production and of 'consumption' or use of human energy, mostly but not solely under the form of labour power.

2 It might be so however that the level of *interaction* could be a fourth, internally consistent level; in which case G.H. Mead would appear on the same foot as the three other leading theoreticians. There are signs that this might happen, for instance the recent rediscovery of Mead by Habermas (1981) and many European sociologists.

In the sixties the opposition was clearly between a class perspective and a 'whole society' functionalist perspective (Bertaux, 1972). The late seventies saw the emergence of the individualist perspective while both other ones receded in the background. But these shifts are only shifts in intellectual interests and cultural centrality of perspectives; the *levels* themselves do not disappear. An excellent analysis of the consequences, for sociological theory, of the existence of three internally consistent levels of social action ('whole society' and institutions; classes; individuals) is developed in Tripier (1984).

3 Such investigations have been undertaken in most developed countries. It is the author's view that some of the best statistical studies are those that have been conducted in France by the INSEE, and by the INED on the causes of differential performances of school children according to social origin (*Population* et l'enseignement, 1970). Britain, Sweden, West Germany and Hungary have also produced high quality data – markedly better than those for the United States.

4 Taking this metaphor one step further, one might also say that while photographs of the Pont des Arts are at least objective representations of it, drawings or paintings are not. How is it then that the latter may capture, better than the photographs, the 'meaning' or the 'essence' of this romantic bridge? Because when we think of it we do not relate to it as engineers but as city dwellers; its technical materiality is thus less relevant than its perception in the 'imaginaire collectif' of Parisians. To represent this perception – and not the object *per se* – is what drawings or paintings can best achieve.

But if, for a given bridge, the global perception in the collective mind's eye is more important than the details of the real object, then is it different for *social processes*? Does any sociologist seriously believe that statistical knowledge about a given process – i.e., the 'objective' knowledge about its objectal reality – is all that matters?

References

Bertaux, Daniel, (1972), 'Two and a half models of social structure', in Walter Müller and Karl Ulrich Mayer, (eds), *Social Stratification and Career Mobility*, Paris/The Hague: Mouton and Ecole Pratique des Hautes Etudes, pp. 117–52.

Bertaux, Daniel, (1974), 'Mobilité sociale biographique. Une critique de l'approche transversale', *Revue Française de Sociologie*, XV(3) (juil.–sept.): 329–62.

Bertaux, Daniel, (1977), *Destins Personnels et structure de classe*, Paris, Presses Universitaires de France.

Bertaux, Daniel, (1981), 'From the life-history approach to the transformation of sociological practice', in Daniel Bertaux (ed.), *Biography and Society*, London and Beverly Hills: Sage Publications, pp. 30–45.

Bertaux, Daniel, (1983), 'Production anthroponomique et nouvelle classe', in Christine Buci-Gluckmann (sous la dir. de), *La Gauche, le Pouvoir, le Socialisme*, Paris: Presses Universitaires de France, pp. 222–34.

Bertaux, Daniel and Bertaux-Wiame, Isabelle, (1981a), 'Artisanal bakery in France. How it lives and why it survives', in Frank Bechhofer and Brian Elliott, (eds), *The Petite Bourgeoisie. Comparative Studies of the Uneasy Stratum*, London: Macmillan, pp. 155–81.

Bertaux, Daniel and Bertaux-Wiame, Isabelle, (1981b), 'Life Stories in the Baker's Trade', in Daniel Bertaux (ed.), *Biography and Society*, London and Beverly Hills: Sage Publications, pp. 169–89.

Bertaux, Daniel et Bertaux-Wiame, Isabelle, (1988), 'La patrimoine et sa lignée: transmissions sur cinq générations', *Life Stories/Récits de vie*, 4: 8–26.

Bertaux-Wiame, Isabelle, (1990), 'Ruptures et continuités familiales dans les trajectoires de mobilité', paper to be presented at the Family Histories session of the XIIth World Congress of Sociology, Madrid, July.

Cachon Rodriguez, Lorenzo, (1989), *Mobilidad social o trajectorias de clase?*, Madrid, Centro de Investigaciones sociologicas y Siglo XXI de Espana.

Courgeau, Daniel, (1985), 'Interaction between spatial mobility, family career and life cycle: a French Survey', *European Sociological Review*, 1–2: 139–62.

Courgeau, Daniel, (1987), 'Pour une approche statistique des histoires de vie', *Annales de Vaucresson*, 26(1): 25–35.

Darbel, Alain et Schnapper, D., (1972), *Les Agents du système administratif*, Paris/ The Hague: Mouton.

Davis, Kingsley and Moore, Wilson, (1945), 'Some Principles of Stratification', *American Sociological Review*, 10: 242–9.

Geertz, Clifford, (1973), *The Interpretation of Cultures*, New York: Basic Books.

Gerritsen, Danielle, (1987), 'Limites de l'Indépendance et mythe de l'autonomie. Bateliers et chauffeurs de taxi', *Annales de Vaucresson*, 26(1) (n° spécial Histoires de vie, Histoires de Familles, Trajectoires sociales).

Gerritsen, Danielle, (1989), *Du fleuve à terre. Les bateliers: mobilité professionnelle, mobilité sociale?* Paris: Institut de Recherches sur les Sociétés Contemporaines-CNAS.

Gotman, Anne, (1988), *Hériter*, Paris: Presses Universitaires de France.

Habermas, Jürgen, (1981), (1987), *Théorie de l'agir communicationnel*, Paris: Gallimard.

Leomant, Christian and Leomant-Sotteau, Nicole, (1987), 'Itinéraires de vie et Trajectoires institutionnelles de jeunes délinquants', *Annales de Vaucresson* 26(1): 199–222.

Marx, Karl, (1867, 1879), (1969), *Le Capital*, Editions Sociales.

Muxel, Anne et Percheron, Annick, (1988), 'Histoires politiques de famille. Premières illustrations', *Life Stories/Récits de vie*, 4: 59–73.

Paradeise, Catherine et Vourch, Françoise, (1982), 'Problèmes de régulation d'un marché du travail corporatiste; la marine de commerce', Nantes: Lersco.

Population et l'enseignment, (1970), Paris: Presses Universitaires de France.

de Singly, François et Thélot, Claude, (1988), *Gens du Privé, gens du public. La grande différence*, Paris: Dunod.

Strauss, Anselm, (1967), *Qualitative Analysis for Social Scientists*, Cambridge: Cambridge University Press.

Thélot, Claude, (1980), *Le Poids d'Anchise*, Nantes: INSEE.

Thélot, Claude, (1982), *Tel Pers, tel fils ?* Paris: Dunod.

Thompson, Paul, (1990), 'Family as a factor in Social Mobility', paper to be presented at the Family Histories session of the XIIth World Congress of Sociology, Madrid, July.

Tripier, Pierre, (1984), *Approches sociologiques du marché du travail.* Thèse d'Etat, Université de Paris VII, to be published under the title *Du Travail à l'emploi*, Bruxelles: Presses Universitaires de Bruxelles.

Weber, Max, (1920), (1968), *Economy and Society*, New York: Bedminster Press.

Zarca, Bernard, (1988), *Les Artisans: gens de métier, gens de parole*, Paris: L'Harmattan.

Handling work history data in standard statistical packages

Catherine Marsh and Jonathan Gershuny

Introduction

In this chapter we make a pitch for the retention of the Renaissance model of the social scientist – one who not only dares to ask big questions about the nature of the world, but who also tries to answer these same questions using his or her own craft skills. Data analysis is too important to be left to statisticians and computer programmers; dogs should wag their own tails.

The standard statistical package is a major part of the Renaissance social scientist's fight against creeping loss of perspective. This is well illustrated even in the life event field, where the literature appears to require the researchers to come to grips with specialist software. There are several problems with this specialist software: 1) it is usually badly documented 2) it tends to offer a particular rather than a general environment and 3) industry standards have not been set, and everyone has their own different pet program (usually the one they wrote themselves).

It is important not to take these arguments too far and decry new software developments in general. It is also important to recognise that new packages take a long time to master, and may often not represent a good human capital investment for the generalist researcher. In this chapter we intend to illustrate the different ways in which we have found it productive and illuminating to manipulate work and life history events data using a combination of SPSSX, the most popular statistical package in use by social scientists, and SIR, a widely used database management package for handling hierarchical datasets. Using these packages in an exploratory fashion has enabled us to go a long way towards an understanding of work event data even without specialist packages. Nevertheless, the models derived should often be tested in some of the more sophisticated specialised software packages.

The ESRC SCEL initiative

In the middle of the 1980s, the Economic and Social Research Council commissioned a large programme of research into the interaction between Social Change and Economic Life (SCEL). This research initiative studied changes in six urban labour markets in Britain: Aberdeen, Coventry, Kirkaldy, Northampton, Rochdale and Swindon. One thousand individuals between the ages of 20 and 60 in each of these localities were interviewed in the spring and summer of 1986, and detailed questions were asked covering many different areas relevant to labour markets and labour market participation.

The interview began with respondents giving interviewers details of their life and work history. The method of recording the information was different for each. In the life history, the interviewers laid out a diary grid organised into years (Figure 1), and asked respondents to go through it separately for several different aspects of their lives; first, recording any moves and housing status changes between the ages of 14 years and the time of interview; then qualifications, marriage, living arrangements, partners and marriage, and finally birth and departure of children. For each of these separate domains of life, events were recorded as *status changes* at a particular year and month.

The work history then followed: it was found in piloting that having established the dates of such things as births of children, respondents often remembered the dates of various job activities more easily. There was however only one pass through time with the work history. (The work history grid is shown as Figure 2.) The work history started with the time at which the respondent left full-time education. A change of 'job' was taken as either a change of employer or a change of job within an organisation or a move between economic activity statuses (from being a housewife into being a student). When the episode was a form of employment, a dozen different characteristics of the job were detailed: the precise nature of the job, the nature and size of the employer's business, the hours per week, whether it was a job mainly done by men or women and so on.

The aim was to date all the events, on the life or work history, to monthly precision. When respondents could not remember the month in which something happened, they were prompted for a season if possible. Such estimates were given special codes instead

PAS
SCELI
MAIN SURVEY
(JUNE–JULY '86)

LIFE HISTORY

RESPONDENT'S NAME ____________

ASSIGNMENT NO: | ADDRESS NO:

N.B. "DON'T KNOW" IS CODED AS 7 OR 77 AS APPROPRIATE

OFFICE USE ONLY

AREA | QUESTIONNAIRE NO: | CARD NO: | NO. OF EVENTS (END FIRST CARD ONLY)

(1) (2) (3) (4) (5) (6) (7) (8) | FIRST CARD (79) (80)

1

		AGE→	14	15	16	17	18	19	20	21	22	23
		ENTER YEAR →	19	19	19	19	19	19	19	19	19	19
*SHOW CARD												
A	WHERE LIVED (ALL MOVES)	TOWN/ CITY										
		COUNTY/ DISTRICT										
		(COUNTRY)										
		O.U.O										
*B	YOUR HOME	CODE										
*C	ALL QUALIFICATIONS	CODE										
*D	MARRIAGE	MONTH										
		CODE										
*E	LIVING ARRANGEMENTS	CODE										
*F	PARTNER'S ACTIVITY	CODE										
G	BIRTH OF OWN CHILDREN (or return, if aged under 18)	MONTH										
		NAME										
		NO.										
H	ARRIVAL OF OTHER CHILDREN (or return, if aged under 18)	MONTH										
		NAME										
		NO.										
I	CHILDREN LEAVE	NAME										
		NO.										

Figure 1

SCELI MAIN SURVEY (JUNE–JULY '86) 3

WORK HISTORY (CONT.)

RESPONDENT'S NAME : - - - - - - - - - - - - - - - - - - -

FOR EACH EMPLOYED/SELF-EMPLOYED EVENT (CODED 01-03, 06 AT K) ASK– P Q R S T U V W X

FOR EACH EMPLOYER OR SELF-EMPLOYED PERIOD AT N ASK– Y Z

CARD NO.	EVENT NO.	J START OF EVENT MONTH YEAR	K ACTIVITY CODE	L JOB TITLE AND BRIEF DETAILS OF WORK DONE (BUT FULL DESCRIPTION FOR CURRENT/LAST JOB)	M SUPERVISORY RESPONSIBILITY YS(1) NO(2) DK(7)	N NAME OF EMPLOYER	O END OF EVENT MONTH YEAR	P HOURS PER WEEK	Q PAY COMPARISON	R NO. OF EMPLOYEES	S WORK WITH MEN/WOMEN	T TRADE UNION MEMBER YES(1) NO(2) DK(7)	U PROMOTION PROSPECTS? YES(1) NO(2) DK(7)	V JOB SECURITY	W HOW CLOSELY SUPERVISED	X WHY LEFT?	Y NATURE OF BUSINESS	Z PUBLIC OR PRIVATE PUB(1) PRI(2) DK(7)
1	09			O.U.O.	1 2 7							1 2 7	1 2 7					1 2 7
1	10			O.U.O.	1 2 7							1 2 7	1 2 7					1 2 7
1	11			O.U.O.	1 2 7							1 2 7	1 2 7					1 2 7
1	12			O.U.O.	1 2 7							1 2 7	1 2 7					1 2 7
(6)	(7)(8)	(9)(10)(11)(12)	(13)(14)	(15)(16)(17)(18)	(19)			(20)(21)	(22)	(23)	(24)	(25)	(26)	(27)	(28)	(29)	(30)(31)	(32)

Figure 2

of the numbers 1–12: e.g. 33 was Spring, 44 was Summer and so on. Of course some respondents could not remember when something had happened even to the nearest year, and the most perverse of all could remember the month but not the year. Handling this sort of missing data produced some headaches at the analysis stage which, with hindsight, could have been prevented if the interviewers had been asked to do the recodes that were eventually done by computer; they should have been instructed to enter Spring as month 3, Summer as month 6, year unknown as month 7 and so on. It is perhaps more arguable, but we feel that it would also have been good to get the interviewers to interpolate midpoints between the previous and next activities when respondents could not remember their dates – it might even have led to better estimates if respondents saw what they were doing and disagreed (though this procedure might subsequently have misled researchers about the quality of the respondents' recall).

But, in retrospect, the biggest error we made was to collect monthly data for all the events but to fail to ask the month of birth. Thus we can date very exactly where in the recessionary cycle of the early 1980s a particular unemployment episode occurred, but we have errors averaging six months when we look at things like age of first entry into the labour force. Fortunately for us, in the sort of labour market analysis we are engaged in, keeping the exact period correct is more important than keeping exact biological age correct.

The natural structure of the event history dataset as originally recorded was therefore as follows. Each respondent had as many work history records as they had had 'jobs' in the sense just defined; the number of records ranged from 0 to over 50. One of the items of information was the starting and finishing date of the record. Information from the life history was stored as one line of data for each life domain. For example, the migration line started with information on where the respondent had lived was stored as location at 14, followed by the date and destination of the first move, and then the date and destination of the second move and so on.

Analysis: the choice of software

Over sixty academics from eight different universities were involved in the SCEL initiative, and some purpose-built software was designed to handle the work and life event data. A suite of Fortran programs at Warwick have been written to perform data management functions (IDEAS). The SABRE package has been developed at the University of Lancaster for the modelling and analysis of this type of data. A volume devoted to discussion of the various methodological issues in the analysis of the SCEL history data has been prepared (Elias and Davies, 1991).

This sort of developmental work is obviously important to keep a discipline changing and alive. But for practitioners the methodology is a tool and not the end product. It is very hard to make realistic life decisions about how many new systems one is going to learn per year, and which are going to be the ones where investment will pay off in a general arena. Independently, the two authors came to the conclusion that we were going to get as far as we could exploring the data with the software that we had facility with, perhaps at the end testing the models which we felt best described the data using some of the more elaborate techniques.

In what follows, we describe a couple of the most useful ways we have found to explore the information in life event data and get to the point where we feel we even have a model to test. The first data structure involves maintaining a SIR database and using it as a pre-processor to derive different SPSS files for analysis. The second involves preparing the data for SPSS from the start.

SIR as a database management tool

SIR stands for Scientific Information Retrieval. It is a set of programs designed to handle data which is not rectangular, where one record can meaningfully be thought of as 'owning' another: in our example, one respondent may 'own' ten job history records, for example. It has several features which make it attractive as a management system for event history data (Ni Bhrolchain and Timaeus, 1983).

First, SIR has the built-in ability to handle different record types. It also has procedures for looping around records of a particular type and around cases which makes it a very natural and flexible way of storing data. These features make SIR very attractive for the manipulation of life event data, especially in comparison with packages like SPSS which were designed in the first instance for rectangular data structures.

Second, it is supported on a wide variety of different computers.

It has been established as a mainframe standard for university database computing in Britain, and is thus found at several different locations, and PC versions exist. This makes possible a productive style of work: developmental work can be done on a subsample of records on the PC version until the researcher is satisfied that the program does what is intended, and then the resulting program can be run on the full file on the mainframe version.

Third, it is tolerably well-documented. The main manual is a little unwieldly (SIR, 1986), but with version 2.2 comes a new SIR Light manual in A5 format which is extremely well-written and which covers all the important principles (SIR, 1988). The main manual can then be used to refer to the full range of options, statistics or whatever. There is a useful primer for introducing SIR to the novice, written by Angela Dale (1986). Finally, the distributors of SIR run periodic instructional courses and maintain a reasonable backup service in the UK for answering queries.

Careful attention has been paid to communication with other common software, and the resulting records can easily be read out as SPSS, BMDP or SAS system files. SIR does offer some statistical facilities – principally tabular forms of analysis, but these are not as extensive or as flexible as in other packages. It has only limited graphics facilities. It is thus best thought of as the housekeeping system which is used to write records for other programs to analyse.

This ability to communicate with other software packages is necessary to get access to more sophisticated statistical procedures, but it also may be needed to avoid some of the drawbacks which exist with SIR. First, it has no built in procedures for handling weights. Thus sample data which may have either been collected deliberately on a disproportionate stratification design or subject to unforeseen response biases which one needs to correct for, is best processed at the last stage in a software package which can handle this. And secondly, its method of handling missing data is pretty primitive and nothing like as flexible as in packages such as SPSS.

Units of analysis

Once event history data are in a SIR database, the researcher has considerable flexibility over what type of statistical analysis to do and how to conceptualise the very unit of analysis; one can experiment with alternative approaches – whether, for example to consider individuals or events as the focus of investigation.

The traditional unit in social research is the individual. The variables used to characterise the individuals may then be of different types: current states (e.g. whether in a trade union or not), past events (such as counts of spells or summaries of durations of previous unemployment), sequences of past events (e.g. whether separated having been married) or constants (sex, parents occupational class at age 14). We have used many such variables in our work on unemployment. However, sticking with the traditional unit in this way does not use the full potential of the data, which is capable of telling us about sequences, and whether the spells of unemployment came after spells of employment or whether they were mainly experienced before the person became established in the labour market, for example.

Furthermore, these individual summary variables are strongly related to age: the older you are the more chance you have had to have a spell of unemployment, a long job duration and so on. These problems with durations can be got round in one of two ways. One could consider the *proportion* of one's life since 15 that has been spent in unemployment, instead of the absolute *number* of days. Or one could consider the length of the longest spell of work, unemployment, economic inactivity or whatever. But these measures do not remove the age bias entirely, since the duration of all kinds of events increase with age; thus the chances are that the longest duration of any activity is the one that the respondent is currently engaged in. This current event is 'right censored': it is not yet complete and we do not know how long it is going to last.

Another possible unit is the event itself. When, as in our database, the data were organised as one event per record, it was very straightforward and natural to start looking at features of these events: what was the average duration of a job or a bout of unemployment, and how had this varied over time? What were the reasons people gave for leaving jobs, and how had the rate of involuntary quits varied for men and women over time? While it was an illuminating exploratory tool, and enabled some hypotheses to emerge, it was not very satisfactory for reasons that will be discussed with the next type of unit.

If we can treat the event as a unit, what about treating the change from one type of event to another as a unit? Transitions from employment into unemployment, or from full-time into part-time work were interesting from many points of view. They helped us to discover, for example, that transitions from part-time into full-time work were rare at all ages: once a person has tasted the freedom of a part-time job it is perhaps hard to give it up – or once off the full-time ladder it may be hard to get back on. (Burchell (1991) has used this technique to examine the relationship between job changes and size of establishments.)

But there are difficulties with conceptualising either an event or a transition between different types of event as a unit to be treated as a separate case in statistical analysis. First, we can arbitrarily vary the number of events, and thus sequences by changing the definition of an event; it was our decision, for example, to include changes of task with the same employer as a job change. Secondly, we may be unhappy about treating all events or transitions as having equal significance when some events last two months and others twenty years. Thirdly, the dating of events is problematical: for example, if we want to plot the average duration of unemployment events, do we plot a spell lasting from 1981 to 1983 at 1981, 1982 or 1983 (dating transitions is of course easier).

Another very useful way of getting a picture of change over time is to construct summary measures of what is happening within a 'window'. These windows can be defined either with respect to chronological time or biological age. We might, for example, construct a file of the latter type, with one case for every five years of life (up to the time of interview) of every person in the survey, and within that time window document some developmental features we were interested in. We shall spend some time considering an example of analysis of the SCEL work history data using the windows based on chronological time.

For a lot of labour market analysis, we found it particularly useful to have a file of person-years – i.e. one case for every calendar year (January to December) of the respondent's adult life. The variables in this file summarized either states during the year or events which occurred during the year. Using such a file, many different forms of data analysis became possible, and useful graphical displays were constructed.

Time windowing

One of the questions we set out to answer was how the rapid rise of unemployment at the beginning of the 1980s affected different people. The theoretical interest and hypotheses related to specific periods of time, so we constructed chronological time windows. These were accurately constructed within the limits of respondent recall.

For this purpose, the SIR database, with one record for each event which records its start and finish date, can be transformed into a rectangular file to be read into a statistical and graphical package such as SPSS. We created a rectangular file with one record for every person-year. To ensure that we worked in whole and similarly defined years, the first year considered was the calendar year in which the respondent was first 16, and the last was the one before the interview, i.e. the calendar year 1985.

We opted for windows one year wide, but we could have made other decisions. If we had made them wider, then much of the resolution capable of showing up rapid changes in the labour market might have been lost; in general the narrower they are the better. But the narrower they become, the more intractable becomes the task of looking at the duration of events inside the window. For example, if you ask for how many days in this year people were unemployed, most of the population will take a value of zero, and of those who were unemployed at all during the year, the single most common value was 365 days.

While there may still be substantive interest in this duration variable, if we then calculate the mean number of days spent in unemployment across various subsamples or over time, we are averaging across two rather different things: the risk of being unemployed at all during the year, and the duration of unemployment spells, the latter variable being truncated at 365 days.

However, a neat solution is possible. Duration in an activity can be thought of as a conditional probability of leaving the event given that you have entered it. In other words, if as well as risk of entering an event type in each year in question we also consider the risk of leaving the event type in that year, we have something that will often act as the conceptual equivalent of duration. Moreover, we have the solution to the problem with durations discussed above in the section on different units of analysis: if we are trying to trace trends in the durations of different events, where in time should these events be centred? We instead ask two analytically distinct questions: what is the risk of becoming unemployed in each year? and what is the risk of getting out of unemployment in each year?

Writing a SIR program to create a time-window file

The SIR program to create a time-windowed file is quite complex, so it is very important to write the structure of the program first in outline, making absolutely sure that the records and cases are initialised and processed in the correct sequence.

Figure 3 shows the structure for a time-window SIR program to write out how many times in each year from age 14 to 1985 that the person flowed into and out of non-employment, and how long the person spent in various different types of activity.

```
collect together all the variables that will be needed
process cases
     initialise the first year to the one when aged 14
     begin the loop
          define the beginning and end of the time window
          set durations and flows to be 0
          process records
               count flows and durations during the year
               write out the results
          end process records
          add one year to both age and calendar year
          if calendar year is now greater than 1985, exit loop
     end loop
end process cases
```

Figure 3
Structure of a time-window SIR program

Once the structure is clear, one can work on getting the various parts of the program right. The heart of the program involved delineating precisely how much if any of each event record should be considered within the window, and then calculating various states and events.

There were seven logical possibilities of the relationship between the time-window (the calendar year) and the event in question. A pictorial representation of each type is shown in Figure 4, together with a type number that can be included in the program comments to remind us what various parts of the program are designed to do. (For the sake of brevity, the terms 'bow' and 'eow' are used in Figure 4 to denote the beginning of the time window and the end of the time window respectively.) The event

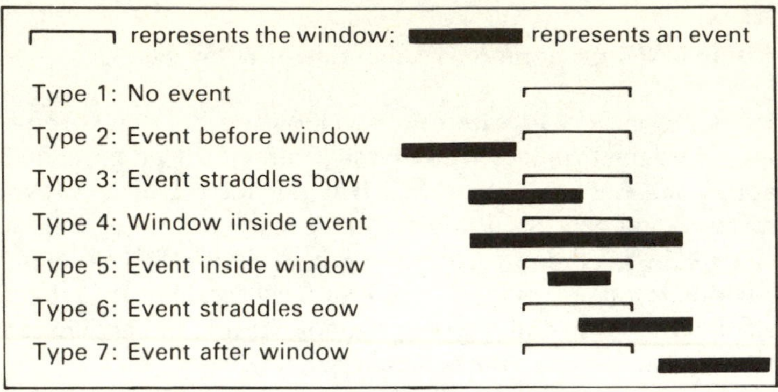

Figure 4
Relationships between events and time-windows

might, if short, fall completely within the window, or, if long, it might straddle it completely. The event might fall entirely before or entirely after the time window under consideration. It might overlap it at the beginning but end during the window, or overlap at the end, starting before the window end but continue beyond it. Finally, because the work history did not begin until the respondent left full-time education, it was possible that there would be years at the beginning for which there was no event at all in the time window; such periods of time had to be correctly recorded as time spent in education.

Once the programming task is broken down into these seven conceptual components, it becomes manageable. It is clear, for example, that with type 3 events, we should count only the period between the beginning of the window and the end of the event when cumulating durations spent in various activities inside the time window. Similarly, if we consider the type of change by comparing this event with the previous one, we are only going to need to calculate flows in types 5 and 6, as it is only in these two types that the transition occurs inside the window.

Debugging and checking programs of this complexity is extremely important. It is useful to begin work on a very small number of cases, and to instruct SIR to write what it is doing at every stage. At the heart of the program, SIR should be asked to write out a message about every record every time it encounters it. The message might say the starting and finishing date of the event, the type of activity that the event is, and the type number as in Figure

2. The debugging program should also write out the identification number and age at time of interview each time it loops through the 'process cases' instruction (i.e. every time it moves on to a new case), and, within that, the value of the year and the person's age in this year every time it loops round calculating the appropriate values for this time window. To check the correct placement of the line which instructs SIR to now write a case to the SPSS system file, it is useful to add a line which instructs it to write out the value of the variables as they are written to the output file.

The only other part of the program that is in any way tricky is to set up a variable into which you put the current value of employment status (0 if not employed, 1 if employed) to enable the program to recall this value and compare it with the employment status of the next record.

The full program required to create this SPSS file is available from the authors. From a SIR database containing information about 600 20–60 year olds, this program creates an SPSS system file with over 14,000 person-year cases. The file will contain a disproportionate number of cases at the younger ages and the more recent periods in time: only the older members of the sample have experienced being over 50 and employment during the 1950s, but everyone has employment records relating to when they were 20 and in 1985.

The advantage of using SIR as a pre-processor in this way is that we retain the ability to change our minds about what it is we are interested in and how this might be calculated. If we decide we are interested next in transitions into and out of education, or between full-time and part-time employment, we only need change a few lines of the program to achieve this.

Using the facilities of SPSS to explore this file

Two illustrations will now be given of the way in which this data can now be further manipulated inside SPSS.

Although the graphical features of SPSSX have not been implemented on many university mainframes, SPSS-PC interfaces with Microsoft Chart and gives the social researcher access to a very powerful and flexible set of graphical routines from inside the SPSS environment. One of the first exploratory tasks in the person-years file might be to plot the probability of inflows and outflows against both lifestage and cohort. The GRAPH instruction in SPSS allows a line graph linking the mean values of a dependent variable within categories of the X-axis variable to be constructed. Thus to plot the probability of inflow into non-employment by age, the instruction is:

graph/line mean (inflow) by thisage.

The resulting graph can be manipulated within Microsoft Chart to alter default labelling, line type or whatever. Finally, the graph itself can also be captured by a proprietory program such as Inset and inserted into a text file that is being word-processed. Thus the data analyst has access to high quality aids during the thinking and exploring stage of the research; without this, it was often the case that only when the final version of a paper with a professionally drawn graph appeared that a relationship or even an error was noticed for the first time in the data.

To illustrate this, compare the risk of inflow and outflow by age. Two remarks are needed about the variables themselves. The idea that the unemployed 'inflow' into the unemployment state (usually onto the unemployment register) and 'outflow' from that state when they leave the register is so well-established that it would be perverse not to use it. However, we are interested in all forms of non-employment for whatever reason; particularly when looking at women, we want to ask a behavioural question about their activity in the past, not an essentially attitudinal one. We are therefore left with the awkwardness of a double-negative: people inflowing into non-employment and outflowing out of non-employment. Secondly, although in theory more than one inflow or outflow is possible in any one year, in fact only 0.1 per cent of people have more than one of either event in any given year, so repeated events within the year will be ignored. The different shape of the risk of inflow and outflow broken down by different ages and different points in time is shown in Figure 5.

It will be important in due course to perform multivariate analysis, where both life course and period are considered together. Only at that point will bias in these graphs in favour of the more recent times and younger ages be corrected. We will also want to investigate whether the link between age and risk of non-employment has changed as unemployment has risen. But it is an important principle in all data analysis that one should be thoroughly conversant with the shape and form of bivariate relationships before proceeding to anything more elaborate.

These graphs suggest strongly that the changes that have

occurred over time have affected the rate of inflow rather than outflow. In other words, the chances of entering a period of non-employment in any one year have grown sharply whereas the probability of getting out of that period have remained stable. This finding contradicts the results obtained by Pissarides (1986) based on aggregate data that the rise in unemployment during the 1980s was mainly due to the decline in outflows rather than the rise in inflows. The graphs also seem to refute the idea that employers do not like taking on older workers; the graph of outflow is relatively flat when plotted against age, once the initial flows into employment have been taken into account.

This file with the person-year as the unit is now in a form where discrete-time models can be constructed within SPSS with ease. Allison, in his excellent introduction to regression in event history and analysis, says that this approach 'is eminently practical and can be applied in a great many situations' (1984: 15). Essentially, we can do regression using the standard facilities available in SPSS. The dependent variables can be the probability of having an inflow or an outflow event in the year in question, and the independent variables can be dummies to represent different periods of time or ages of the respondent (or covariates if graphical inspection suggests that the relationship is linear), qualifications, sex, partner's economic activity status during the year and so on. Thus both constant and time-varying explanatory variables can be introduced with ease. For exploratory purposes, OLS regression can be used, saving the more costly maximum likelihood estimation required for logit modelling to be used to calculate unbiased estimates of coefficients.

Working directly with a purpose-built SPSS file: The time-period vectors approach

One significant reason for using a database package such as SIR is the asymmetry in the narrative data. The younger SCEL respondents may have had only a few years of life since the age of 14, but the very oldest group of respondents entered the workforce in 1942; an efficient database management system will store these records in a form that is at once easily retrievable and economical in its use of computer space.

If we are willing to forego the economy, however, it becomes possible to spread this data into a symmetrical rectangular file. We

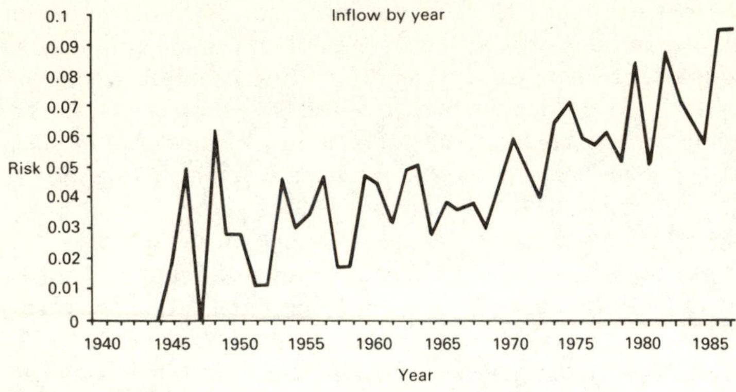

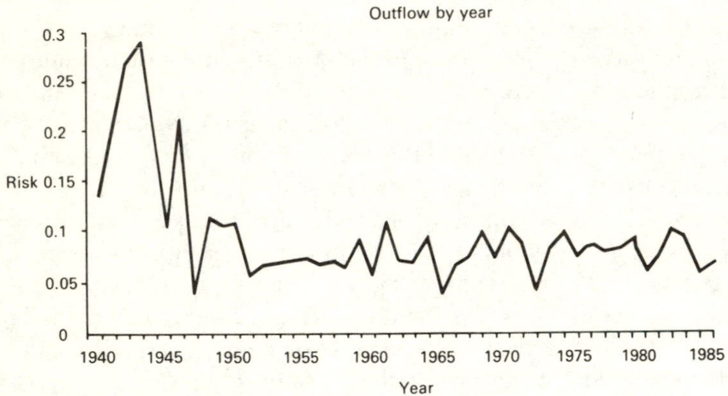

Figure 5
Inflow and outflow by year

have constructed a rectangular SPSSX system file, which takes the individual respondent as the case, and contains details of various employment and family attributes for each two-month period in chronological time since January 1927; a total of 356 periods. We take this starting date as the earliest entry in the work histories of those partners of SCEL respondents who provided material to the 1987 SCEL household survey; none of this partner's data is however used in what follows. So for each category of work history information we have a 356 element vector, with element 356 providing information about March–April 1986. (For those SCEL

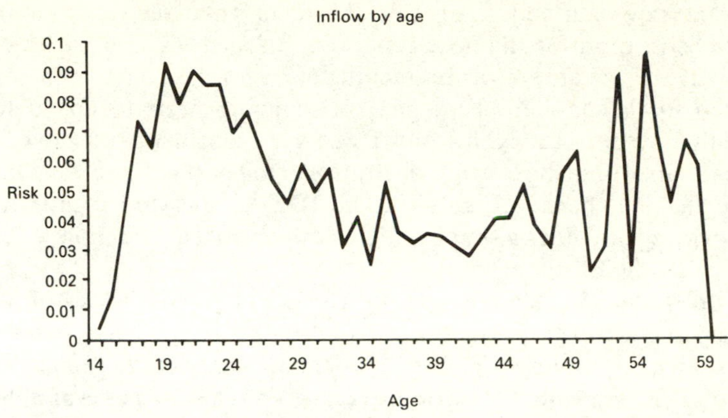

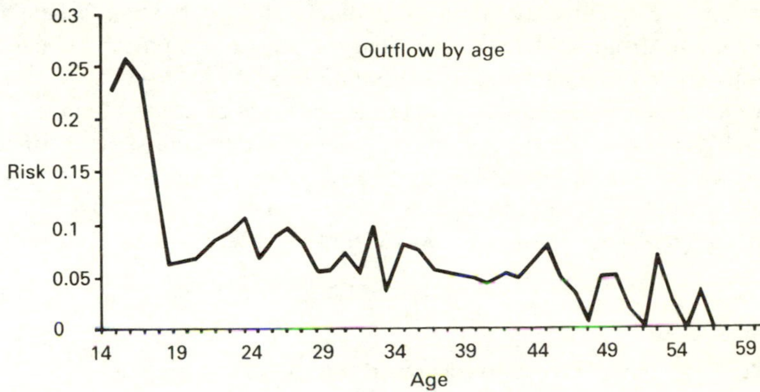

Figure 5 cont.
Inflow and outflow by age

respondents who participated in the household survey we have a further 7 elements, but these are also ignored in the following analyses.) With this arrangement of data, just about half of all the elements are blank (i.e. coded as missing) since they relate to a period before the respondents reached the age of 14.

The decision to use a two-month unit rather than the one-month unit as in the raw data may reduce the usefulness of the rectangular file for certain purposes (though it is perfectly appropriate for all the illustrations given in this paper). If monthly units turn out to be required, we have no alternative but to return to the raw data and regenerate the rectangular file in the more extensive form for the next generation of analysis. This signals a relative disadvantage of the rectangular vector file approach: the need for a considerable degree of planning prior to any data-analysis. But to set against this is the very considerable analytical flexibility within the overall constraints of the particular rectangular file that has been generated. (The IDEAS software mentioned previously provides a simple means for generating one-month files from the SCEL data.)

From the 356-element vectors we have derived a series of 45-element vectors, representing attributes on a yearly basis with the first element representing the respondents' first year in the labour force. (It is possible to produce year-by-year summary variables from the two-month vectors, by taking modal values for the year, taking the occurrence of a particular status or change in status throughout the year, by registering the status at a particular fixed point in each year, or by a combination of these; in what follows we use inter alia, variables for the occurrence of unemployment in each year, and for the modal occupational prestige score.) Since we know the respondents' ages and years of first entry to the labour force, we can look separately at 'cohort groups' selected on the basis of the historical year of entry to the labour force.

Are previously unemployed men differentially subject to unemployment?

We can illustrate the use of the vectors file with a simple example, again drawn from our work on employment in the SCEL sample. We know that people in relatively low-status occupations are disproportionately at risk of unemployment. It is also suggested that a history of unemployment increases the risk of subsequent unemployment, either because of the erosion of job skills while out of work, or because of the effect of a record of unemployment on prospective employers' perceptions of candidates for jobs. We can explore the interrelations between these factors using two of the vectors from the master file. In what follows we use the vector of months of unemployment for each successive year in the workforce, and a vector giving the respondents' modal occupations for each year. (We have in fact taken the Hope-Goldthorpe (H-G) occupational prestige score for each occupation, which allows us to rank occupations from lowest, which score in the range 10–20, to highest which score 80–90).

We start by constructing a series of new composite variables that combine information about educational level, the occupational level of the first job and the level of the most recent job. For each successive year we set the value of the relevant composite variable to equal 0 if the respondent's first job on entry to the labour force had an H-G score below 30, and to 1 if 30 and above; and if (after year 1) the H-G score of the job held in the immediately previous year was above 40, the derived variable was set to equal 2; and for all those respondents still in full-time education after age 18 (i.e. those with some higher education) the derived variable was set to equal 3. So our new variable vector combines some attributes of the original characteristics of the SCEL respondents, with some evidence of the occupational trajectory through the life-course. It is of course possible to construct more complex composite variables using more of the work history imformation.

Our example uses the very simplest data presentation technique, cross tabulation. We take the constructed yearly occupational trajectory vector as a predictor (in the SPSS system file this is the variable list OCCTR1 TO OCTR45). We recode the 'months unemployment per year' vector (UNEMP1 to UNEMP45) into a binary form indicating whether or not the respondent experienced any unemployment in the course of each year. Then, to produce the results summarised in Table 1, we select those male respondents whose first job dated between 1961 and 1971, and issue fifteen instructions of the form:

```
CROSSTAB OCCTR1 BY UNEMP1
. . . . . .
CROSSTAB OCCTR15 BY UNEMP15
```

The first part of Table 1 shows the proportion in each occupational category who experienced any unemployment in each successive year. Consider for example year 15. We see that 24 per cent of those who entered at a low occupational level and have remained there were unemployed during the year; also unemployed were 13 per cent of those who entered at a level scoring above 30 but have not subsequently risen to a level scoring above 40, 5 per cent of those entering or achieving an occupational level scoring above 40, and 1 per cent of those with higher education.

Certainly the composite predictor variables were put together on a pragmatic basis, dichotomising each of the component

Table 1

SCEL work histories – men, entry cohort 1961–71

Years since entry	*Unemployment rate by years since entry*														
	1	*2*	*3*	*4*	*5*	*6*	*7*	*8*	*9*	*10*	*11*	*12*	*13*	*14*	*15*
Model 1: Entry and achieved occupational characteristics															
low entry hgc	.07	.10	.09	.05	.07	.09	.08	.11	.11	.13	.16	.13	.23	.30	.24
high entry hgc	.03	.01	.03	.03	.03	.05	.06	.06	.06	.06	.08	.07	.08	.13	.13
last hgc high		.01	.01	.02	.04	.04	.05	.03	.03	.04	.03	.04	.04	.05	.05
education high	.03	.02	.01	.01	.03	.02	.01	.02	.01	.03	.01	.03	.03	.01	.01
Total	.03	.02	.02	.02	.03	.05	.04	.05	.04	.05	.05	.05	.07	.08	.08
Chi-square Prob	.21	.00	.00	.41	.21	.10	.04	.01	.00	.01	.00	.01	.00	.00	.00
Uncert.Reduct.	.01	.12	.08	.02	.02	.02	.04	.04	.05	.03	.08	.03	.08	.12	.10

Model 2: Entry and achieved occupational characteristics plus unemployment history

Employed last year:															
low entry hgc	.07	.07	.03	.01	.04	.06	.03	.05	.03	.08	.06	.04	.11	.13	.08
high entry hgc	.03	.01	.02	.02	.02	.03	.02	.01	.03	.03	.02	.03	.02	.06	.04
last hgc high		.01	.00	.02	.03	.02	.03	.01	.03	.02	.01	.03	.03	.02	.03
education high	.03	.01	.01	.01	.01	.01	.00	.01	.01	.02	.00	.02	.01	.01	.00
Unemployed last year:															
low entry hgc		.50	.63	.43	.75	.43	.57	.83	.63	.57	.78	.60	1	.75	.58
high entry hgc		.14	.67	.14	.29	.57	.57	.69	.57	.43	.73	.53	.79	.88	.75
last hgc high		.00	.50	1	.50	.67	.57	.71	.17	.43	.83	.63	.40	.70	.50
education high		.25	.33	.50	1	.50	.33	1	.33	1	.40	.50	.75	.25	1
Grand mean	.03	.02	.02	.02	.03	.05	.04	.05	.04	.05	.05	.05	.07	.08	.08
Chi-squared P	.21	.00	.00	.00	.00	.00	.00	.00	.00	.00	.00	.00	.00	.00	.00
Uncert. reduct.	.01	.22	.37	.20	.23	.24	.34	.51	.28	.23	.52	.29	.43	.42	.44

Key
hgc = Hope-Goldthorpe categories.

variables at the level that served best to predict unemployment. But the results correspond to our prior (theory based) expectations of the operation of the labour market, and the vector does seem to predict successfully. Regularly throughout the first fifteen years in the labour force (which is all that is available for this entry cohort) those least advantageously placed in terms of their initial and subsequently achieved occupational characteristics, are regularly and reliably the most at risk of unemployment. The extent of the risk of unemployment of the least well placed increases remarkably through this period. Admittedly, this was a period of generally rising unemployment: 2 per cent of our sample experienced some unemployment of more than one month's duration in their first year in the labour market, and this proportion rose to 8 per cent by their fifteenth year. But our least advantaged group faced a risk of being unemployed, for each of years 9 to 15, around three times as high as the average, while those more advantaged in terms of our predictor variable, faced a considerably lower than average risk of unemployment throughout this period.

Variance reduction statistics are not appropriate for a very seriously skewed-distribution binary variable such as the yearly rate of unemployment. But statistics concerning the 'reduction of uncertainty' (i.e. the extent to which the value of the dependent variable may be predicted by knowledge of the independent) are usable. (We have used the uncertainty reduction coefficient described in the SPSS manual (1975: 226–7)). The statistics for uncertainty reduction using the composite advantage variables to predict unemployment rates in Table 1 are somewhat unstable. But it does seem that towards the end of the period our composite predictor variable reduced uncertainty, or 'explained', about 10 per cent of the occurrence of unemployment.

This leaves quite a lot of the unemployment in our records unexplained. But now we add in to our crosstabulation the respondents' previous history of unemployment. The second part of Table 1 shows what happens when we split each of the values of the derived predictor variables by whether or not the respondent was unemployed during the previous year. This new 8-value derived predictor is very much more effective at reducing uncertainty: the coefficient is still unstable, but lies in the range 30–50 per cent. Broken down by previous unemployment in this way, origin and occupational achievement seem to make less difference. Those who entered the workforce in low status occupations who have not risen far in status terms and who have not had previous experience of unemployment, are still more at risk than others who have not previously experienced unemployment – but the margin of difference of risk is now very much smaller.

Or to put it another way, a very large part of what might otherwise appear to be an occupation-related risk of unemployment, may alternatively be interpreted as a previous-unemployment-related risk of unemployment. Unemployment is certainly concentrated among those in low status occupations. But within the low status occupation groups (as in the other groups), most of those who become unemployed in a given year have also been unemployed in the previous year.

There are two serious potential problems with the analysis so far. Spells of unemployment often last for more than a year, so what we see here may in principle be no more than a consequence of a large number of long term unemployed who are continuously unemployed year by year. Potentially even more subversive of our tentative conclusion is the possibility that it is not previous unemployment that determines present unemployment, but some third, so far unidentified, characteristic of the individual that predicts both this year's unemployment and last year's. We can in fact go some way to answering both of these problems.

We can cope with the first of these problems very directly, by excluding the longer-term unemployed. Our original unemployment vector, remember, registered months of unemployment per year. Table 2 is constructed by taking, for each year, only those respondents who had some employment during the previous year.

Table 2

Alternative predictors of unemployment – SCEL men cohort entering employment 1962–71, for each year, excluding cases with continuous unemployment through the previous year

Years since entry	*7*	*8*	*9*	*10*	*11*	*12*	*13*	*14*	*15*
	Uncertainty reduction coefficients								
Unemployed:									
1 During previous 5 years	.17	.36	.04	.10	.30	.06	.19	.17	.16
2 since entry	.19	.23	.04	.08	.22	.04	.17	.13	.13
3 previous year	.16	.41	.10	.08	.35	.13	.22	.16	.22
Row 1/Row 2	.87	1.55	1.11	1.26	1.36	1.68	1.17	1.31	1.30

Of around 70 unemployed people in this cohort's year 15 in the labour market, for example, 25 are excluded by this procedure.

Having extracted all of the cases where the previous year's unemployment continues into the subsequent year, we still find (row 3) a quite considerable reduction in uncertainty about each year as a result of knowing whether or not the respondent was unemployed in the previous year. Part of the result in the previous paragraph does reflect no more than the continuity of long-term unemployment; the uncertainty coefficient of 0.22 in year 15 for example does correspond to a 0.39 coefficient when the longer-term unemployed are included. But more than half the effect remains when they are excluded.

The second objection can only be approached somewhat indirectly. If indeed there is some such unidentified characteristic, it must presumably inhere in the individual's background or personality, and apply through the life-course. Let us hypothesize that any such hidden characteristic has its effects randomly through the life course; then, presumably, the more of the previous life we include in a predictor variable for the present state, the better should be our prediction. Compare rows 1 and 2 in Table 2. Row 1 uses a binary unemployment experience/no unemployment experience variable calculated, for each year, from the previous five years as a predictor; row 2 uses a similar variable, but calculated for the whole work history (in both cases excluding, on a yearly basis those with no employment in the previous year). Contrary to our null hypothesis, the five-year variable performs substantially better than the whole-life variables. (Only in year 7 does the 'whole career' variable perform better than the five year variable; but the 'whole career' is in this case just six years long.)

We conclude for the moment, therefore, that part of the explanatory power of recent history of unemployment on current unemployment probably relates to the unemployment exercise itself rather than to some prior state of the individual. We presume the existence of some mechanism of disqualification of the sort we have previously outlined. The evidence is not yet conclusive: we need in particular to attach some extra controls to allow for the influence of historical changes in labour demand in the economy.

But though we cannot yet be completely certain of the mechanism, we do certainly have a definite conclusion at the descriptive level: men of the 1962–71 entry cohort who have been recently unemployed, are greatly more at risk than men of otherwise broadly similar occupational background who have not been recently unemployed. Unemployment is thus concentrated more narrowly than on simple occupational groups. The result is not restricted to this entry cohort. Table 3 estimates the same model over the longer time span available for the 1946–55 entry cohort. Very similar results emerge. It is largely those who have been unemployed who become unemployed.

It is however not these tentative conclusions themselves that we would commend to our readers, but the mechanics of the analysis. We are able to use the most straightforward data presentation and statistical techniques, and the most widely available data analysis package, to explore this most complex data collection. Our conclusions are not yet entirely solid. But our next steps – for example adding information on our respondents' external economic environment in the form of yearly unemployment rates – may proceed along the same straightforward lines.

Conclusion

Many projects have collected event data that has remained under- or even un-analysed. The sheer complexity of the data is often not appreciated at the time when research timetables are drawn up. The potential of life event data is exciting. We should be able to come up with answers about the enduring effects of early labour market experiences, for example (preliminary analysis seems to confirm the view that early unemployment is not very strongly associated with later unemployment). It may be that we end up concluding that the things that have the most impact are those that are proximate in time – but we cannot know this without access to this sort of data over a lifetime. One contributory factor which helps to explain why life event data has not yet lived up to its promise of rich reward is, we feel, the relative under-development of exploratory, browsing techniques for this material.

If we are to achieve more than painting in the fingernails on the ceilings of our Social Sistine Chapels, we have to find ways of doing this sort of analysis within the statistical and computing environment with which the general researcher is familiar. Sophisticated techniques and special purpose software will certainly be necessary on occasion; but they should only be used where they *are* really necessary, and will repay the not inconsiderable personal investment required to use them.

Table 3

SCEL work histories – men, entry cohort 1946–56

	Unemployment rate by years since entry																													
Years since entry	*1*	*2*	*3*	*4*	*5*	*6*	*7*	*8*	*9*	*10*	*11*	*12*	*13*	*14*	*15*	*16*	*17*	*18*	*19*	*20*	*21*	*22*	*23*	*24*	*25*	*26*	*27*	*28*	*29*	*30*
Model 1: Entry and achieved occupational characteristics																														
low entry hgc	.04	.04	.08	.03	.05	0.4	.06	.04	.04	0	0	.02	.04	.04	.02		0	.03	.03	.03	0	0	.01	.04	.03	.04	.04	.03	.08	.09
high entry hgc	.02	.02	.01	.01	.00	.02	.01	.03	.00	.03	.03	.03	.03	.02	.03	.03	.02	.02	.02	.01	.03	.03	.03	.03	.03	.02	.04	.04	.04	.08
last hgc high		.01	0	.02	.02	.01	.01	.01	.01	.01	.01	.00	.01	.02	.01	.00	.00	.01	.00	.01	.01	.01	.01	.02	.02	.02	.04	.04	.04	.05
education high	.05	.02	.03	.03	.03	.02	.02	0	0	0	0	.03	0	.02	.02		0	0	.02	0	0	.03	.02	.02	.02	0	.03	.05	.03	.03
Grand mean	2.6	2.2	2	1.8	1.8	1.6	1.6	2	.8	1.6	1.4	1.8	1.8	2	1.8	1.2	1	1.4	1.4	1.2	1.4	2	1.8	2.6	2.6	2.2	4.2	4.0	4.7	6.5
Chi-square P	.21	.48	.00	.52	.05	.49	.09	.42	.08	.22	.31	.30	.22	.68	.57	.11	.21	.47	.42	.46	.21	.20	.63	.75	.84	.44	.99	.91	.54	.40
Uncert. Reduct.	.02	.02	.13	.02	.08	.03	.05	.04	.10	.07	.07	.05	.06	.01	.02	.10	.09	.04	.04	.04	.08	.06	.02	.01	.01	.04	.00	.00	.01	.01
Model 2: Entry and achieved occupational characteristics plus unemployment history																														
Employed last year:																														
low entry hgc	.04	.00	.03	.00	.02	.00	.06	.00	.00	.00	.00	.02	.02	.00	.00	.00	.00	.02	.02	.01	.00	.00	.01	.03	.00	.00	.01	.01	.05	.05
high entry hgc	.02	.00	.00	.00	.00	.02	.01	.02	.00	.02	.02	.01	.01	.00	.02	.01	.01	.01	.01	.01	.02	.02	.02	.00	.02	.01	.03	.01	.02	.05
last hgc high		.00	.00	.01	.01	.00	.01	.00	.00	.01	.01	.00	.00	.01	.00	.00	.00	.01	.00	.01	.01	.01	.01	.02	.01	.01	.03	.02	.01	.03
education high	.05	.00	.03	.02	.04	.02	.02	.00	.00	.00	.00	.03	.00	.02	.02	.00	.00	.00	.02	.00	.00	.03	.00	.00	.02	.00	.03	.02	.00	.02
Unemployed last year:																														
low entry hgc		1	1	.50	1	.67	.00	.67	.67	.00	.00	.60	1	1	.33	.00		1	.50	1	.00	.60	.33	1	.67	.75	.67	.25	1	.50
high entry hgc		1	.43	.67	.50	.00	.00	1	.00	1	.33	.50	.60	.50	.33	.80	.40	.25	.67	.00	.50			1	.40	.33	.50	.75	.57	.75
last hgc high		1		1	.67	.50	.50	1	.33	.50	1		1	1	.67	.00	1		.50	.50	.00	.00	.50	.50	.50	1	.50	.71	.75	.83
education high		.33	0	.50	.00	.00	.00	.00					.00		.00	.00				.00			.50	1	.00	.00		1	.67	.50
Grand mean	2.6	2.2	2	1.8	1.8	1.6	1.6	2	.8	1.6	1.4	1.8	1.8	2	1.8	1.2	1	1.4	1.4	1.2	1.4	2	1.8	2.6	2.6	2.2	4.2	4	4.7	6.5
Chi-squared P	.21	.00	.00	.00	.00	.00	.00	.00	.00	.00	.00	.00	.00	.00	.00	.00	.00	.00	.00	.00	.00	.00	.00	.00	.00	.00	.00	.00	.00	.00
Uncert. reduct.	.02	.96	.55	.48	.49	.30	.14	.55	.56	.24	.31	.35	.43	.49	.34	.54	.49	.20	.43	.27	.14	.22	.26	.57	.28	.47	.15	.49	.41	.29

Key

hgc = Hope-Goldthorpe categories.

References

Allison, Paul, D., (1984), 'Event history analysis: regression for longitudinal event data', Sage University Paper series on Quantitative Applications in the Social Sciences, 07–001, Beverly Hills and London: Sage Publications.

Burchell, B., (1991), 'Job changes and size of establishments: sources and destinations', in Elias and Davies, (1991).

Dale, A., (1986), *A Teaching Package for the Database Management System SIR*, University of Surrey, Department of Sociology.

Elias, P. and Davies, R., (1991), *Life and Work Histories*, Oxford University Press.

Ni Bhrolchain, M. and Timaeus, I., (1983), 'A general approach to the machine handling of event history data with special reference to employment histories', *Centre for Population Studies Working Paper*, 83–1, London School of Hygiene and Tropical Medicine.

Pissarides, C., (1986), 'Unemployment and vacancies in Britain', *Economic Policy*, (October): 499–559.

SIR, (1986), *SIR/DBMS User's Manual: Scientific Information Database Retrieval System*, Version 2.

SIR, (1988), *SIR/Light; Scientific Information Retrieval Database Management System: Quick and Easy Guide to SIR*.

SPSS, (1975), *Statistical Package for the Social Sciences*, second edn.

Ageing and life history: the meaning of reminiscence in late life

Peter G. Coleman

Introduction

In this paper I would like to consider whether there are, in later life, special psychological influences acting upon individuals' constructions of their life histories. The questions raised by such enquiry are close to the heart of a developmental psychology of ageing and also have important sociological implications, not least for the collection of life history data from individuals. Is the tendency to reminisce itself a characteristic of old age? Whether it is or not, are there particular characteristics that distinguish the content of an older person's story? Which external circumstances shape the nature of reminiscence in later life? Are there individual differences among older people that we should be attentive to if we are to gauge the psychological relevance, and thus also see more clearly the social relevance, of a person's story?

This paper is divided into four main sections. The first section considers a variety of influences acting on the construction of an individual's life history, including personality, culture, major turning points in life, individuals' search for meaning as well as their need to explain and defend their actions; this material indicates that the psychological study of memory has only just begun to tackle issues concerning life histories. The following section focuses on old age and the different theoretical viewpoints that have been expressed about the functions of reminiscence in late life. On this basis, the third section develops a differential approach to individuals' involvement with their life histories and describes the characteristics and consequences of the different types that have been identified. It is stressed how important it is for the researcher of life histories to be aware of the different needs and dilemmas that people can express in attempting to tell the story of their lives. The final section illustrates the interaction between individual development and the depiction of social history.

The construction of an individual's life history

A life history, at any age, is the particular construction of an individual person in a particular context. Even the most superficial consideration of life histories, both autobiographical and biographical, demonstrates the importance of individual differences, in the selection of events and experiences which make up the content of the story, and in the extent to which this material has been integrated and restructured. A life history is the product of a variety of factors, some social and cultural, but others more individual, and involving both motivational and cognitive factors. There is also the influence of the immediate context to be considered, in particular the role of individuals who have directly or indirectly stimulated the telling of the story. There is an interplay between what people are able to tell about their lives and what they perceive to be of interest to their audience.

There are people who grow up without seemingly having had the opportunity to make more than the most rudimentary assessment of their life course. In such circumstances the very attempt to describe it can lead to new insights. Grimes (1988) refers to therapeutic work with criminals in North America; individuals' accounts of their life histories are built up by systematic questioning about their reported actions. This leads to the development of new material and also the perception of recurrent themes i.e. simplification as well as amplification.

Individual differences in ability to formulate a life history are also apparent in old age, and seem relatively independent of general mental ability. Formal tests have been the focus of most previous work on age and memory, but experimental psychologists who have come to take an interest in the natural contexts in which memory functions in everyday life have also noticed striking individual differences in the development of skills for reconstructing personal histories. For example Rabbitt, reviewing the recent work of his own research unit comments on the lack of memory for life history in many people he has investigated: 'the fact that many healthy, active elderly people seem to recall only the most general outlines of most of their life experiences and social roles must mean that they now inhabit a strange conceptual universe, in which most of the data on which the rest of us base our public and private self-definitions have become inaccessible' (Rabbitt, 1988: 506).

While individual differences are stressed, it is important not to forget the role of culture in shaping the form of life histories. The idea that there are stages in life is common to many cultures, although the actual categories employed may differ. In both biographies and autobiographies individuals refer more or less explicitly to culturally shared norms and expectations which provide a framework to the depiction of a particular life course. These may be accepted stages of life, such as childhood, adolescence, adulthood, old age. They may also make use of standard mythical scenarios, such as the archetypal story of 'the hero', which can have great power in structuring an account e.g. 'the call . . . the journey . . . the battle . . . the return'. Sometimes it is society's rituals which provide the framework e.g. birth . . . going to school . . . beginning work . . . getting married . . . retirement . . . the funeral. Only rarely do people compose their own structures as well as content. Indeed often the structure can impinge greatly on the content. For example, it is striking how in various cultures the stories of 'saints' have common themes.

Culturally shared notions of stages of life do not always determine the structure of an individual's story. Some life histories are less focused on the multiple stages of an entire life but rather focus on one or two major turning points. Marcoen's work at the University of Louvain on important life ideas shows that many people can respond to questioning about the emergence of meaning and commitments in their lives (Marcoen, 1988). In his sample of Belgian university students, their parents and grandparents, 24 per cent of the important ideas named were considered turning points in the person's life course, and 52 per cent were characterised as very important and having lasting effects on the person's life. It is not surprising if such gaining of insight forms a crucial part of a person's story.

However compelling a particular structure of a life story may appear, there can be no such thing as a final account of a person's life. Any coherent account is shaped by an underlying and continuing search for meaning, whether on the part of the subjects or their biographer. Most of the earliest surviving life history accounts come from the realm of religious biography, and they focus on particular themes such as conversion. Analysis of them can provide illustrations of the dynamic forces at work in the construction and reconstruction of life histories, because much of the material that influenced their formulation, namely sacred texts, are available for inspection.

An excellent example is provided by one of the most celebrated of autobiographies, the 'Confessions' of St Augustine. It contains a reconstruction of his conversion experience, written fourteen years after the events it depicts. This has recently been subjected to analysis (McGuckin, 1986). The passage is striking for its vivid narrative which appears at first sight to guarantee its authenticity. Augustine, provoked by the conversation of friends who have come to visit him, enters an 'agony of indecision' as to the way of life he should follow. He runs into the garden outside his villa, throws himself weeping under a fig tree, hears the sing-song voice of a child in a neighbouring house calling 'take and read', interprets this as a sign from God, picks up the copy of St Paul's letters which he has to hand, and finds in the passage he first puts his finger on the answer to all his doubts. A close examination of this episode, however, shows many parallels with the biblical passages to which we know Augustine subsequently became very attached. There are obvious similarities with the passage of the conversion of St Paul in Acts (which itself retraces the earlier biblical account of the conversion of Helidorus). Allusions to the psalms also figure in the account. Even the fact of the fig tree seems to echo the passage in John's gospel where Nathanael is drawn bewildered to Christ: 'I saw you under the fig tree' (St John 1.49).

The aim of such a scholarly investigation of Augustine's narrative is not to deny the authenticity of Augustine's experience of conversion, but rather to draw out how the account – in the stylised conventions characteristic of historical and personal narrative of his time – is constructed around biblical concepts. It is through an understanding of the Bible that Augustine has found meaning in his own life story. He places his own conversion in the stream of God's providence for sinful man throughout time. It is also a good example of the 'literary' use of reminiscence and life history.

A somewhat different influence on the construction of an individual's life history is provided by the need to explain and defend one's actions. A good example, again from the realm of religious autobiography, is provided by John Henry Newman's 'Apologia Pro Vita Sua'. The changing use of memory for particular events which Newman presents in the course of justifying his leaving the Church of England for the Roman Catholic Church has recently been analysed (Thomas, 1988).

Earlier periods of life do change their character when remembered, in ways that may surprise us if we have preserved a record of their previous character, in writing or even in memory itself. For example I can distinctly remember saying to myself when I left school for the last time 'never forget how terrible these school years were'. But now I find it difficult to recapture that degree of negative feeling towards my schooldays. The content of my memories for school is more positive than I could have predicted twenty four years ago.

The systematic study of autobiographical memory within psychology has only recently begun to encompass the reconstruction of the personal past (Neisser 1982, Rubin 1986). This is part of a movement in psychology away from the investigation of unnatural laboratory situations to more real world concerns. The purposeful use of memory in a variety of contexts has become the subject of study, not just accurate recall of information under defined conditions. This requires new ways of thinking about memory. Concepts, such as the memory + race, have to lose their simplistic connotations. In ordinary life the same events have to be remembered within various contexts and the 'content' of a memory will accordingly change with the precise demand that provoked it. The 'storage' of such a memory trace has to be flexible enough to allow for multiple use.

Such considerations have made psychologists aware of the complexity of the issues involved in the study of autobiographical memory. For example the concept of 'pseudomemory' has its use in referring to situations where pressure is applied to an individual to enhance recall. Well-intentioned subjects may claim strongly that the pseudomemories refer to episodes that, in fact, did not exist. How can such memories be distinguished from other genuine personal memories or from generic personal memories, where repeated exposure to a set of related experiences gives rise to a generic image? It appears that people are well aware of such distinctions themselves and can introspect about them, when searching for the reality behind their memories (Crovitz 1986). Moreover we should not allow the presence or absence of accurate details to determine our evaluation of the significance of an episode that an individual recalls. 'The specification of details "from memory" may seem convincing, but details may be intentionally or unintentionally fabricated . . . even when details are wrong, the meaning behind a claimed episode may be quite correct' (Crovitz, 1986: 288). This conclusion corresponds with the comments made earlier about St Augustine's account of his conversion.

Considerable powers of discernment may therefore be required in evaluating the status of a memory, both on the part of the person remembering and the person listening to or reading what is remembered. Similar issues are raised to those concerning personal insight generally, which have been set out recently by two cognitive psychologists, Watts and Williams. The achievement of personal insight is difficult to assess. There may be a requirement to look beyond what is obvious and what is easy to accept. The search may involve our emotions but not in an unrestrained way. Stereotyped ruminations may need to be set aside. An attentiveness is required that is 'broad, sustained and penetrating' (Watts and Williams, 1988: 152).

One last point to be stressed is the influence on the speaker's choice of material of the perceived potential interest in it which is attributed to the listener. Similar considerations apply to the writer of a biography or an autobiography. Everyone has a story to tell but not everyone is certain of its interest to others. How some people do come to consider their story interesting while others remain unsure depends on such personal characteristics as self confidence, but also on the reactions shown by others. Some people need to be coaxed to speak about themselves. This may result in a fresh evaluation of their own lives, as in the work with criminals reported above. The influence of the stimulator of the narrative upon the narrative itself has not yet been given much consideration by psychologists but remains a potentially important area of research.

Old age and reminiscence

Old age has traditionally been regarded as a special time for reminiscing, speaking and thinking about the past. This has not always been given a positive connotation however. Aristotle observed in a telling sentence which he included in his treatise on 'Rhetoric': 'they live by memory rather than by hope, for what is left to them of life is but little compared to the long past'. In part this reflected Aristotle's own rather negative emphasis on the physical and mental deterioration he observed among older people. This is quite a different frame of mind to the one reflected for example in Cicero's panegyric, 'De Senectute', where the author looks to serenity, reflection and wisdom as rewarding features of old age.

Such opposing views of old age have been continuous themes in Western culture up to the present day, and have also characterised the debate on the meaning of reminiscence in recent times. Twenty years ago reminiscence often tended to be discouraged by professional staff working with elderly people as a result of attitudes which associated it, falsely, with mental deterioration. Now, partly due to a growing interest in individuals' oral history, the pendulum has swung completely around and reminiscence currently forms one of the most popular approaches to therapeutic and diversionary work with older people, particularly in residential settings. Only recently have some authors begun to question whether this emphasis too is exaggerated; for example Coleman (1986a), and Thornton and Brotchie (1987).

Generally speaking, those theorists who have sought normative development through adulthood and have seen old age as being characterised by special new tasks, potentials or powers, have also conceptualised reminiscence in a positive light. This applies to psychologists and psychiatrists as Buhler (1935), Jung (1933), Erikson (1959), Erikson *et al.* (1987), Butler (1963), Neugarten (1964; 1979) and Gutmann (1987). But there have also been those who on the basis of empirical research and clinical experience have argued that there is no evidence for maturational change in personality in adulthood and ageing (e.g. Costa and McCrae, 1980; Siegler *et al.*, 1979). Such authors claim that what is special to old age are the situations in which older people more often find themselves; those of declining physical abilities and loss of social roles, etc.

The implication of the latter view is that younger people would behave similarly in similar circumstances. Also to be considered is the less directly measurable but all-pervasive influence of differences between generations in the formative experiences which have affected their life expectations and attitudes. Some psychologists have claimed reminiscence to have as important a function with younger people in certain situations e.g. of loss and relocation (Hogman, 1985; Galante and Foa, 1986; Bender, 1989). Others, however, have pointed to the lack of evidence for the efficacy of encouraging people to reminisce other than its merely diversionary character (Thornton and Brotchie, 1987).

It has also been pointed out that there is little hard empirical evidence, over and above general stereotypes, even to associate increased reminiscing *per se* with old age. Studies which have investigated and not found age differences in the temporal content of thinking are often cited (e.g. Cameron, 1972; Giambra, 1977; Lowenthal *et al.*, 1975). Also, as Rabbitt (1988) has pointed out, older people do not always have a life story to tell. However, more recently the traditional association between reminiscence and old age has been reasserted from surprising directions. Writing from a sociobiological perspective Mergler and Goldstein (1983) have argued that there is a preparedness in old age for the transmission of culturally important information based on life experience, and this contribution helps explain the emergence and survival of old people within human societies.

From a different perspective cognitive psychologists have argued that the study of autobiographical memory requires a life-span approach, including both childhood amnesia and late life reminiscence (Rubin *et al.*, 1986). In general memories decay with time but a simple retention function is insufficient to explain recall in subjects over the age of about 35 years. Then reminiscence proper seems to begin, defined by 'an increase in early memories above what would be expected by a monotonically decreasing retention function' (p.208). A number of studies indicate recall of a disproportionate number of memories from the earlier stages of an individual's life. Just as childhood amnesia is a phenomenon which requires special attention in the study of autobiographical memory, so too does reminiscence of distant events in later life.

Whereas some contemporary research adds weight to a social and cultural conception of the role of reminiscence (e.g. Gutmann, 1987), other considerations relate more to the Aristotelian view of memory in late life as a solace and a refuge. Thus Rabbitt seeks to explain why cognitively intact institutionalised elderly people, in contrast to those living in the community, remember more incidents from their early years and less from the recent past. His answer reflects a consideration of the different purposes of memory in the two groups. While the young and active old need frequently to review the recent past in order to plan the immediate future, 'the institutionalised, but cognitively alert, elderly do not have to plan the routine lives which they share with all their immediate acquaintances. In this static, communal, environment rehearsal of everyday minutiae makes poor conversation. When the theatre of the mind becomes the only show in town, archival memories begin to be actively explored for scripts. Remote memories are increasingly rehearsed for recreation, and the pattern of memory accessibility across the life-cycle is changed' (Rabbitt, 1988: 503).

Although exciting in the new perspectives it offers for the study of autobiographical memory, cognitive psychology has only just begun to touch such questions of function. Therefore for a discussion of the uses of reminiscence by older people we have to rely upon developmental and social psychological theories. From a review of the existing literature on reminiscence in old age it seems possible to define a number of possible functions all reviewed below; these include 'changing social roles', the 'process of life review' and 'the maintenance of self esteem'. All, it should be noted, assume that there is a tendency for reminiscence, as an interior as well as social activity, to increase in late life.

Changing social roles

Increased reminiscence on the part of older people reflects their changing social roles. There is both a negative and positive form of this theory. The negative form is associated with the so-called 'disengagement theory' (Cumming and Henry, 1961). On the basis of a cross-sectional survey of people of different ages living in Kansas City, it was proposed that there was a tendency with age towards diminution of and withdrawal from social activities and contacts and an increase in 'interiority' reflected in increased introspection, reverie and thinking about the past. Such 'disengagement', the theory argued, was not necessarily accompanied by any loss of subjective well-being. The original theory was heavily criticised, for neglecting the effects of social and physical constraints on activity in old age as well as failing to consider generational differences in attitudes to social activity. But it is often forgotten that the theory was set up as a conscious reaction to the dominant American norms of the time which regarded the maintenance of youthful activities as the criterion of successful ageing. The theory denied this to be so.

A more positive view of changing social roles is that claimed by anthropologists for older people in traditional societies (e.g. Simmons, 1945). They were observed to take on the roles of story-teller and guardian of cultural habits and values. In both of these functions reminiscence served them well. In the most recent form of this theory, powerfully expressed in his book *Reclaimed Powers*, David Gutmann (1987) claims that there are intrinsic psychological changes which prepare older men and women to take on these new roles as 'culture tenders' and 'emeritus parents'. These include increased passivity and detachment from 'pragmatic power' on the part of men. In turn these developments have the effect of increasing their hold on the sources of 'sacred power'.

Disengagement from practical affairs thus is a prelude to engagement with the higher, more abstract, level of cultural values. Rather than merely preparing the rest of society for their demise, as in the original functional theory of disengagement, this transition enables older people in traditional societies to 'help to provide young men with the powerful meanings that they require in exchange for giving up the temptations of barbarism and random procreation in favor of civility and fatherhood' (Gutmann, 1987: 233). In this role the capacity of older people to exploit their memories over a long period of life experience is put to good use.

A process of life review

Reminiscence in old age constitutes a process of life review necessitated by the awareness that life is coming to an end. This view was eloquently expressed by the American psychiatrist Robert Butler in a paper first published in 1963. He drew on examples from his own clinical experience, as well as from a variety of relevant literature. There are also distinct parallels with the final stage or task of life, as the achievement of 'integrity', depicted by Erik Erikson in his psychosocial theory of the life course (Erikson, 1959). This involves the acceptance of one's past life without regrets. The life review can be seen as a way of reaching such an attitude of mind by sifting through memories and putting right what still can be corrected. Interestingly both Butler in his original article (1963) and Erikson in a later commentary (1978) refer to Ingmar Bergman's film *Wild Strawberries* to illustrate their ideas. This depicts an egocentric professor who through a process of life review, prompted first by disturbing dreams and later by more conscious recollections, comes to realise his inadequacies and finally to intervene sympathetically in the life of his family. Although a necessary process, both Butler and Erikson point to the possibility of failure, of a sense of despair over a life that has had serious faults for which time is too short to make amends.

As an important potential task of later life this theory has received much approval, but most commentators have come to disagree with Butler's stress on the life review as a necessary task that cannot be avoided. Some older people with unsatisfactory pasts seem able to avoid reminiscing by remaining active in the present. A more telling criticism is provided by studies of older people in critical situations as in relocation to institutional care. Reminiscence may figure greatly in people's thoughts and conversations at this time, but it is unlikely to have a 'life review' character. The inner motivation and/or supportive network for a search towards a more accurate and objective account of one's life is lacking. Older people under stress are much more likely to use reminiscence to confirm to themselves a more constant and positive image of their lives (Lieberman and Tobin, 1983).

Maintenance of self esteem

Reminiscence contributes to the maintenance of self concept and self esteem in old age. This view of reminiscence was expressed in the gerontological literature at the same time as Butler's 'life review' article. McMahon and Rhudick (1964) published observations of veterans of the Spanish-American war who were impressive both for their high levels of adjustment and for their tendency to reminisce. The reminiscence they observed also did not have the characteristics of reanalysis of the past but of stressing its value. They criticised Butler for generalising from cases of psychological pathology. Their subjects claimed to have seen the best, and seemed to gain a renewed sense of self esteem by confirming their link with their past lives.

Other studies have suggested similar uses of reminiscence. The studies reported by Lieberman and Tobin (1983) of older people being moved into American institutional settings probably provide the best examples of an identity maintenance view of reminiscence. What emerges so strikingly from their work is the variety of ways, including the use of 'myth', whereby the self is maintained in the face of loss of sources in the outside world. 'The sense of self does not change; rather what we see is the utilization of strategies by the elderly to maintain this sense of selfhood. At its most general level, the strategies represent myths – the myth of control, the myth of self-constancy – and the blurring of the boundaries between the past and the present' (Lieberman and Tobin, 1983: 348).

By their sympathetic formulation of the issues Lieberman and Tobin promote a sensitivity to the ways in which older people, in situations that threaten their sense of self, may 'bend' reality and how this may be a necessary strategy for them. This may include emphasising the presence of the past in the present. Quite a different strategy, although equally extreme, is illustrated by Hazan's study of elderly people in a Jewish day centre in London. In this context most features of the past and present were denied. What was emphasised was the shared reality of present life in the day centre, and the only parts of the past that were recalled readily were to do with shared experience that did not divide or single out individuals (Hazan, 1980).

It is probably this view of reminiscence, as a means of maintaining the identity and self respect of elderly people whether as individuals or as a group, which underlines much of the current reminiscence work in institutional settings. By putting people in touch with their past lives, and by confirming to them that their lives have been interesting and valuable, it is hoped to maintain people's sense of self-esteem. Certainly many people may come to disregard their past lives as of little interest to others and thus also to themselves. Demonstrating that this is not so may have surprising and uplifting results.[1]

Types of reminiscence in older people

Older people's attitudes to reminiscence

These different theoretical views as to the functions of reminiscence are also evident in older people's own accounts of what they are doing. The author has carried out research in a variety of settings on older people's attitudes to reminiscence (Coleman, 1986b). In the most detailed of these (Coleman, 1986a), a study of fifty people living in council owned sheltered housing schemes in five London boroughs, I also collected recordings of individuals' reminiscences over a period of ten years. In my earlier analysis of the first year's data (Coleman, 1974) I looked for associations between 'types' of reminiscence. In those who had a negative view of their past lives an association was apparent between the absence of self-analytic reminiscing and maladjustment. There was also an association, among the men in the sample, between high morale and conversation which was informative (for example speaking about important historical events or expressing views about general world issues).

When the views that older people expressed themselves, about what they were doing when they were reminiscing and why, were analysed, a more useful set of distinctions began to emerge. I started by dividing those who said they reminisced a lot from those who said they did it very little. When I further looked at what the former group had to say about what reminiscence meant to them, again a further clear division appeared between those who found it a pleasant and those who found it a disturbing experience. Fourteen people described reminiscence in wholly positive terms as giving them 'a good feeling', gaining for them 'appreciation of their life' or a sense of 'fulfilment' and helping them in 'making sense of things'. A number said it was also 'a comfort', a help in 'getting over difficulties', although four people said it was not sufficient help in coping with the present difficulties they were currently facing.

The remaining four people who reminisced a lot described it in quite different terms. One man said that he 'argued' with himself and that some of his thoughts were 'terrible'. Another said that thoughts about the past obsessed him and 'drove him mad'. The other two spoke about troubling thoughts. One said 'there is nothing harder than the past'. These four seemed to be involved in an active life review process in which they were confronting parts of their life which they found difficult to accept.

Among those who said they reminisced very little, a similarly evident split in attitudes appeared. The majority, thirteen people, expressed themselves more or less neutrally, saying that reminiscence was of little or no help or had 'no point or purpose'. But the remaining four expressed a much more disturbed attitude to reminiscence, stating or implying that they personally had to avoid thinking about the past because it made their present situation worse. Comments such as the following were made: 'it makes me feel more miserable', 'it gives me a sad feeling', 'it makes it harder for me to bear this life', and 'it makes it more difficult for me to accept the present'.

It was not difficult to place the remaining fifteen people who said they reminisced to some degree within this basic four-fold distinction – whether they valued reminiscence, were troubled by unhappy memories, saw no point in reminiscing or had to avoid it. Of the 15, seven had a predominantly positive attitude to reminiscence as an enjoyable activity which brought them a sense of appreciation of their life, four stressed the regretful and hurtful nature of their memories, two saw reminiscence as a minor activity which had no relevance to their present situation and a further two saw reminiscence as something they really would prefer to avoid because comparison with the present was too depressing.

Altogether then, twenty-one people in the sample could be described as valuing their memories, eight people as having disturbed memories, fifteen as seeing no point in reminiscing and six people as having to avoid reminiscing because of the sense of loss it produced in them. Not surprisingly, the second and fourth groups had significantly lower morale than the first and third groups. Six of the eight people who were disturbed by reminiscence that they could not avoid, presented symptoms of depression, and of those who felt they had to avoid reminiscence because the comparison with the past made them sad, five appeared depressed.

This breakdown already indicates why reminiscence in itself is not associated with good adjustment. Reminiscence can be a sign of successful ageing and high morale, and so can absence of reminiscence. Compulsive reminiscing can be a sign of psychological disturbance as can deliberate avoidance of reminiscing. I would not want to suggest that the above distribution is representative of attitudes to reminiscence in the elderly population as a whole. Evidence collected from larger samples elsewhere would indicate that this sample contained a higher than average number of people who did not enjoy reminiscing (Coleman, 1986b). It is interesting to speculate why this might be. Perhaps as a predominantly lower socio-economic group they contained more people whose experience of life had been harsher. Certainly a number expressed appreciation of the better living conditions and opportunities that the post-war welfare state had produced. Better housing and pensions were emphasised and also opportunities for adult education. Many however did not appreciate that their own life histories had value in themselves. Most died before the current interest in oral history had begun to flourish (Thompson, 1978). One man did live though to see his account of his involvement in the relief operation from Dunkirk properly recorded.

A differential approach to the use of reminiscence in old age

A differential approach to people's use of memories in late life has been taken further in recent research in Canada by Watt and Wong (in press). In their study they distinguish six types of reminiscence: integrative, instrumental, informative, narrative, escapist and obsessive. Their findings indicate that greater amounts of integrative reminiscence (in which the speakers are achieving a greater sense of meaning and coherence in their life stories) and instrumental reminiscence (where they are recalling past attempts to cope with difficult situations and thus perhaps achieving a greater subjective perception of control) characterise the better adjusted in their samples.

These distinctions have important implications for those seeking to use reminiscence in a therapeutic way with older people. But they are also relevant to those whose principal aim is the collection of life histories. Question marks must be raised about the unreflective use of reminiscence which does not consider its psychological significance for the individual. For example an encounter with a person in the process of life review needs to be handled sensitively. Although talking about the past in itself may not have any particular therapeutic merit, the encouragement of structured life-reviewing on a one-to-one basis, and where difficulties are faced, does appear to be beneficial (Fry, 1983; Haight, 1988). The creative and healing potential of the life review process in late life may in fact have been submerged by its confusion with other uses of reminiscence. Its characteristics need to be better understood (Molinari and Reichlin, 1985).

It is counterproductive to rush in to sensitive areas of a person's life without preparation. For example the presentation of World War One slides, in some of the original material produced for stimulating reminiscence, has been known to trigger reactions of extreme disturbance in men who were not properly informed what was happening. In those with evident emotional vulnerability, for example with some types of psychiatric patients, therapists have often found it more constructive deliberately to focus on positive memories to the exclusion of negative ones (Lowenthal and Marrazzo, 1990). This recognises that adjustment to emotional upsets may be prolonged or even never fully resolved. When memories of self blame predominate in an individual's reminiscences it is important to try to make the distinction between justifiable and unjustifiable self accusations. Depressive reactions may be accompanied by unreasonable feelings of blame and guilt which need to be counteracted. However a person's sense of guilt may be well founded and in these circumstances, where actual wrong has been done, it has to be accepted not disputed.

In other cases one may be confronted by unresolved grief reactions. As I have already mentioned, I noticed in my study on elderly people in sheltered housing that there was a group of people, whose past lives had been happy, but who could not bear to reminisce because the contrast with their present situation was too great. In considering grief in old age it is important to bear in mind that loss is an essential part of ageing. Psychologists such as Neugarten (1979) and Gutmann (1980) have stressed how older people acquire strengths, notably a well-developed capacity to introspect, which may enable them to deal better with loss. In this context the prolonged depressed reaction of someone who remains in a grief stricken state and is unable to gain comfort from his/her memories has to be seen as abnormal and requiring therapy (e.g. Worden, 1982).

In cases of disturbing life review and prolonged grief it is important to be able to seek professional help from professional therapists as well as spiritual counsellors. The most recent handbooks on reminiscence work take these problems into account, as well as more common problems encountered with frail elderly people such as sensory loss and speech handicaps.

A quite different and neglected problematic aspect of reminiscence is the socially objectionable conversation of those who use their own memories to boost themselves at other people's expense. In group work such a situation must be handled well, otherwise the aim of group reminiscence as a sharing rather than dividing activity can be torpedoed. Ideally such people need to be taken aside and some consideration given to why they find it necessary to behave in this way and whether there are not outlets which are less anti-social that they can use to assert themselves. Sensitivity is needed. The study of Lieberman and Tobin (1983) has well illustrated how older people in difficult and demeaning situations may be driven to such extreme strategies to defend their sense of identity and self importance.

Such behaviour also places a question mark against our society if it forces some older people to resort to such tactics. We should take note of the findings from traditional societies (e.g. Gutmann, 1987) where older people come to take on important roles concerning the transmission of information and values. There the potential of older people's reminiscence is seen to its best effect. But it requires an audience. Recently commentators have come to emphasise more the importance of the social context to reminiscence (e.g. Tarman, 1988). Older people in part tell us what they want to say, in part what they think we want to hear. Study of the interaction between the reminiscer and the interviewer would be of great interest to life history users.

Life history and social history

The main emphasis of this paper has been to impress the reader of the importance of an analysis of the personal thoughts and feelings behind a person's account of her or his life history in late life. A life history is not a static product of an individual at a particular point in time, but a developing process reflecting a changing view of the life course. We need to consider the point the individual may have reached in this development. Is she searching for a more coherent, integrated and meaningful picture of her life? Has he maybe already reached a synopsis with which he is happy to rest? Is she still preoccupied with disturbing events that she witnessed or maybe was responsible for? Or maybe he really cannot see any rhyme or reason within his past, perhaps because the task of integrating his experiences within a broader context is beyond him. He may not be able to consider his own life to be of significance. Is she overwhelmed by a sense of loss and of painful nostalgia for a lost world? If the significance of the interpretation of the social history through which a person has lived is to be properly assessed, such analyses must accompany it.

My research suggests that those who have been successful in finding order in their own life are also more likely to have observed patterns in the world around them. Of the material collected from recorded interviews with older people living alone (Coleman, 1986a), the most striking social comment came from those who had clearly been able to achieve a good measure of integrity in their own lives. It was striking because it vividly depicted individual experience yet also transcended the particular situation described. Some examples may illustrate what I mean.

Mrs Parsons had been a great worrier all her life caring both for a sick only child and husband, both of whom had died young, yet in old age in her isolation she had achieved a measure of peace and serenity. When she looked back it was without bitterness or nostalgia, but rather with a calm eye:

> 'I think people were happier, they weren't so self-centred, as they are now, and they weren't flying about trying to find pleasures, they were simpler I suppose. I'm talking about the working class, not about the rich, because they had their pleasures all the time, didn't they? But the working class I think, they didn't get much and they didn't expect much, and if they

got their daily bread, well they thought they were lucky. Of course you don't know the hungry 1930s, do you? It's a good thing you don't. They used to parade the streets with banners, give us work, you know, just starving with no dole, nothing, no relief of any kind, and men used to form a column and walk through the streets – "the hungry '30s", I expect you've heard of it. People were hungry, they really were. Margarine was only threepence a pound in those days, and you know they couldn't afford to buy it, it just shows you, doesn't it. And yet the rich went on in the same old way, enjoying everything, wasting enough that would have kept a family for a week. Used to go to the dustbins. I know, I've heard it. It all seems very wrong doesn't it. But as I say, that doesn't bother me any more. That's all gone, yes, it's all gone, as though it's never been. Like a dream, good thing too, isn't it. Because you could harp on those things and get really unhappy, couldn't you.'

Mr Norton was also an isolated man without being lonely. But he had thought a lot about life and had much to say about the world. He had never really got over horrific experiences in the First World War. But he had accepted at least that it was not reasonable to expect him to forget them. He was 'not constituted that way'. At the same time these experiences had enabled him to recognise a lot of human pretension.

'I try to be logical if I can, reasonable. I am not out to reform the world, accept it as it is and try to adapt myself to it. I think that is the most reasonable point of view. Any person who thinks they can reform the world, I think is living under a delusion. You see the problem is so vast, people don't realise. They are misled by these politicians and various other people who know better, but are using them for their own advantage. You will see them in full spate before long, leading up to another election . . . instead of playing down to the public they ought to be trying to lift them up. Instead of that, they use them to their own advantage. No-one believes them anymore really. It's gradually breaking through you see to the man in the street that these people are only playing a game. At least that's the way I like to look at it. . . . But the ordinary man has sunk into a sort of apathy. He has been deceived that many times. You try to get them to reason intelligently and apply a bit of logic. They have never heard of it, they have never been taught that way. . . . It's a case of suppressing the knowledge which ought to reach the man in the street. . . .'

'. . . Lloyd George, he made millions out of armaments with his feed the guns campaign. There was an old woman there in Manchester. She said, "Terrible feeding the guns," she had a big bag of teacakes, she said "I'm going to feed the gunners". . . . Feed the guns! Welsh wizard! I know what I'd have done with him if I'd got hold of him. He did very well out of the war. So did Stanley Baldwin, the big steel people. So did the clergy too. "Praise the Lord my dear Augusta, we've won a battle, such a muster. Ten thousand Germans sent below. Praise God from whom all blessings flow!" There is nothing like a bit of soldiering to buck your ideas up, you see life in the raw then.'

Mrs Manners by contrast was a much visited person, admired by all who knew her because of the uncomplaining way she coped with a painful and crippling disease. She did not speak much but liked to listen to others. When pressed though she would describe how she had been transformed by a strong religious faith she had gained in mid-life. She looked for good where it was to be found both in the past and in the present, and tried to achieve a balanced viewpoint.

'. . . there weren't the things to have and do when I was younger. We were perhaps more satisfied than the younger people are today, though no doubt if there were the opportunities that there are now, we would have been exactly the same. I think it's the decade that you're brought up in that you live in, really. . . .'

'. . . it's a different life for women nowadays. I often wonder how so many young women manage to combine work and a home. I don't think, well I suppose I could have done, but I would have hated to have done it. When I was young I found a three bedroomed house and my husband and two children were quite enough for me to do, and I can honestly say that I was never bored. I could always find something to do. We used to make our own jams and pickles and things like that you know. Of course today there are so many more things to have, and everything is so expensive that I suppose the girl just thinks she's got to go out to work. And then things like holidays. Holidays were not generalized in my day, you were lucky if your husband had a job and you got a holiday with pay. But of course now it's possible to go abroad and all these things are very nice but of course they are all so expensive.'

'. . . the days when we could get out and walk a lot in the countryside before the advent of cars, that was a lovely time. I do go now on the rare occasions that my son-in-law takes me to the beauty spots, but the beauty of it for me is spoilt by so many cars and charabancs and that kind of thing, and I remember it of course when there wasn't, but this must be with progress, I mean I do realise that. More people can now enjoy it. It's just that when you've seen it, you know, as it used to be, it's not quite so good now, but as I say that's rather a selfish view, because so many more people now can enjoy these places.'

There was a strong tendency on the part of people in this sample to denigrate modern society and glorify the past. Another sample of older people that were interviewed living in sheltered housing in Southampton exhibited the same attitudes (Coleman and McCulloch, 1990). As the illustrations above suggest this was not the case with many of those who had achieved a considerable degree of harmony in themselves. They sought to tell the most truthful story they could. This is surely one of the greatest benefits older people can confer on younger people, to present the lesson of experience. This is not to imply that all those who decried the present were not trying to be helpful. Some genuinely hoped and campaigned, for example within their families, for a return to the values they remembered. No doubt such people received much respect in return. But many seemed satisfied simply to criticise and retreat into a self-satisfied citadel of 'moral siege'.

Unfortunately modern society has given older people the idea that it is quite permissible for them to retreat into their own self-contained interests and activities. We should not let them. They have much to tell us from their life experiences and we should ask them to try to tell us what it is useful for us to know. Old age does appear to provide both the capacity and the opportunities to reflect on life and draw lessons. Older people have traditionally been looked upon to provide guidance, to help prevent the younger generation from being submerged by the demands and pressures of daily life, and to point to underlying values and continuity of culture. This is the wisdom we must ask older people still to provide. They, and we, should not rest content with mere gossip and complaint. We should expect more.

Conclusions

This paper has attempted to review and integrate current thinking about the psychological influences on the telling of life stories in late life. Although the evidence collected on the subject is still slight there are good reasons to accept the common view that ageing is associated with an increased tendency to reminisce about life experiences. In traditional societies this appears to provide the older generation with an important teaching role. Old age is also by definition the last stage of life and the awareness of approaching death requires that people come to a summing up of their lives including both achievements and failures. This can be another reason why a person feels impelled to reminisce. Quite different in character is the use of reminiscence to maintain self esteem. This is especially relevant to older people in situations where they have experienced considerable loss of role and ability, as after institutionalisation. The former task is that of the explorer who in the face of death tests the validity of a life as it has been lived, the latter that of the conserver who holds on to well established proofs of worth and value.

Research investigations have been cited which confirm that individuals can vary considerably in the type of involvement they show in their memories. Integrative and instrumental reminiscence appear to characterise the better adjusted. Uneasy relations with the past shown by obsessional and avoiding attitudes are signs of maladjustment and must be handled sensitively. Researchers of life histories will inevitably be confronted with individuals who have not (yet) been reconciled with their past lives. They must have some guidelines to help them to respond to individual dilemmas, and to take psychological factors into consideration in interpreting the significance of social comments made by subjects; both those who have not found as well as those who have found order in their own personal stories.

Reminiscence is not an exclusive characteristic of old age. With the development of a life-span psychology we are better equipped to consider how the impetus to make sense and order of one's life changes with differing circumstances. Observations from a variety of fields need to be incorporated; historical autobiographies as well as twentieth-century oral accounts. Surprisingly neglected by psychologists has been the consideration of the influence of the social context upon the formulation of a life story. People can formulate, analyse and record their stories on their own, but often others provide the necessary catalyst, whether a spiritual director, a friend or the proverbial stranger on a long train journey. How they react to a person's initial self expressions is important in determining the nature of the story that is told. Our ignorance of this interaction is another unfortunate result of the separation of social from developmental psychology. Particularly interesting questions arise about the role of the old person as story-teller which would also benefit from cross-cultural comparisons.

Note

1 The organisation Help the Aged has pioneered the development of reminiscence work and has produced a number of booklets and training packs for workers in this area; see Help the Aged, Educational materials for adults, Education and Research Department, Help the Aged, 1989.

References

Bender, M., (1989), 'Reminiscence: applications and limitations', *Bulletin of the Psychologists' Special Interest Group in the Elderly*, (British Psychological Society), 29: 22–7.

Buhler, C., (1935), 'The curve of life as studied in biographies', *Journal of Applied Psychology*, 19: 405–9.

Butler, R.N., (1963), 'The life review: an interpretation of reminiscence in the aged', *Psychiatry*, 26: 65–76.

Cameron, P., (1972), 'The generation gap: time orientation', *The Gerontologist*, 12: 117–19.

Coleman, P.G., (1974), 'Measuring reminiscence characteristics from conversation as adaptive features of old age', *International Journal of Aging and Human Development*, 5: 281–94.

Coleman, P.G., (1986a), *Ageing and Reminiscence Processes: Social and Clinical Implications*, Chichester: Wiley.

Coleman, P.G., (1986b), 'The past in the present: a study of elderly people's attitudes to reminiscence', *Oral History*, 14, 50–59.

Coleman, P.G. and McCulloch, A.W., (1990), 'Societal change, values and social support: exploratory studies into adjustment in late life', *Journal of Aging Studies*, 4, 321–2.

Costa, P.T., Jr and McCrae, R.R., (1980), 'Still stable after all these years: personality as a key to some issues in aging', in P.B. Baltes and O.G. Brim, Jr (eds), *Life-Span Development and Behavior*, vol. 3, New York: Academic Press.

Crovitz, H.F., (1986), 'Loss and recovery of autobiographical memory after head injury', in D.C. Rubin (ed.), *Autobiographical Memory*, Cambridge University Press, Cambridge, pp. 273–90.

Cumming, E. and Henry, W., (1961), *Growing Old: The Process of Disengagement*, New York: Basic Books.

Erikson, E., (1959), 'Identity and the life cycle', *Psychological Issues*, 1: 18–164.

Erikson, E., (1978), 'Reflections on Dr Borg's life cycle', in E. Erikson (ed.), *Adulthood*, New York: Norton.

Erikson, E., Erikson, J. and Kivnick, H., (1987), *Vital Involvement in Old Age: The Experience of Old Age in Our Time*, New York: Norton.

Fry, P.S., (1983), 'Structured and unstructured reminiscence training and depression among the elderly', *Clinical Gerontologist*, 1: 15–37.

Galante, R. and Foa, D., (1986), 'An epidemiological study of psychic trauma and treatment effectiveness for children after a natural disaster', *Journal of the American Academy of Child Psychiatry*, 25: 357–63.

Giambra, L.M., (1977), 'Daydreaming about the past: the time setting of spontaneous thought intrusion', *The Gerontologist*, 17: 35–8.

Gibson, F., (1989), *Reminiscence with Individuals and Groups: A Training Manual*, London: Help the Aged.

Grimes, R.L., (1988), 'Scenario analysis: ritual and religious biography', paper presented at the 12th International Congress of Anthropological and Ethnological Sciences, Zagreb, Yugoslavia.

Gutmann, D.L., (1980), 'Psychoanalysis and aging: a developmental view', in S.I. Greenspan and G.H. Pollock (eds), *The Course of Life: Psychoanalytic Contributions Toward Understanding Personality Development. Vol. III. Adulthood and the Aging Process*, US Department of Health and Human Services, Washington DC, pp. 115–27.

Gutmann, D.L., (1987), *Reclaimed Powers: Towards a New Psychology of Men and Women in Later Life*, New York: Basic Books.

Haight, B.K., (1988), 'The therapeutic role of a structured life review process in homebound elderly subjects', *Journal of Gerontology*, 43: 40–4.

Hazan, H., (1980), *The Limbo People: A Study of the Constitution of the Time Universe among the Aged*, Routledge and Kegan Paul, London.

Hogman, F., (1985), 'Role of memories in the lives of World War II orphans', *Journal of the American Academy of Child Psychiatry*, 24: 390–6.

Jung, C.G., (1933), *Modern Man in Search of a Soul*, New York: Harcourt.

Lieberman, M.A. and Tobin, S.S., (1983), *The Experience of Old Age: Stress, Coping and Survival*, New York: Basic Books.

Lowenthal, M.F., Thurber, M.E. and Chiriboga, P., (1975), *Four Stages of Life*, San Francisco: Jossey Bass.

Lowenthal, R. and Marrazzo, R., (1990), 'Milestoning: evoking memories for resocialization through group reminiscence, *The Gerontologist*, 30, 269–72.

Marcoen, A., (1988), 'Important life ideas and meaning giving in life-span perspective', paper presented at the 3rd European Conference on Developmental Psychology, Budapest, Hungary.

McGuckin, J.A., (1986), 'The enigma of Augustine's conversion', *The Clergy Review*, 72: 315–25.

McMahon, A.W. and Rhudick, P.J., (1964), 'Reminiscing: adaptational significance in the aged', *Archives of General Psychiatry*, 10: 292–8.

Mergler, N.L. and Goldstein, M.D., (1983), 'Why are there old people? Senescence as biological and cultural preparedness for the transmission of information', *Human Development*, 26: 72–90.

Molinari, V. and Reichlin, R.E., (1985), 'Life review reminiscence in the elderly: a review of the literature.' *International Journal of Aging and Human Development*, 20: 81–92.

Neisser, U., (1982), *Memory Observed: Remembering in Natural Contexts*, San Francisco: Freeman.

Neugarten, B. and associates, (1964), *Personality in Middle and Later Life*, New York: Atherton.

Neugarten, B., (1979), 'Time, age and the life cycle', *American Journal of Psychiatry*, 136: 887–94.

Rabbitt, P., (1988), 'Social psychology, neurosciences and cognitive psychology need each other; and gerontology needs all three of them', *The Psychologist: Bulletin of the British Psychological Society*, 12: 500–6.
Rubin, D.C., (ed.), *Autobiographical Memory*, Cambridge University Press, Cambridge.
Rubin, D.C., (ed.), (1986), *Autobiographical Memory*. Cambridge: Cambridge University Press, pp. 202–21.
Siegler, I.C., George, L.K. and Okun, M.A., (1979), 'Cross-sequential analysis of adult personality', *Developmental Psychology*, 15: 350–1.
Simmons, L.W., (1945), *The Role of the Aged in Primitive Society*, New Haven: Yale University Press.
Tarman, V.I., (1988), 'Autobiography: the negotiation of a lifetime', *International Journal of Aging and Human Development*, 27: 171–91.
Thomas, S., (1988), 'Newman and Heresy: The Anglican Writings', Ph.D. thesis, University of Durham.
Thompson, P., (1978), *The Voice of the Past: Oral History*, Oxford: Oxford University Press.
Thornton, S. and Brotchie, J., (1987), 'Reminiscence: a critical review of the empirical literature', *British Journal of Clinical Psychology*, 26: 93–111.
Watt, L.M. and Wong, P.T.P., (n.d.) 'Successful aging: typologies and themes of reminiscence', forthcoming in *International Journal of Aging and Human Development*.
Watts, F. and Williams, M., (1988), *The Psychology of Religious Knowing*, Cambridge: Cambridge University Press.
Worden, J.W., (1982), *Grief Counseling and Grief Therapy*, New York: Springer.

Life histories and the cultural politics of historical knowing: the *Dictionary of National Biography* and the late nineteenth-century political field*

David Amigoni

I Introduction

The late nineteenth century was a time when many collections of life histories in the form of collective biographical projects were initiated. It can be both interesting and instructive to examine these projects from a number of perspectives; involving first the people who were included in the collections, and the nomination process by which they came to be included; second what is written about them; and third what the authors of the collections saw as their purpose, and how these collections should be read and used. What can be learned from such an investigation? An historical exercise such as this might throw interesting light on the recent efforts of social scientists in collecting life histories; in particular, it might pose questions about the recent contemporary data collection exercises which have not been considered; for example, questions which relate to the ways in which it is necessarily selections of data which are collected; and the ways in which readers or users of these data are positioned in relation to the data by the rhetorical systems that are used to communicate it. Some of the implications have already been explored. For example, there can be nothing new in showing how forms of social and cultural bias pervade the collections of life histories that have been assembled by social groups in Western cultures. Nor would it be original to trace a connection between representations of cultural insiders and blocks of institutional power; or for that matter a link between the selective slice of history offered by such a collection of biographical representations and a coded quest to legitimate blocks of cultural power. Such insights are usually articulated with a view to simply exposing a particular bias. However, it might be more valid to investigate the strategies by which some collections of data rather than others are able to disguise their partiality and make it acceptable.

It is in this context that Colin Bell's paper 'Some comments on the Use of Directories in Research on Elites' (1974) is interesting. Bell began to address the issue of partiality in the nomination process in the case of one great British life history project of the late nineteenth century, the *Dictionary of National Biography* (*DNB*). Bell's point was to:

> remind readers that entries in a dictionary are the end product of a social process of nomination that can be studied in its own right . . . for these nomination processes are good data and may be as significant for studying the elite as is describing the entries in directories.[1]

Bell went on to demonstrate that a nomination process initiated through and dominated by upper-middle-class literary intellectuals produced a collection of dictionary entries that significantly prioritised and thus contributed to the status of this group. Bell's point was that the *DNB* constituted a mirror image of the elite power exercised by the group. However, his analysis separates the 'hidden' yet revealing nomination process from the content of the 'visible' Dictionary. Bell's separation of the nomination process from the *DNB* itself is implicitly modelled on a particular conception of the distribution of hegemonic power; hegemony, in Bell's understanding, is secured *prior* to the consumption of the Dictionary.

One of the broad aims of this paper will be to rethink models of the means by which cultural hegemony is secured, and the role played by collections of life histories in helping to construct the cultural relations of hegemony. This will involve looking at the *DNB* as a complex communicative act. To begin with, part II will address the question of the nomination process; for what purpose was it initiated? by whom was it initiated? who did the nominating and what exemplary lives did they nominate? Many of these questions have been posed and answered by Bell. However, the paper will take its consideration of the nomination process beyond that of Bell's by thinking about the way in which the communication of information relating to the process helped to legitimate the *DNB* and the set of values that it sought to uphold. In part III, the theme of communicative self consciousness will be further elaborated, and the paper will ask how the *DNB*, in association with certain authoritative commentaries, attempted to ensure the transmission of these values by constructing a socially and culturally specific reading position through which, it was hoped, the life history data would be digested. These questions will be approached and conceptually unified by following in the illuminating footsteps of Michel Foucault. For as Hubert L. Dreyfus and Paul Rabinow point out:

> Foucault has shown at length that official biographies and current received opinions of top intellectuals do not carry any transparent truth. Beyond the dossiers and the refined self-consciousness of any age are the organised historical practices which make possible, give meaning to, and situate in a political field these monuments of official discourse.[2]

In part II, the paper will look at the nomination process that defined the scope of the original *DNB* (sixty-three volumes, 1885–1900) as a strategy of refined self-consciousness, legitimating it over and above less refined, or partial and sectarian rivals – in this context, the paper will particularly draw upon Frederic Harrison's *New Calendar of Great Men* (1892); in other words, the paper will argue that the nomination process is an organised historical practice with an ideological function. In part III, the paper will show how a variety of texts, from the entries in the Dictionary itself to an essay written by its main editor, Leslie Stephen (1899), attempted to persuade the reader of the *DNB* into observing certain conditions of its use; that is to say, in situating readers among certain cultural assumptions when seeking historical knowledge, the *DNB* projected itself as a monument of official discourse, which resisted forms of fugitive or subversive discourse believed to carry the potential to undermine established institutions. Throughout both sections, the paper will be concerned to show how these insights situate the biographical Dictionary in a political field making bids for cultural power; an issue which leads back to the paper's concern with models of cultural hegemony.

II The nomination process: the nature of the '*DNB*' as a cultural project

Late Victorian Britain saw a sustained programme aimed at building cultural authority through projects creating and promoting a sense of national identity. The construction of dictionaries of various kinds was a contribution to this programme. It is helpful to compare the *DNB* alongside *The New English Dictionary* (*NED*) which was being assembled at the same time.[3] While the *NED* sought to codify and settle a version of the English experience at the level of the word, the *DNB* sought to do the same in respect of biography or the life history. It was claimed that the project had 'once and for all rescued national biography from the dungeon of public apathy'.[4]

It will be appropriate to consider first the intellectual personnel who coordinated these projects. Like the *NED*, whose production was coordinated by the indefatigable James Murray, the emergence of the *DNB* owed a lot to one very industrious man, Leslie Stephen. Neither, however, were alone in their respective endeavours; Murray depended on an army of readers who sent him definitions of words, drawn from English writings with which they were engaged; and Stephen relied upon an extensive network of dispersed contributors, researching and writing the lives that he, as editor, would eventually tailor for inclusion in the *DNB*. Indeed, a consideration of the lists of contributors that preface the published versions of both projects suggests that in a number of instances, the same personnel were contributing to the production of the *NED* and the *DNB* simultaneously.[5] In this respect the *NED* and the *DNB* were characteristic cases of a particular model of late Victorian intellectual production.

What does this model say about late Victorian intellectuals and the politics of intellectual production in which they were engaged? First, that the intelligentsia were decentralised and working across the institutions of civil society (journalism, the law, the church) rather than in one concentrated block; though for the most part its members were the educational products of Oxford and Cambridge, few contributors were academics in a professional sense.[6] This contrasted with, for instance, German models, where intellectuals were perceived to be employees of the centralised state. Second, and as a result of this, the distinction between professional and lay was not so marked. Both of these factors helped produce a mode of self-identification amongst intellectuals which stressed their independence. However, this independence was to be exercised within a common public sphere of rational discourse; and it was an intellectual duty to initiate the uninitiated into its procedures. There had been, throughout the nineteenth century, a quasi-evangelical impulse attached to much intellectual activity.[7] The *DNB* can be seen as an extension of this tradition.

Principles of nomination

Before a collection of life-histories could enter into this tradition, it had to be put together by a process of nomination and selection; different strategic approaches to this process will now be considered in relation to some of the collective biographical projects that proliferated from the 1850s and 1860s.[8] Many of these collections presumed to represent universal history, while others were frankly more localised in their claims of coverage. However, both types were commonly organised round a closed selection and nomination process. That is to say, autocratic editors of universal biographical histories determined their selection of lives according to an arbitrary point in the present, leading to a partial reckoning of 'where we are now';[9] while localised biographical histories determined their selection of lives on the basis of a fixed, sectarian category of identity.[10] The *DNB*, it could be argued, was able to command a cultural field and secure a hegemonic status by claiming its stance towards the selection and organisation of the life histories it embraced was open, flexible and thus impartial. In order to make clear the nature of this effect, the *DNB* shall be compared to *The New Calendar of Great Men*. The latter collection of life histories appeared to utilise an authoritarian or closed process of selection, determined by arbitrary assumptions relating to first a narrative of universal history, and second, rigid, sectarian categories of identity. Each collection sought to establish an authoritative relationship with its readers, but based on different principles; the authority of the *Calendar* was located in the dogmatic and deterministic paradigm of historical and societal development organising its biographical entries; while the authority of the *DNB* was founded on its objectivity and impartiality, or values that filtered through the project as a result of its open and democratic nomination process. However it will be argued that any legitimacy conferred on the *DNB* on the grounds of its open nomination process was an ideological effect generated by the rhetoric of presentational strategies which concealed a dogmatism every bit as deterministic as that organising the *Calendar*.

The nominators: pedagogy v. participation

Frederic Harrison's *The New Calendar of Great Men*[11] was developed out of a highly schematic version of Comtean Positivism; its biographical sweep embraces all periods of Western and some

Eastern history; it works explicitly with a *theory* of political and societal development. This clearly contrasts with the British national focus and the absence of explicit theoretical commitment underpinning Stephen's *DNB*.

The *Calendar* was very explicitly organised around Comtean categories that generated a deterministic master-narrative; the progress of Western Civilisation organised from an arbitrarily fixed point, but conceived none the less as having a universalising perspective. Each month of the *Calendar* represented a branch of human knowledge or practice, arranged according to its sequential importance to an historical telos (Month one: Theocratic civilisation; Month thirteen: Modern science);[12] each day of the calendar was represented by the biography of a particular worthy whose work had advanced the knowledge or practice represented by the particular month in which they figured; for example, Theocratic civilisation: Mahomet; Modern science: Newton.[13] The representativeness of these figures was determined in the first instance by Auguste Comte, but subsequently taken up by an exclusive group of intellectuals who related to Comte as disciples.[14] These intellectuals were totally responsible for composing the individual biographical entries that went to make up the *Calendar*; and in this role they effectively acted as priests.

The authoritarian nomination process was replicated in the very structure of the entries that resulted. These entries adhered to a standard pattern; a brief life history, outlining the subject's date of birth, education, and the scope of their work; on the basis of this they were assigned a fixed identity, which functioned by advancing the inevitable progression of a scientific branch of knowledge or practice, and in turn the entire master-narrative. The life history was not supported by a reference system citing sources. Instead, the reader was invited to take the details uncorroborated, on authority. This authority was buttressed by an approved text, and the reader was referred to this for confirmation of the priest's judgemental commentary.[15] As such, both nomination process and life history related to the reader in the manner of an authoritarian pedagogue. As Harrison's editorial commentary makes clear, the *Calendar* is not a Dictionary to be consulted willy-nilly; rather it is intended to be read in sequence, in order that a 'vivid impression of the *synthetic* or organic character of man's general progress' might be inculcated.[16]

If the *Calendar* was rather negatively received as a form of 'scientific hagiography',[17] suppressing data and debate in the interests of deterministic categories, then the *DNB* outwardly eschewed such practices. Its contributors were under strict instructions (editorially imposed by Stephen) to limit their narratives to only that which the relevant historical record yielded; speculation and extraneous hindsighted comment was, as far as possible, to be eschewed.[18] The model stressed the active participation of the reader;[19] the free-thinking reader was supposed to be presented with the salient facts relating to the life, a list of sources against which the facts could be independently checked, and a chronological list of unevaluated works (if any) authored by the subject. Again, this discipline of biographical construction appears to follow directly from the set of principles underwriting the nomination process that brought the *DNB* into being. The independence granted to the reader of the *DNB* was the corollary of a nomination process founded on open and flexible participation. However, the rhetorical presentation of the 'reality' of this process, and the sense of legitimacy to which it gave rise, can be read as an ideological strategy.

This ideology of open participation has a bearing on two themes raised earlier; first Colin Bell's concern with the nomination process, and second the conditions of intellectual production from which the *DNB* emerged. As Bell has shown, the nomination process is an important register of the limited embrace of a life history project such as the *DNB*. However, the Dictionary self-consciously discusses its own nomination process in the 'Statistical Account' which appeared in the sixty-third volume and summed up the achievement of the project; this account can be viewed as serving the purpose of legitimating a certain mode of intellectual production.[20] In this context, the alphabetical dictionary form of the *DNB* becomes very important. Contrary to priests deciding which life histories are fit for the laity to be familiar with in the case of the *Calendar*, for the *DNB*, a community is invited to deliberate democratically. After George Smith had appointed Leslie Stephen as editor of the project, it was decided that an alphabetically arranged provisional list of names that might comprise each volume would appear in the *Athenaeum* periodical prior to beginning the research, writing and editing of each volume. Readers of the *Athenaeum* were thus invited to comment on and amend the lists.[21] In practice, this meant that the profile of the *DNB* altered little; readers of the *Athenaeum*, with a common educational background, were more likely to be of a similar mind as not. Still, the symbolic legitimacy that open participation bestowed on the *DNB* was the functionally important aspect of the practice. As Leslie Stephen asserted in a separately published essay entitled 'National Biography', it was the rational character of the Dictionary that was culturally significant;[22] and part of that rationality is generated by its emergence from a public sphere of discourse ('submitted to public criticism'),[23] where questions of the inclusion of individual life histories were held to be rationally debated amongst free-thinking, free-speaking equals.

However, from a genealogical perspective the 'Statistical Account' can be read as a document that helps to critically historicise the *DNB*; at the precise moment that the results of the Dictionary's 'refined self-consciousness' are subjected to statistical and taxonomic scrutiny, the organised historical practices that locate the project's functions in a political field become plain. For the 'Statistical Account' is a contradictory text which articulates, on the one hand, a sense of the politics that would ideally follow from the open participation model of intellectual production, and on the other, a commitment to deterministic categories that circumscribe the 'openness' and uncover the Dictionary's refined self-consciousness as ideological. The 'Statistical Account' is premised on the assumption that there has been an absolute level of distinction to which individuals have historically needed to aspire in order to win recognition by the Dictionary; thus, the rhetoric of the 'Statistical Account' speculates:

> When we compare the total of thirty thousand memoirs in this work with the total number of persons who are believed to have reached adult life (i.e. their twenty-fourth year) in these islands through the historic ages, it appears that as many as one in every five thousand has gained a sufficient level of distinction to secure admission to this Dictionary. If the calculation be based on the whole number of births, and not on the number of persons who have reached the mature age of twenty-four, every infant's chance of attaining the needful level of distinction has been one in ten thousand.[24]

Notably, this rhetoric ascribes the recognition by the Dictionary to the question of chance, and suggests a sense of equality of opportunity; every infant has had the chance of attaining the needful level of distinction, and even though the odds against them doing so are ten thousand to one, those odds are none the less *quantifiable*. Accordingly, the rhetoric of the 'Statistical Account' is a further extension, and legitimation, of the open participatory model of intellectual production underpinning the *DNB*. For it suggests first that the needful level of distinction qualifying a subject's life history for a place in the Dictionary has been rationally defined and agreed within the sphere of public debate, and second that public debate has successfully brought to public attention the precise proportion of the population who have figured as worthies. Ultimately, this rhetoric and the participatory model that it legitimates define the Dictionary's position within the late nineteenth-century political field. The participatory model of intellectual production stresses a broad commitment to democratic organisation; while the rhetoric of chance, or opportunity, in the 'Statistical Account' communicates a meritocratic understanding of the history and current structure of social relations, wherein every subject starts with a chance, and a few struggle to prominence (and so into the Dictionary). This implied position on meritocracy was buttressed elsewhere by a commitment to the mechanisms that were held to guarantee it; free-market economics and the science of political economy. These commitments were made explicit in the publicity material celebrating the *DNB*, which was always keen to point out that the *DNB* as a publishing venture was the product of free-market enterprise, and not the State, the institution which sponsored many comparable projects of national biography in late nineteenth-century Europe.[25] But was a specific political commitment to free-market economics evident in the structure of particular biographical entries? And if so, how effective was the rhetorical presentation of the nomination process, as the embodiment of rationality, openness and disinterested thought, in making these entries appear acceptable and above politics?

Politics and biographical content: two versions of the life and works of Adam Smith

In order to answer these questions, it will be instructive to compare the contrasting representations of the life of a single historical subject, Adam Smith, as set down by the *DNB* and the *Calendar* respectively. As a worthy whose surname began with a letter falling towards the end of the alphabet, Adam Smith did not make it into the *DNB* until volume 53 (1898), after the principle of the nomination process had been observed through the pages of the *Athenaeum*. Whereas in the *DNB* the subject figures as one Smith among many others, in the *Calendar*, Adam Smith is included in the month given over to 'Modern Philosophy'. Undoubtedly we might expect to infer certain conclusions from these two different positions. On the one hand, the hagiographical *Calendar* merely made Adam Smith function as a component of a deterministic master-narrative, which assigned him a sectarian identity policed by rigid categories; while on the other hand, the *DNB* projected Smith disinterestedly, without recourse to a reductive theory and a predetermined view of the course of history. However a reading of the texts indicates that alternative conclusions can be drawn.

In Leslie Stephen's view, the purpose of the individual biographical entries comprising the *DNB* were to be a logical extension of the values upheld by the nomination process; in reading the Dictionary, users were to be as active and discriminating as the *DNB*'s nominators; they were to be allowed to 'put the dots over the i's' for themselves in Stephen's memorable phrase.[26] However, Stephen's own biography of Adam Smith for the Dictionary, it might be argued, was an account that closed down the reader's capacity for critical activity. For the narrative immediately classified Smith as a 'political economist',[27] and, as the author of *The Wealth of Nations*, a text which is 'an authority both with statesmen and philosophers'. Crucially, the narrative identifies Smith as the founder or 'originator of the study of political economy as a separate department of scientific enquiry'.[28] By giving Smith the title of the founder of a concrete object of study, that object of study (political economy) was endowed with a precise point of origin and a developmental history, following the best present-centred traditions of Positivist historicism, which elsewhere in the *DNB*, the legitimating rhetoric of the nomination process contained in the *DNB* was self-consciously careful to eschew. The *DNB* contains, therefore, statements in individual biographical entries that contradict the values of intellectual openness and flexibility signalled by the rhetoric of the nomination process and its organisational strategies.

However similar reversals permeate the *Calendar*. Thus, although one might expect Harrison's biography of Adam Smith to be ruled by the master-narrative that framed it, such expectations are here overturned. Significantly, the *Calendar* disagrees with the *DNB* on the value of *The Wealth of Nations* by denying it the status of an originary point: 'the *Enquiry into the Wealth of Nations* has little in common with the numberless so called treatises of Political Economy which succeeded it'.[29] In denying that Smith's text was the founding statement of an immutable body of scientific law, the biography goes on instead to project Smith's book as a treatise exploring the unequal and contestable economic relations between classes; 'the inequality of the law which permitted combinations of masters, while repressing those of men, is exposed'.[30] In contrast to Harrison's biography, Stephen's biography of Smith thus represents political economy as an inevitable part of the late nineteenth-century landscape, to a degree which sought to put the discourse beyond political contestation. By this means Stephen and the *DNB* were attempting covertly to defend a position in the political field while making it read like a transcendence of politics. In this sense, the *DNB*'s broader legitimating strategies were not a part of the *Calendar*'s complexion.

The contrasting complexions of the *DNB* and the *New Calendar of Great Men* were, as this section has shown, closely connected to the contrasting principles and processes of nomination that constituted them as collections of life histories. We should not see the nomination process merely as the hidden agenda behind a collection of data, at least as in the simple sense proposed by Colin Bell. For as the argument here has been concerned to show, in the case of the *DNB* particularly, the explicit rhetorical presentation of the nomination process sought to generate expectations in the reader regarding the intellectual disinterestedness of the data to be inspected. However, a more critical perspective on aspects of the data has suggested that such expectations could only have been partially satisfied because of the covert political commitments displayed by the entries comprising the *DNB*. Rather than being a hidden agenda itself, the nomination process served to hide the political agenda structuring the biographical content of the *DNB*.

III The '*DNB*' and the 'cultivated reader'

Having started to look at the specific content of the *DNB* in the last section, this section will continue to examine selected biographical entries, while simultaneously extending the analysis of their place within late nineteenth-century cultural and communicative politics; as such, the purpose of the authors of the *DNB* will be examined, focusing in particular on how they intended the collection should be read, and by whom. As argued in the last section, the *DNB* was an ideological project in so far as the positions in the political field that it occupied were presented as disinterested and *non*-political. However, in addition to presenting itself as a provider of materials supporting the practice of disinterested enquiry, the *DNB* saw itself as a disseminator of useful knowledge in the form of concrete historical knowledge. This life history project was conceived as a massive and enduring representation of the national experience articulated through biography. Accordingly, the project was intended to be accepted as a monument of official discourse. In line with this aim the *DNB* constructed a particular reading position that claimed to provide authoritative access to historical knowing. Simultaneously, this reading position denied authority to other forms of discourse claiming knowledge of history. This section will go on to consider how such a reading position was constructed.

Obviously the collection of thirty thousand biographies comprising the *DNB* amounts to a potentially complicated and diverse reading experience, especially when the collection was designed for dictionary use; that is to say as a source of reference that had limited control over the use to which its data were put. This clearly contrasts with the *Calendar*, which demanded the reader consult its biographies in sequence, an activity which would lead to the reader acquiring an organic sense of history (though the argument assembled at the end of part II should urge caution in asserting the necessity of this). It is in response to this potential for the occupation of a plurality of positions within the rambling structure of the *DNB* that a unified reading position was thought to be necessary. The nature of the reading position was explicitly formulated in Leslie Stephen's essay 'National Biography'; this essay will be discussed in relation to some particular biographical entries in the *DNB*, where the explicit formulation as set out in the essay can be seen working implicitly.

Stephen's essay was a detailed statement on the rational principles that held the diverse content of the Dictionary together.[31] Stephen sought to ensure that readers would observe these principles by two means. First, Stephen couched his essay in the form of the Preface that the first volume of the *DNB* never had.[32] As such, the essay set itself up as an authoritative statement about the *DNB*, or a reading frame through which the Dictionary might then be read and used. Second, the parameters of this frame were constructed and set through the use of the persona of 'the cultivated reader'. Who were the 'cultivated readers'? 'Cultivated readers' constituted a pre-existing constituency that the Dictionary sought to serve; in offering a particular biography or life history to this constituency, '[t]he aim should be to give whatever would be really interesting to the most cultivated reader, though leaving it to the reader to put the dots over the i's'.[33] Significantly, the cultivated reader is a reader with the capacity of independent judgement; or a reader interpellated by the strategies of refined self-consciousness that characterised the production of the *DNB*.

The fact that the 'cultivated reader' was an interpellated role as opposed to the occupant of an independent space is revealed by the way in which readers are persuasively hailed at the level of individual entries to the Dictionary. For example, in the life of the mid-Victorian autodidact historian H.T. Buckle, one of Stephen's contributions to the *DNB*, the reputation of the Buckle's most renowned text *The History of Civilisation in England* (1857) was negatively assessed by the biographer-guide in the following terms: 'The reasons [for this waning of reputation] are obvious. Buckle's solitary education deprived him of the main advantage of schools and universities – the frequent clashing with independent minds – which tests most searchingly the thoroughness and solidity of a man's acquirements'.[34] Notably, independence is not held to be compatible with a process of self-education; for the reader was invited to find it 'obvious' that independence of mind was conditional upon a university education, or the defining entry-qualification to the Victorian intelligentsia. The cultural dominance of this group is finally confirmed by the biographer-guide's judgement that 'though his [Buckle's] conclusions are neither very new nor valuable to serious thinkers, they are put forward with a rhetorical power admirably adapted to impress the less cultivated reader'.[35] A number of naming devices and exclusionary strategies were at work here producing a determinate reading position; 'serious thinkers' are named, and the sophistication of these readers was meant to place them above the 'rhetorical power' of Buckle's historiography, which will titillate the 'less cultivated'. In seeing 'rhetoric' named as the property of a domain of otherness, the readers were encouraged to identify the Dictionary text as rhetoric-free, and in being free of the machinery of persuasion, an independent zone. By means of this further act of exclusion, and because the zone of 'rhetoric' is the zone of the 'less cultivated', the reading position here was to be reserved for 'the cultivated reader'.

In relation to the practice of claiming historical knowledge, what does this reading position exclude, and what does it promote and enable? The position of 'the cultivated reader' resists '*synthetic* or organic' models of the historical process (to quote *The New Calendar of Great Men* again.)[36] The participatory form of collecting life histories signified a self-consciously critical and *elaborated* approach to questions of selection and nomination, which sought to elevate itself above closed, partial collections; so in the matter of an approach to the past, the 'cultivated reader' was to seek for *elaborate* complexity, while the 'less cultivated reader' accepted simpler patterns. On what basis did this distinction lead to the discrimination against certain historical subjects and their contribution to culture? Buckle's significance to late nineteenth-century culture provides at least part of an answer. In respect of Buckle, the 'cultivated reader' had cause to be assertive. For as Stuart MacIntyre has shown in his study of pre-marxist autodidact culture, Buckle's writing was an important component in the independent working-class construction of a desired synthetic narrative of materialist history.[37] To validate Buckle would have been to legitimate his contribution to this practice, and the popular-radical aims of this practice. For this reason the position of the 'cultivated reader', enshrined in the narrative perspective of the biography of Buckle, invites the rejection of Buckle's historiography. The implicit message is that it would be *illegitimate* to attempt to reproduce culture on the basis of acts prompted by Buckle's model of the historical process.

If the reading position implicitly excludes some contributions to historical knowing on grounds of competence, the sort of historical knowing that it promotes is grounded in first a specific and narrow sense of agency, and second in the adherence to a set of disciplinary parameters. Both of these features can be seen clearly in Stephen's essay and through the structuring of specific life history entries in the *DNB*.

Agency and the broad lines of history

In the essay on 'National Biography', Stephen makes explicit reference to the relationship between biography and broader processes of history:

> History is of course related to biography inasmuch as most events are connected with some particular person. Even the most philosophical of historians cannot describe the Norman Conquest without reference to William and Harold.[38]

History here figures as the arbiter of practical action and its effects upon the world, functioning as disciplinarian upon more abstract modes of enquiry such as philosophy. These effects can be traced to the actions of individual subjects which can then be transcribed into biographies and preserved. Stephen's essay thus suggests that the reader of the Dictionary will have privileged access to the precise conditions of agency that have structured particular historical events constituting the nation's history. The reader is positioned in relation to the individual biographies so that they become the basic data enabling complex historical accounts to be built.

Although apparently dispersed and uncoordinated, these data preserve and support the grand narrative of developmental history, exemplified through the account referred to earlier of the biography of Adam Smith. In the case of Adam Smith, the support was effected by means of a closure around the categories of identity (political economist) and uncontestable achievement (founder of political economy); for the support to be truly effective however, certain conditions of use relating to the Dictionary were put before the reader. Again, these are made explicit in Stephen's essay, in the reading space that it marks out. Stephen's essay characterises the *DNB* as a last line of defence. It was to be a defence against an ever expanding archive (in the form of the British Museum, the Public Record Office, and the burgeoning unofficial archive of popular memoirs and writing) which was in danger of confronting the researcher as 'a hopeless labyrinth' which spelled fragmentation for a coherent sense of *telos*:

> The main outlines, which used to be the whole of history, are still the most important, and instead of being filled up and rendered more precise and vivid, they sometimes seem to disappear . . . in any case one conclusion is very obvious, namely, that with the accumulation of material there should be a steady elaboration of the contrivances for making it accessible.[39]

On the one hand then, the reader is to approach the *DNB* as a form of cultural *elaboration*, which projects and celebrates complexity; but on the other, the contrivances that enable this elaboration, life histories, should preserve the 'main outlines' of history. Accordingly, in being given the basic biographical data from which questions of agency in accounts of the past might be settled, the reader is also positioned in relation to the 'main outlines' of the past itself. Thus a biographical identity ('statesman', 'political economist', 'man of letters') designates agency (historically significant action) within a set of disciplinary parameters ('practical politics', 'speculative politics'/'thought', 'literature'/'culture'). The organising categories of identity, agency and a corresponding domain of action are allied according to certain rules in the biographical narratives constituting the Dictionary, and these alliances and rules sought to keep the reader on an acceptable path through the labyrinth of the past.

How did these concepts work together in Dictionary biographies to regulate historical knowing; and what did they set themselves to resist? Their workings shall be dealt with in a moment, for their functions only make sense in terms of what they were resisting. The Dictionary strove to resist other 'contrivances' (Stephen's term) which had previously exercised a hegemony in respect of codifying national relics and historical sources. Particularly prominent amongst such relics would have been the great synthetic historical narrative of the nineteenth century, Macaulay's monumental *History of England* (1848–61) which exercised such power over the process of codifying history after beginning publication in 1848. Again, this resistance can be seen in the reading position delineated by Stephen's essay, and in the text of the *DNB* when Macaulay and his text are cited.

Reference to Macaulay's great narrative is made in 'National Biography' when Stephen specifically sets about defining the use value of the *DNB*. Stephen cites the instance in the *History of England* where 'Macaulay tells a very curious story about a certain intrigue which led to the final abolition of licensing the Press in England'.[40] Its elements and actors do indeed make it a strange story, and they need to be known if we are to understand the point that Stephen is making.

In 1688–9, it remained the case that all material seeking publication had to apply for a Crown License before it could be legally printed. Early in the reign of William III, Edmund Bohun was appointed to the office of Licenser. Although appointed by William, Bohun's political colouring was that of an unreconstructed Stuart; he justified his loyal service to the new regime of William by privately believing that the House of Orange occupied the throne by right of conquest – a view, of course, that ran counter to the official version of legitimate succession. Charles Blount was the author of a pamphlet advocating the freedom of the press; by means of a neat manoeuvre, the pamphlet wove an account of

Bohun's perspective on the current state of politics into its argument. In a moment apparently forgetful of the likely consequences, the Licenser welcomed the appearance of his own views in written form by granting Blount's pamphlet a license. With this heretical pamplet in circulation, seemingly blessed by the Licenser, Bohun was arrested and imprisoned. The regime set about dismantling the discredited Licensing system.

Macaulay's narrative handles the episode in a markedly self-conscious way; 'It may perhaps not be impossible, even at this distance of time, to put together dispersed fragments of evidence in such a manner as to produce an authentic narrative which would have astounded the unfortunate Licenser himself', and it concludes its account in judging that 'the emancipation of the English Press' should be attributed to Blount and his fugitive pamphlet.[41] Macaulay does two things here. Latterly, he assigns Blount the important status of agent in respect of the act securing political and intellectual emancipation; far from being merely the author of a pamphlet, Blount is identified as one of the joint authors of the history of liberty. However, Macaulay also self-consciously implicates the reader in the struggle the enquirer enters into with the archive to reach this 'authentic' judgement.

Stephen acknowledges the importance of this episode as an illustration of 'the conditions under which English writers won a most important privilege', but he asserts that reference to the Dictionary will make the illustration 'more distinct'.[42] In short, Stephen proposes that historical knowing based on the life history model will establish more precise relations between agent and event, and thus isolate the historical significance of the event instead of synthesising it with something greater. Stephen draws upon two familiar justifications to give priority to the Dictionary in a hierarchy of 'contrivances' seeking to codify the reader's relationship to the archive. First, Stephen appeals to a conservationist discourse which expresses a concern for the marginalised or unique, or that which is in danger of being lost to the centralising tendencies of synthesised narrative; 'Charles Blount and Edmund Bohun necessarily vanish from Macaulay's pages as soon as they have played their little drama. But it is natural to inquire what these two men otherwise were . . .'.[43] Second, Stephen makes an appeal to depth-hermeneutic discourse; thus Macaulay 'can only deal with the particular stage at which an obscure person emerges into public . . . [whereas] we can trace his movements *below the surface*' (my italics).[44] 'We', that is to say Stephen's 'cultivated readers' of the *DNB*, were being urged to use life histories to penetrate to the deeper, complex truths of history that lie beneath narratives which only scratch the surface.

A reader referring to the biography of Blount in the Dictionary in order to extract this deeper truth would have encountered a subtly different reading of Blount's relationship to the liberty of the press to that represented by Macaulay. In the Dictionary life, Blount is identified as the author of some freethinking books, and he is specifically located in a line of freethinkers, as 'the successor of Herbert of Cherbury and the predecessor of Toland'.[45] The relationship between Blount's identity, and the field of historical activity within which that identity is held to be significant, restricts Blount's status as an agent, when compared to that which his name enjoys in Macaulay's grand political narrative. The *DNB* entry says:

> The suggestion that the title of the Sovereign rested upon conquest, as Blount had probably foreseen, excited intense indignation. The House of Commons ordered the pamphlet to be burnt by the common hangman, and Bohun was imprisoned and dismissed from his office. Bohun's blunder made objections to the system felt. The Licensing Act was renewed, but after a division, and for only two years, after which it was never revived.[46]

Therefore, Blount is restricted in the *DNB* to 'probably' foreseeing the consequences of his action in pushing his text for Licensed publication; it is 'Bohun's blunder' that causes the restraint on free speech to be examined. Furthermore, the site of that examination is stated to be Parliament, which assumes a privileged role by ordering Blount's book to be burnt. This is important in the sense that the Dictionary portrays Blount's book as having minimal influence on Parliament; Parliament, and the history of the liberty of the press, are shown to be independent of the book's influence; Parliament is portrayed as concluding the episode for itself.

What does this denial of Blount as an active subject of history amount to in relation both to the *DNB*'s stated project, and its less explicit position in a political field? The brief biography of Blount acts as a 'contrivance' to historical knowing in precisely the way in which Stephen's essay claims it will. It provides an elaboration of a particular event while preserving and defining more strongly the 'main outlines' of history and particular conditions of agency; so that ‘intellectual history’, the field within which Blount’s pamphlet has significance, and ‘political history’, the field within which Parliamentary decisions are made, are kept as distinct fields of action whose lines of demarcation do not blur. Important questions relating to the legitimacy of styles of political intervention are thus raised; in the essay ‘National Biography’, Stephen points to a preoccupation in Macaulay’s historical writings with the activities of ‘fugitive literature’, or literature which originates outside or on the margins of established culture and institutions, and which constitutes a challenge to their ascendancy.[47] In this context, the biography of Blount in the *DNB* can be read as an attempt to define the impact of ‘fugitive literature’ on established institutions as ineffectual and non-subversive.

The assumptions that structure the telling of the particular historical event associated with the life of Charles Blount rely on conceptions of order, and the demarcation of domains. The *DNB* account implies that consensus and stability are maintained by an equilibrium of forces, as represented in an act of independent intellectual endeavour whose implications are independently and rationally assessed by the experienced practitioners of the art of statesmanship. The assumptions underpinning this image can be argued to have worked in two ways. At one level, they seemed passively to represent the past; but at another less obvious level, they actively and politically sought to reconstruct the present in which they were circulating.

IV Conclusions

In taking the late nineteenth-century life history project of the *Dictionary of National Biography* as its object of concern, this paper has argued that the *DNB*, through its refined and self-conscious method of selecting entries, and its rhetorical presentation of these methods and entries, hailed a particular type of reader (the ‘cultivated reader’) from a specific position within a field structured by conflicting cultural and political viewpoints. It has also argued that the peculiar durability of the *DNB* with respect to its judgements on historical figures, their works and activities, and its implicit claims about the nature of historical knowing, can be traced to a capacity for eliding the nature of its commitment to positions within this political field. Moreover, it has argued that the rhetoric representing the processes of intellectual production that brought the collection into being, at the same time as disguising biases and making them acceptable, bestowed prestige and legitimacy on the cultural grouping who initiated the processes.

Furthermore, the finished collection of life histories, which this rhetoric framed, were themselves made up of images which sought to promote a particular set of activities held to be beneficial to the British nation-state; simultaneously, these images resisted activities that were believed to pose the nation-state a threat. In stressing the active function of images constructing life histories and biographies, the paper takes issue with Colin Bell. Bell's approach to the *DNB*, which played down the analysis of content, focussed instead on the biased nomination process shaping the Dictionary. This he saw as essentially a *reflection* of preconstituted elite power; according to Bell's analysis, power was always being derived from and exercised within sources extraneous to the *DNB*. In one sense Bell is correct about the location of the sources of power; it would be foolish to underestimate the enabling power vested in economic security and a university education, which constituted the foundations of the intellectual elite that both Bell and this paper are concerned with. However, while valid from the perspective of one model of the means by which hegemonic power is secured, Bell's insight does not represent the hegemonic relationship between intellectuals, discourse and power at its most effective moment; the moment of communication. From a communicative angle, hegemony is never a completed state; instead, it has perpetually to be made and remade.[48] As such, hegemony is to be initially secured in the relationship of power that is established between a formation of intellectual discourse and a reader, and so in terms of the position that the reader is invited to read from. Accordingly, the approach adopted in this paper has emphasised the need to analyse the communicative strategies that make up the various components of the late nineteenth-century *DNB* as a complex life history project; the paper has argued that when examined from this angle the *DNB* becomes a sophisticated *bid* for cultural power. To read the *DNB* in this way is to argue that it had a dynamic role in a history of subtle struggle aimed at *securing* cultural power.

How though does such an historical analysis relate to the concerns of today? Although a new volume of the *DNB* continues to be compiled and published every decade, its concerns are commemorative, and thus very different to the analytical concerns of contemporary social historians and social scientists. However, even present day collections of life history data begin with important decisions relating to the selection and arrangement of that data, and such decisions have, as this paper has argued, a crucial bearing on the use to which this data can be put. To cite in conclusion a contemporary instance of its significance, when David Vincent, John Burnett and David Mayall set out recently to compile their *Autobiography of the Working Class*, they utilised in part a participatory nomination process; those with access to or knowledge of the autobiographies written by working-class men and women were encouraged to correspond with the editors.[49] Of course, there were very good, pragmatic reasons for using radio airwaves for this purpose; it was the best way to ensure reaching the widest possible audience, and bringing in the greatest quantity of data. However, the symbolic meaning of this practice is not cancelled out by such pragmatic concerns. In the way that the *DNB* addressed its nominators from the exclusive preserve of the *Athenaeum*, the *Autobiography of the Working Class* project by contrast addressed its nominators through a medium of popular communication, orientating the project towards a position in the cultural and political field contesting the position occupied by the once hegemonic *DNB*. The degree to which the nomination process is either an explicit or covert part of an operation involving the collection of life histories is thus worth investigating, whatever the context.

Notes

* This was originally presented as a paper to the Inaugural Conference of the Keele Life Histories Centre (October 1986); I am grateful to Gordon Fyfe, Charles Swann and Jim McLaverty for helpful comments, and to Shirley Dex for her patience, encouragement and valuable editorial advice. My thanks are due to Brean Hammond who commented on an early draft; special thanks to Mike Pudlo and Roger Webster who commented on a later version.

1 Colin Bell, 'Some Comments on the Use of Directories in Research on Elites, with particular reference to the Twentieth-century supplements of the *Dictionary of National Biography*', in Ivor Crewe, (ed.), *British Political Sociology Yearbook: Vol. 1 Elites in Western Democracy*, Croom Helm, London, 1974, pp. 161–71.

2 Hubert L. Dreyfus and Paul Rabinow, *Michel Foucault: Beyond Structuralism and Hermeneutics*, Harvester, Brighton, 1982, pp. xiii–xiv.

3 For the history of the formation of the *NED* (later the *OED*), see K.M. Elizabeth Murray, *Caught in the Web of Words: James A.H. Murray and the Oxford English Dictionary*, Oxford University Press, Oxford, 1979.

4 Commemoration of a Dinner held to honour the publisher of the Dictionary, George Smith, (6 June 1894); from '*DNB*'; *Circulars, Menus of Complimentary*

Dinners in Connection with the Undertaking (1888–1894), held in the British Library, Department of Printed Books.

5 Comprehensive lists of the contributors to both the original *DNB* and the original *NED* have been preserved by subsequent new editions of the texts. The overlap is exemplified in the journalist intellectual Leslie Stephen, and the academic intellectual F.J. Furnivall; however, the fact that the great proportion of contributors who were producing material for both projects simultaneously cannot be institutionally identified points to patterns of association that did not depend on one dominant institutional focus.

6 However, when professional academics did contribute, they contributed heavily; for instance, the number of articles contributed by the historians C.H. Firth (Regius Chair, Oxford: 222) and T.F. Tout (Professor of History, University of Manchester: 240) meant that they had, in effect, written an entire volume of the Dictionary each.

7 This quasi-evangelicalism should perhaps been seen less as the inheritance of a Clapham Sect upbringing in the way that Noel Annan represents it in his *Leslie Stephen: the Godless Victorian*, and more as a set of techniques and practices seeking to redefine the content of the categories of the 'moral' and the 'intellectual', which were open to appropriation.

8 The field of collective biography produced at this time can be surveyed through two sources; Phyllis M. Ricks, *An Analytical Bibliography of Universal Biography*, Library Association, London, 1934; and Robert B. Slocum, *Biographical Dictionaries and Related Works*, Galse Research, Detroit, 1967.

9 See for instance J.F. Waller (ed.), *The Imperial Dictionary of Universal Biography*, W. Mackenzie, London, 1863; and Samuel Maunder (ed.), *The Biographical Treasury; A Dictionary of Universal Biography*, Longman, Green, Longman and Roberts, London, 1859, (which went through eleven editions up to 1873).

10 These were often produced by groups facing sustained opposition, and can be seen as attempts to secure legitimacy through the demonstration of a tradition; see for instance Joseph Gillow (ed.), *A Literary and Biographical History: A Bibliographical Dictionary of the English Catholics, 1885–1902*, Burns and Oates, London.

11 Frederic Harrison (ed.), *The New Calendar of Great Men*, Macmillan, London, 1892.

12 Ibid., pp. 1–38, 583–644.

13 Ibid., pp. 37–8, 615–17.

14 See ibid., p. xi for the list of 15 contributors, who, in addition to Harrison, included J.H. Bridges and E.S. Beesly (who held the Chair of History at University College, London).

15 Characteristically, the reader is referred either to an approved text from the series of publications entitled 'Positivist Library', or relevant sections from Comte's *Positive Philosophy*, or *Positive Polity*.

16 *Calendar*, p. vi.

17 See John Morley's description of *The Calendar* in his review for *The Nineteenth Century*, vol. 31 (1892), pp. 312–28; taken from Martha S. Vogeler, *Frederic Harrison: The Vocations of a Positivist*, Clarendon Press, Oxford, 1984, p. 356.

18 Stephen demanded from potential contributors entries drawn up along the lines of a 'business-like form'; he further legislated that there would be 'no room for elaborate analysis' and that 'philosophical and critical disquisition' would be considered out of place; Leslie Stephen 'A New Biographical Brittania', *Athenaeum*, 2378, (23 Dec. 1882), p. 850.

19 The reader, it is claimed, is left to 'put the dots over the i's'; see Leslie Stephen, 'National Biography', in his *Studies of a Biographer*, 4 vols, Duckworth, London, 1899, vol. 1, p. 24.

20 All references to the *DNB* relate to the first edition as published by Smith, Elder and Co., London, in 63 vols between 1885 and 1900; the nomination process is described in the 'Statistical Account', vol. 63, 1900. The 'Statistical Account' was coordinated by Sidney Lee, who ultimately took over from Stephen as editor-in-chief when Stephen's health failed him. It amounted to a retrospective assessment of the scope and achievement of the *DNB*; tabulating statistical information relating to the number of biographical entries contributed by individual contributors; the total number of biographical entries; and the distribution of this total across the succeeding centuries of national history.
21 Ibid., pp. vii–viii.
22 Leslie Stephen, 'National Biography' in his *Studies of a Biographer*, 4 vols, Duckworth, London, 1899, vol. 1, p. 5.
23 *DNB*, 'Statistical Account', vol. 63, p. viii.
24 Ibid., p. xiii.
25 'In Germany, in Austria, in Belgium, such work has been done, or is being done, with the aid either of the National Treasury or state-aided literary societies . . . In this country great undertakings are carried out independently of state aid . . .' Sidney Lee, speaking at a Dinner to George Smith (6 June, 1894).
26 Stephen, 'National Biography', p. 24.
27 *DNB*, 'Adam Smith', vol. 53, 1898, p. 3.
28 Ibid., p. 9.
29 *Calendar*, 'Adam Smith', p. 526. For a recent and more rigorously theorised confirmation of this perspective, see Keith Tribe, *Land, Labour and Economic Discourse*, Routledge and Kegan Paul, London, 1978. Tribe argues at length that Smith has been retrospectively appropriated by, and made falsely identical to, the discourse of classical political economy.
30 *Calendar*, 'Adam Smith', p. 527.
31 Leslie Stephen, 'National Biography', p. 5.
32 Ibid., p. 4.
33 Ibid., p. 24.
34 *DNB*, 'Henry Thomas Buckle', vol. 7, 1886, p. 211.
35 Ibid.
36 *The New Calendar of Great Men*, 'Preface', p. vi.
37 Stuart MacIntyre, *A Proletarian Science: Marxism in Britain, 1917–1933*, Cambridge University Press, Cambridge, 1980, p. 71.
38 Leslie Stephen, 'National Biography', p. 12.
39 Ibid., p. 10.
40 Ibid., p. 15.
41 Lord Macaulay, *The History of England from the Accession of James II*, 3 vols, 'Everyman', Dent, London, 1906, vol. 3, pp. 181–92.
42 Leslie Stephen, 'National Biography', p. 16.
43 Ibid.
44 Ibid.
45 *DNB*, 'Charles Blount', vol. 5, 1886, p. 243.
46 Ibid., p. 244.
47 Leslie Stephen, 'National Biography', p. 14.
48 The importance of the communicative dimension of hegemony is brought home in Antonio Gramsci's very detailed meditations on the dynamics of cultural artifacts; see Geoffrey Nowell-Smith and David Forgacs (eds), *Selections from the Cultural Writings*, Lawrence and Wishart, London, 1985. Raymond Williams deals with hegemony as a process in *Marxism and Literature*, Oxford University Press, Oxford, 1977, p. 113.
49 John Burnett, David Vincent and David Mayall (eds), *The Autobiography of the Working Class*, in 3 vols (vol. I 1790–1890; vol. II 1890–1945; vol. III, supplement), Harvester, Brighton.

Labour markets and industrial structures in women's working lives

Sylvia Walby

Introduction

The analysis of women's position in society is often considered to be particularly affected by their stage in the life cycle. This paper will examine that hypothesis in relation to one aspect of women's position in the labour market. Is the life history method the best way of gaining an understanding and explanation of patterns of women's participation in paid work?

On the one hand it can be argued that women are particularly affected by their stage in the life cycle because of the importance of child birth and child care in their lives. On the other, it can be argued that this overstates the significance of biological events at the expense of the significance of other factors structuring women's lives. In particular, that there is a problematic tendency to use a 'job model' to explain men's work patterns and a different one, 'a gender model', in order to explain women's work patterns (Feldberg and Glenn, 1979). That is, labour market and industrial structures are used to explain patterns in men's work and domestic events used to explain patterns in women's work. The greater tendency to use the life history method in the analysis of women's as opposed to men's labour force experience, thus may push our understanding of women's employment in a different direction from that of men to a greater extent than is warranted.

Domestic versus labour market explanations

There are three parallel debates on women's participation in paid employment which deal particularly with the question of the significance of women's life cycle, and hence the pertinence of the life history method.

First, whether women's disadvantaged position in paid work is due on the one hand to their possessing less human capital than men, or on the other, due to discrimination against them.

Second, whether it is family structures or labour market structures which underlie women's different position in paid work.

Third, supply side versus demand side models of women's participation.

These debates all bear upon the issue of whether longitudinal or cross-sectional methodologies are more appropriate for the analysis of gender relations in employment. These discussions have considerable overlap, as I shall show below.

The first debate, as to whether human capital models can explain the different positions of men and women in paid work has been subject to extensive discussion (see for instance Amsden (1980), Treiman and Hartmann (1981), England (1982), Mincer (1962), Mincer and Polachek (1974), Walby (1988)). On the one hand human capital theorists argue that women's lower wages can be explained as a consequence of women's lesser human capital as indicated by their skill, qualifications and labour market experience. On the other, it is argued that it is discrimination which accounts for the lesser wages and lesser access to occupations of women than men. (An overview analysis by Treiman and Hartmann of tests of this model by human capital theorists suggests that while this theory is able to account for some of the wages gap between men and women, it is unable to explain more than two-fifths of this gap.)

In the second debate, one side argues that women's position in paid work can be understood primarily as a result of their position within the family, while the other emphasises the importance of labour market structures. Here one set of writers has suggested that it is women's role as homemaker, in particular taking care of children and a husband, which means that women have a different relationship to the labour market than does a man whose principal role is that of breadwinner. Women typically spend less time in paid work than men as a consequence of their domestic work and have fewer skills partly as a direct consequence and partly because women's anticipation of this role means that they typically acquire fewer qualifications than men. The other side of this debate stresses instead the structuring of the labour market which leads to women's confinement to those jobs which are paid less and are considered less skilled. Here it is the role of organised men in the labour market as trade unionists or employers which is seen to structure opportunities in favour of men and away from women.

The third debate is constructed around the dichotomy of supply side versus demand side factors. On the one hand women's position in the labour market is considered to be a result of supply side factors, such as the structuring of their human capital by their domestic situation. On the other, women's participation in paid employment is considered to depend crucially on what employers offer, in the context of patriarchally structured industrial relations.

As can be seen these three debates overlap. Indeed in certain circumstances they might look as if they were merely different expressions of the same debate. Thus if it could be argued that women's position in paid employment is different from that of men because they have less human capital because of their position in the family and that this supply side variable is determinant. On the other it could be argued that women's position is different from that of men because of discrimination which is rooted in the labour market and leads to different demand for women as compared to men workers. However, the three debates do not necessarily overlap, although this is often the case. For instance, some Marxist feminists have argued that it is the family which leads to women's disadvantaged position in the labour market, and this is not a human capital approach, although it still focuses on the supply side variable of the family.

The point here is that life histories are of more importance if the first side of each of these three debates is considered to be correct and less important if the second side is taken. Life histories gather data on the factors considered relevant by the first position, and rarely gather data on factors considered central by the second approach. Life histories used in the analysis of employment usually collect information on a person's education and training, periods of labour market participation and withdrawal, geographical and occupational mobility, and life events such as child bearing and rearing. They are not suited to gathering information about the nature and sources of the structuring of the labour market. This is because life histories collect information on individual characteristics.

However, this point should not be overstated, since life histories will necessarily record the effects of labour market structuring. Indeed they provide information about how an individual experiences the labour market. Cross-sectional analyses cannot tell us about how a given individual, or cohort, experiences structural change. Thus life histories provide us with information, which is otherwise unobtainable, about the implications of structural change for individuals or specific social groups. This is the great strength of the life history methodology for analyses of work.

This paper will examine these issues about the life history method in relation to women's employment. The data set which is used to explore these issues is described below.

Lancaster women's work histories

The Lancaster Women's Work Histories was a data set gathered in Lancaster in 1980–1. It contains information on a sample of 300 women aged 18 upwards in the Lancaster travel-to-work-area (TTWA). The data concerned life histories, with an emphasis on employment histories, together with contemporary data on a wider range of issues including the domestic division of labour and political and social attitudes. In addition we asked for the areas in which the women had previously lived.

The most detailed information was on employment. Women were asked to recall all the jobs they had ever held. For each job each woman was asked about the occupational and industrial classification, rate of pay, amount of job specific training and reason for leaving. These were coded using the Census (3-digit) and Standard Industrial Classification (SIC) distinctions respectively, and reasons for leaving a job were coded with our own 19-fold classification.

The sample was obtained from the electoral registers for the area, Lancaster having a near coincidence of administrative and TTWA boundaries. The wards were stratified in order to ensure a balance between the two main urban areas of Lancaster and Morecambe as well as the associated rural area, all of which are part of the TTWA. The women were interviewed by Anne Green using a structured questionnaire, some for several hours.

This is only one of several data sets on the Lancaster TTWA which are available. This local labour market was the focus of intense study by the Lancaster Regionalism Group as part of the ESRC financed initiative on the Changing Urban and Regional System, so we have separate sources of data on structural change from various survey sources, including the Department of Employment Census of Employment, and also on its political history.

Methodological problems

We encountered a number of predictable methodological problems in the collection and coding of these data. Those which are discussed here are the sample size, the recall problem, the unit of data collection and the occupational classification problem.

The typical method of data collection in Britain has been that used in the Lancaster survey – the use of a questionnaire survey conducted by interviewer to obtain retrospective recall of information by the respondent. People's memories are fallible and they are likely to be more fallible the further back they are asked to remember. Thus the early data is likely to be less accurate than the recent data. The question of the degree to which the early data is inaccurate is unknowable, unless the respondent admits to not knowing. Where the respondent admits to not knowing we were able to disregard the question and analysis on that topic. In this study respondents were asked a variety of questions about each job. Some of the answers on detailed issues, for instance pay, were recorded as 'not known' sufficiently frequently for these data to be considered not worth analysing. It is more likely that people will remember the occupation and industry of jobs of lengthy duration held recently, than they will remember short duration jobs held thirty years ago. A repeat interview panel survey in which respondents are asked to report on the present at regular intervals throughout their lives would overcome these problems, but at considerable expense.

It is the issue of selective recall which lends support to the argument that the life history method is inevitably subjective. If we cannot collect data which has a direct correspondence to events in a person's past then should we abandon notions of scientific reliability and settle for a notion of life histories as rich ethnographic data instead? In this view life histories are not irrelevant, but they are not the kind of hard data which is appropriately analyzed with statistics and computers. Instead they give us memories of the past, which are interesting precisely because they are selective. The research work on recall reviewed in the introductory chapter to this volume suggests that it can be reliable for certain topics. Thus the claim that life histories are only subjective goes too far.

A second methodological issue we faced concerned the sample size. The size of the sample needs to be quite large in order to deal with the effects of different cohorts. This makes life history collection even by recall extremely expensive. The Lancaster Women's Work Histories data set is at the limit of acceptable size for the analysis performed upon it. Even so, the aggregations which had to be performed in order to achieve statistically significant results were sometimes less than desirable. Some analytic questions were not considered capable of reliable answer and they had to be abandoned. One way past this problem is to abandon the attempt to gather data on more than one age cohort at a time. For the Lancaster study this was considered an unacceptable limitation since the intersection with the different structural changes was a question of central interest. For other studies it might be an acceptable limitation. Another alternative is to utilise a large sample, but to ask only limited questions, the kind of questions for which a guiding interviewer is not necessary. This is the practice in the OPCS Longitudinal Survey (LS).[1] These LS data were used by Dan Shapiro within the Lancaster CURS study (see Bagguley *et al.*, 1990). The issues which were examined in the above analysis could not have been asked using data from the LS which is restricted to a few pieces of information. Indeed the Lancaster Women's Work History data set is unusual in asking questions about all job changes over a working life, rather than over a limited number of years or a limited number of points in a life time.

These strengths and weaknesses of the life history method so far discussed are common to analyses of work histories for men as well as women, although the data set utilised above concerned only women. Another gendered issue concerns the household. While many analyses of men's working lives assume that the nature of a man's co-residents is of only marginal interest, the opposite assumption is usually made about women. An open-minded analysis would, of course, ask the household questions about men as well as women, in order to test, rather than merely assume, that the household is of significance to women's employment and not to men's.

Our data set contained some questions about household composition. However, it was not possible, given the limited time available for the interview, to ask many questions about other household members over time. While it is reasonable to ask about the occupational and financial status of current household members there was not time to ask about this for the respondent's lifetime, nor would it have been likely to be accurate. This is partly because recall about others is less likely to be accurate, even if the respondents had once known the information. There is a particular difficulty about asking about ex-household members, whose absence may well have been due to a traumatic event, such as death or divorce. Interviewee co-operation is likely to cease in a sufficiently large proportion of these cases to make any data collected unreliable. Thus retrospective collection of household data is particularly difficult. Our data set was based on individuals. If, however, the hypothesis that women's employment patterns are significantly determined by that of their husband and household were being adopted, then it would be logical to make the household rather than the individual the data collection unit. The amount of interviewee co-operation to achieve this significantly increases. This is particularly difficult over time, given the propensity of households to change membership. Retrospective questioning would have to deal with the issue of which household is under analysis, while panel interviewing would be faced with the alternate dissolution and extension of the unit under study. Given the current rates of divorce in Britain, never mind 'simple' issues such as marriage and death, longitudinal analysis of employment taking the household as the unit would be bedeviled with methodological difficulties. It should be noted however, that the current study takes the individual as the unit on theoretical grounds, not that of methodological ease.

An additional problem faced was that of the choice of occupational coding. Analysis of women's occupations is fraught with classificatory difficulties. The conventional classifications have been based upon male occupations; using such categories, women are classified into a few categories only. The heavy preponderance of clerical work and semi-skilled service sector work among women and the small presence of women in skilled manual work are in sharp contrast with the balance of occupations among men. Various alternative approaches and categories have been suggested (see, for instance, Dex, 1987).

In this study we decided to proceed pragmatically and to see how the occupations grouped. We worked on the now standard assumption that people are more likely to move between jobs which are similar than they are between those which are dissimilar. We had the data on job changes and so could discover which were the jobs between which our 300 women moved most frequently. We placed in the same grouping those occupations between which there was most movement, and drew distinctions from other occupational groupings between which our 300 women moved less frequently. This analysis was done under the direction of Prof. Richard Davies, using techniques described in Goodman (1986) and Green (1989). This does have the disadvantage of not being directly comparable with the classification of men's jobs, but men were not in this sample anyway.

This procedure produced an eightfold classification: professional; intermediate; clerical; skilled manual; factory manual; service workers; sales; and unskilled. This was very similar to the occupational groupings classified as profiles produced using a similar method by Dex on the 5,230 women of the DE/OPCS Women and Employment Survey in 1980. This classification is different to that typically used for men in a number of ways. Firstly, the classification splits factory and service workers (both either subsumed under semi-skilled or scattered), which reflects the distinctiveness of the service sector niche especially for part-time women workers. Secondly, it separated sales from clerical workers; this separation is now widely commented upon where sales workers have worse rates of pay and conditions than clerical workers, that is, sales jobs have circumstances more akin to manual workers than white-collar ones.

In a separate exercise the industries in which the women worked were grouped into two: production and services, the former involving a conflation of manufacturing and the tiny extractive sectors.

Domestic versus labour market explanations

As I have suggested earlier the classic divide in the literature on women's employment is that between domestic/human capital and labour market/discrimination models. I have argued that the life history methodology has an inbuilt imperative towards the former and away from the latter explanations. Thus the data set outlined above would often be analysed by examining correlations between domestic events and labour market events. For instance the standard questions would include: Does a greater number of departures from the labour market for child- or husband-care lead to lower labour market status and lower earnings? Does a longer absence from the labour force for such unpaid work lead to a similar outcome? The answer to these questions is, on average, an unequivocal affirmative as a multitude of studies of similar data sets have shown. For instance, this is the clear outcome of the analysis of the nationally representative sample of women in the Women and Employment Survey (Martin and Roberts, 1984). Hence it would appear to confirm the domestic/human capital model. However, Martin and Roberts were careful to consider other elements in their analysis, asking questions, for instance, about the extent of occupational segregation.

The contrary thesis emphasises the importance of labour market structures, discrimination and the demand side of the economy. Indeed the Lancaster economy had undergone major structural change, especially over the period 1960–80. The Lancaster Women's Work History data set was gathered in the same TTWA as a range of cross-sectional data sets which point up a range of other possible hypotheses. The Lancaster TTWA underwent early de-industrialisation in the 1960s and 1970s, so that by 1980 the structure of the labour market was heavily weighted towards the service sector. The manufacturing sector, which had been based on the production of lino more or less closed down during the 1970s and 1980s, apart from those firms which were able to diversify into plastic covered wallpaper. Textile mills, not cotton but artificial fibres, similarly were closed down by multinationals which moved production abroad to cheaper sources of labour.

The period 1960–80 saw the collapse of the sector of the economy which had traditionally employed many men, manufacturing, and the growth of the sector which today employs many women, services. During this period Census data shows an enormous increase in the paid employment of women.

One question here is which had greater effect on women's patterns and experiences of paid employment – the life cycle, or de-industrialisation? Do we conclude that the enormous increase of women workers is due to these sectoral shifts in the economy? Or do we conclude that despite the overall increase in women's employment the life cycle effect remains the overwhelming feature structuring women's experiences of work?

Since the answer is, obviously, that both are significant, the question becomes – can we disentangle the different implications of these developments for women? In particular, what happens at the intersection of life and work trajectories on the one hand and industrial and labour market change on the other?

In this context I hope to have shown that the study of life history data by itself is problematic. It pushes us towards certain explanatory hypotheses, even if the authors of the study are careful to add appropriate qualifications. Rather we need to utilise both longitudinal and cross-sectional data sets. The most interesting results are at the intersection of the two.

The Lancaster data set on Women's Work Histories is strongest on the issue of job changes. Changes in jobs are a routine aspect of all working lives. The point of change potentially gives us some important indication of the social and economic processes at work. We can analyse the direction of change and the various correlates of this. We can examine the nature of the changes which women made from job-to-job and on the point of entering and leaving the labour market. We can examine these changes by occupational group, by industrial sector, and by full-time and part-time working.

My question is whether the changes correlate better with aspects of domestic structure or with labour market structures. Many women do take a break from paid work in order to work at home looking after children and husbands for certain periods of their lives. But how important is this break for the nature of the paid work that women take? The domestic or gender model suggests that it is the overwhelming structuring event, while the 'job' model would focus on the nature of the labour market structures.

The complexity of a data set such as this one on Lancaster is that domestic events are occurring simultaneously with changes in labour market opportunities. When women re-enter the work force after a break they are not entering the same labour market, but rather one which has been changed by industrial restructuring. Over the period of study the nature of the Lancaster labour market was significantly changed by the de-industrialisation of the local economy. The manufacturing sector underwent significant decline, as both the product market changed and also production was moved abroad by the multinational owners, while the service sector underwent considerable expansion.

De-industrialisation and the experience of the labour market

This process of de-industrialisation occurred in Lancaster a little earlier than in many other British cities, but otherwise is similar to the change undergone in the rest of Britain in the early 1980s. The Lancaster economy had been dominated by a few large manufacturers, but these largely closed down in the 1960s and 1970s. These firms were part of multinational conglomerates. In the textile sector, the product was artificial fibres. This process was first run down by a failure to invest in the newer forms of technology; it then moved abroad to sources of cheaper labour. In the case of linoleum the product itself was one of the problems as the market changed and carpet became the preferred and affordable alternative. Chemicals was a further manufacturing sector to suffer serious contraction. The main types of occupations in these plants were manual, involving various levels of skill. They were jobs held predominantly, but by no means exclusively, by men.

At the same time as the manufacturing sector was collapsing the service sector was expanding. Lancaster had been from the nineteenth century a centre for health care, from its early period as the county town. Even after it lost its status as the centre for county level government its hospitals remained. These included not only general physical hospitals, but also those for the mentally ill and mentally handicapped. This sector expanded during the 1960s and 1970s. Further, Lancaster became a centre for education, with the founding and expansion of the University from 1964, together with the development of a college of higher education. This service sector was primarily in the public rather than private sector. In addition there was the development of the retail sector as Lancaster became more of a regional shopping centre; that is, there was growth in the private sector services. The occupations in this service sector were at all levels of skill, including a more significant professional component than those of the declining manufacturing sector. A higher proportion of these jobs were held by women than had been the case in the declining manufacturing sector. The changes in the economy of Lancaster are explored in more detail in Bagguley *et al.* (1990).

At this aggregate level the changes in industrial structure and gender composition of the work force appear to go neatly together. But the aggregate level data cannot tell us whether individuals themselves directly experience de-industrialisation in their own personal work lives. We do not know whether, for instance, the typical worker moves from manufacturing to service sector during the course of their lives. An alternative possibility is that it is new entrants to the workforce who take the new service jobs while the ex-manufacturing workers become either retired or unemployed. In the former case workers experience and are able to compare both sectors. In the latter they cannot. This has important implications for peoples' experience and consciousness of social and economic change. Also, changes of this kind must have implications for local politics.

The work history method then adds something to the analysis of de-industrialisation which cannot be gained from the aggregate data alone. These changes have massively different implications for consciousness and action according to how individuals move through these industrial and labour market changes.

The analysis of job changes enables us to answer some of these questions about the way individuals experience these changes. Do people stay within the industrial sector and occupation? If they change does this have a pattern, or does it appear random?

An examination of the job changes of our 300 women shows that 75 per cent of job changes were within an industrial sector. Of movements between sectors a slight majority were from production to services rather than from services to production. The change from production to services at the structural level of the Lancaster economy was directly experienced in terms of a change directly from a production job to a service job in only 15 per cent of job changes, as Table 1 illustrates.

Table 1

Job movement by sector for Lancaster women

	1960–80		*All working life*	
	No.	*%*	*No.*	*%*
Production to service	36	15	188	24
Service to production	25	10	121	16
Service to service	123	51	278	36
Production to production	57	24	186	24
Total	241	100	773	100

These figures show that despite the very considerable restructuring of the Lancaster economy during the period 1960–80, the number of job changes which followed the direction of change from production to service was not very great.

This initial analysis examines the impact of structural change only, following the suggestions of the 'job' rather than 'gender' model. In the second approach we would expect to analyse the impact of domestic events. We know from other sources that a period out of the labour market has a detrimental impact on women's occupational position in work. For instance the Women and Employment Survey showed that women who re-entered the labour force after such a period were likely to come back at a lower level than that at which they had left. This effect is exacerbated if women return to part-time rather than full-time work. Some women do slowly regain their original occupational level, but others never do, and few better it (Martin and Roberts, 1984).

My question here is how women negotiate this break through the changing industrial and occupational structure. The labour market is different on their return. Do they go with this change, or are the women committed to their earlier work identifications? This is a question about women's commitment to work. Are they committed to particular forms of work, or not? Is women's attachment to their occupations firm or flimsy? This question is difficult to answer directly since women's options are highly constrained. If women wish to return part-time rather than full-time, then their options are even more constrained, since part-time jobs are concentrated in the lower levels of the service sector. If domestic considerations were paramount then we might expect women re-entrants to be flexible in their industrial sector and occupation in order to maximise compatibility with domestic needs.

We divided job changes into two categories. The first, 'job-to-job', entailed a direct movement from one form of paid employment to another with no intervening break. The second, 're-entrants' involved a break in paid employment. This enabled us to compare the nature of the job changes between these two types of behaviour.

Interestingly we find a high degree of attachment by women to their industry and occupation. Indeed this attachment is quite striking over the duration of the break from employment. Shifts between industrial sectors are more likely to occur on job-to-job changes than they are over a break in employment. Re-entrants typically return to the industrial sector which had previously employed them. This occurs among workers in both the production and the service sectors as Table 2 illustrates.

The most important change from the perspective of the de-industrialisation thesis is that from production to service. This represents the structural changes in the economy. The majority of women who make this move during the course of their working lives do so directly from one job to another without a break.

So the majority of women returners take employment in the

Table 2
Sectoral change of re-entrants compared to job-to-job changes

	Numbers of changes	
	Job-to-job	*Re-entrant*
Production to service	65	33
Service to production	64	11
Service to service	79	199
Production to production	70	116

same sector as that which they left. Most changes between sectors involve job-to-job moves not involving a break from employment. That is, the employment break is of little significance in understanding the shift of women from the manufacturing to the service sector.

These findings are different from those by Dex (1987) on industrial mobility over the life course. Dex's results suggested that women did experience de-industrialisation over the life course and suggests that the sectoral shift occurs particularly frequently over the first break from the labour market during child bearing. This difference may be due to sample differences, for instance, that Lancashire women are more attached to their industrial niche than women over Britain as a whole. Alternatively it may be that the analysis of the Lancaster Women's Work Histories used a different operationalisation of the employment break for child rearing. The Lancaster analysis used a very precise separation of the various job changes according to whether it was job-to-job or whether there was a break, while the Dex analysis used a simpler operationalisation of employment profiles in terms of age and jobs pre- or post- birth of first child.[2] The Lancaster anlaysis of 'breaks' thus included those for second and any subsequent children, while these were not included by Dex and it may be that the first break is more likely than second or third breaks to lead to a shift in industrial niche.

Part-time, full-time and industrial sector

Most women who return to employment after a break for child care do so part-time rather than full-time. This might be considered to be a pattern determined by domestic factors. But even this can be shown to be significantly affected by the industrial and occupational structure because part-time jobs are not randomly distributed through the industrial and occupational structures. Instead they are concentrated in the service sector and in lower level occupations. Thus the return to work might be thought to drive women towards the lower level jobs of the service sector, since this is where the part-time jobs are located.

The Lancaster data shows, as expected, that returners are more likely than job-to-job movers to move from full-time to part-time work during a job change event. However, the extent to which the return is of this type of change from full-time to part-time is itself significantly affected by the industrial location of the former job. Women returners who stayed within the production sector were more likely to return full-time, while women returners who changed from production to service were the most likely to change from full-time to part-time. See Table 3 below.

Table 3
Full-time to part-time changes

	% Full-timers in the original sector moving to part-time in the destination sector	
	Job-to-job	*Returners*
Production to service	17	48
Service to production	4	31
Service to service	8	24
Production to production	5	5

These patterns reflect the lack of availability of part-time work in the production sector in Lancaster and its presence in the service sector. They indicate the significance of the industrial and occupational structure in determining women's patterns of full-time and part-time work. The domestic model alone is insufficient.

Occupational change

The analysis has so far concentrated on the division between industrial sectors. This is the aspect of the employment structure which is most directly related to the industrial restructuring. However, it is the change in the occupational structure which is usually considered to have a more direct bearing upon a person's work experience. The work history data has the advantage of enabling us to ask about the relationship between industrial-occupational change and individuals work histories, and not merely about relationships for aggregate populations. We can ask whether workers who change their industrial sector also change their occupation. In this way we can ask about the impact of de-industrialisation upon occupational experience.

The most interesting group, from the point of view of the de-industrialisation thesis are those who moved from the manufacturing to the service sector. We have already noted that returners in this category were the most likely to make the transition from full-time to part-time work. Women who were clerical workers in the manufacturing sector tended to stay within this occupational grouping after a transfer into the service sector. That is, for this group, one of the largest occupational groups for women, the change in industrial sector is likely to have made little difference to their experience of employment since they stayed within the same occupation. The skilled and unskilled factory workers who changed sector logically changed occupation. The skilled workers were more likely to experience downward than upward mobility though a significant minority made an upward move. Sales work was the biggest recipient of these workers followed by unskilled work (often cleaning). See Table 4 below.

The reverse sectoral movement, from services to production, involved less people. Again the large grouping of clerical workers tended to cross the sectoral divide without changing occupational category. This stability in attachment to clerical work happens again in the production to production and service to service transitions.

Indeed the overall picture from the analysis of industrial and occupational change is the resilience of women's occupational attachment despite job changes even if these involve sectoral shift. We see here that the 'job' model rather than the 'domestic' model is more useful in understanding these aspects of women's employment.

Table 4

Occupational changes for those moving from production to service industries

From production	*Numbers of those making transitions: To service*									
	P	I	C	Sk	M	Se	Sa	Usk	Ukn	Total
Professional (P)	2	2	0	0	0	0	1	0	0	5
Intermediate (I)	0	0	3	0	0	0	1	1	0	5
Clerical (C)	1	6	20	0	0	1	1	0	0	29
Skilled (Sk)	3	5	5	1	1	7	12	10	0	44
Manual (M)	8	9	11	0	1	6	23	19	0	77
Services (Se)	0	0	0	0	0	0	1	0	0	1
Sales (Sa)	1	1	1	0	0	1	2	2	0	8
Unskilled (Usk)	0	0	3	0	0	2	4	7	0	16
Unknown (Ukn)	0	0	1	0	0	1	0	1	0	3

The experience of de-industrialisation

Most of the workers in the service sector were new entrants to the labour market. The figures for those who first entered the labour market in the 1970s show that the majority did enter the service rather than the production sector – 74 per cent entered services and only 26 per cent production.

This means that the direct experience of de-industrialisation by having the sectoral shift over the lifetime is less than one might have expected from the aggregate figures. Not so many workers make the transition from manufacturing to service work. The new service jobs are taken by new workers. Even those workers who did make that sectoral transition are unlikely to have experienced a major transformation of their work experience, since the largest group did not change their occupation during this transition.

Political and legal changes

Data sets on life histories and employment necessarily contain data from the viewpoint of individuals. I have discussed the analysis of these data in interaction with data on structural changes in employment and argued that it is this intersection of analyses which is the particularly important addition to our knowledge. However, there are still other social factors which have not been taken into account. These types of analysis may well lead readers to think that industrial and occupational patterns determine employment patterns, and that the economic factors recorded in such data sets constitute a complete causal system. However, this omits such relevant changes as those in the legal and political structure. For instance the rise in the number of married women in paid employment might be attributed solely to changes in the economic system, such as the increasing demand for cheap labour. This would ignore an important change not visible in the data – that of the removal of the marriage bar. Changes in patterns of economic participation by women have also been affected by legislative changes for instance the introduction of equal opportunity legislation; and the introduction of legislation which gave rights to full-time workers, but not part-time workers, making the latter more attractive to employers. That is, political struggles have been important in the restructuring of labour market opportunities for women. Obviously, these do not appear in the data sets, so analyses of these data for correlations necessarily miss important variables. In short, the life history method has difficulty incorporating an appreciation of political struggle and legal change into its causal analysis. This is not an argument against doing life histories, merely a plea for modesty in its claims.

Conclusions

The life history method does add much valuable material to the analysis of employment patterns. However, there are some serious problems if these data are falsely assumed to contain sufficient information by themselves to explain such employment patterns. The strengths are that life histories enable us to understand the implications of structural change at the actual individual level, and prevents false assumptions that the individual experience is represented by aggregate change. This was demonstrated most clearly in relation to the de-industrialisation thesis in the Lancaster economy where it was shown that it was rare for individuals to have moved jobs from manufacturing to the service sector despite the change in the structure of the aggregate economy. Instead we were able to see women's attachments to particular occupations and industries, even across breaks in employment due to child bearing. The new service sector jobs were taken primarily by new young workers, not those displaced from the collapsing manufacturing sector. It would be false to think that the majority of individuals directly experienced de-industrialisation in their own employment histories.

My argument is that life history analysis is at its strongest when used together with a data set on structural change, such as in this example. It is weakest when it is used by itself, since there is a tendency to presume incorrectly that the data contains all the variables necessary to explain its patterns. In relation to women's employment the problems arise when it is incorrectly assumed that interruptions of employment by domestic work are the main determinant of women's patterns of employment, neglecting structural factors in the labour market and political and legal factors.

Women's employment patterns are determined by many factors of which their location in the life cycle with its different domestic demands is merely one. Insofar as there is a tendency within life history analysis to overemphasise the significance of this factor then the methodology has serious shortcomings. Insofar as it is used in conjunction with other data sources which capture other aspects of social and economic structure then it can lead to significantly improved analysis of women's employment.

Notes

1 This is a one per cent sample survey from the Census. Records are linked across the decade long gap, in order to build up a set of longitudinal data. The strengths are the size of the sample and the reliability of the sampling frame. The restrictions include the limitation of the range of questions which can be asked on the Census form, and also that data is collected only at 10 year intervals, missing many changes. A further current restriction is that only the last two Censuses have been so linked.

2 This is a discussion of issues raised by Shirley Dex in a personal communication.

References

Amsden, Alice H. (ed.), (1980), *The Economics of Women and Work*, Harmondsworth, Penguin.

Bagguley, Paul, Lawson, Jane Mark, Shapiro, Dan, Urry, John, Walby, Sylvia and Warde, Alan, (1990), *Restructuring: Place, Class and Gender*, London: Sage.

Dex, Shirley, (1987), *Women's Occupational Mobility: A Lifetime Perspective*, London: Macmillan.

England, Paula, (1982), 'The failure of human capital theory to explain occupational sex segregation', *Journal of Human Resources*, 17 (summer): 358–70.

Feldberg, Roslyn and Glenn, Evelyn Nakano, (1979), 'Male and female: job versus gender models in the sociology of work', *Social Problems*, 26(5) (June): 524–38.

Goodman, L.A. (1986) 'Some useful extensions of the usual correspondence analysis approach and the usual log-linear models approach in the analysis of contingency tables' in *International Statistical Review*, 54, 243–309.

Green, M. (1989) 'Generalisations of the Goodman association model B, the analysis of multi-divisional contingency tables' in A. Decarli, B.J. Francis, R. Gilchrist, G.H.H. Seeber (eds) *Statistical Modelling Lecture Notes in Statistics* 57, Springer-Verlag, New York, pp. 165–71.

Martin, Jean and Roberts, Ceridwen, (1984), *Women and Employment: A Lifetime Perspective*, London: HMSO.

Mincer, Jacob, (1962), 'Labor force participation of married women: a study of labor supply', in National Bureau of Economic Research, *Aspects of Labor Economics*, Princeton: Princeton University Press.

Mincer, Jacob and Polachek, Solomon, (1974), 'Family investments in human capital: earnings of women', *Journal of Political Economy*, 82(2): S76–S108.

Treiman, Donald and Hartmann, Heidi, (1981), *Women, Work and Wages: Equal Pay for Jobs of Equal Value*, Washington DC: National Academy Press.

Walby, Sylvia (ed.), (1988), *Gender Segregation at Work*, Milton Keynes: Open University Press.

Unemployment incidence following redundancy: the value of longitudinal approaches

Leslie Rosenthal

Introduction

The period of unemployment following after redundancy has been studied by a number of researchers. The literature contains a number of studies which are longitudinal or at least retrospective over a reasonably extended period. Some of these studies are by economists (MacKay and Reid, 1972; Edlin, 1988; Andersen, 1989) and others are by sociologists (Walker *et al.*, 1985; Harris *et al.*, 1987; Davies and Esseveld, 1989; Wood, 1984). There are some differences in the focus of areas of interest, depending upon the discipline of origin of these studies, but there are also overlaps in interest. Sociologists have examined the social production of redundancy and have documented the way the labour market is not dichotomised into employment and unemployment, but has informal 'grey' areas which are highlighted in some post redundancy careers; sociologists have also contributed a perspective on the way reactions to redundancy are influenced by prevailing managerial profiles and strategies in the decisions about who is to be made redundant, social networks, and structures of authority in a firm, as well as the available and perceived job opportunities in the local labour market. Economists have concentrated more narrowly on the redundant groups' return to work, the actual job opportunities and the workings of labour markets.

Studies of redundancy have had in common an interest in the post redundancy careers of the redundant. What has tended to happen is that these careers are classified according to some simple criteria, up to the point at which the study ceased to follow them up. So we are often told, as in the case of Harris *et al.* (1987), that one third of the sample remained continuously unemployed over the follow-up period, 23 per cent remained continuously employed and 42 per cent had a chequered career. This gives us the beginnings of a picture of post redundancy careers, but it is a very static picture and there is a lot further one could go to explore the over time and dynamic nature of this experience; also, an exploration within a multivariate context could give us clues to the determinants of the various types of experiences.

Empirical analysis of economic phenomena such as the incidence or duration of unemployment spells and other work history events are usually undertaken by the use of either cross-section data, collected across individuals at a single fixed point in time, or time-series data, collected usually for a large and often varying aggregation of individuals viewed at a number of different points in time. Either one of these methods of collecting such information may, however, be subject to a number of problems. In particular, pure cross-sectional data on the uncompleted unemployment spells of the currently unemployed will typically overestimate the length of completed unemployment spell the average individual may expect to spend between employments. This problem arises because those with relatively long periods of unemployment are disproportionately more likely to be among the unemployed at any particular point in time, which increases the average measured length of unemployment spell. One-off cross-sectional studies are also unable to identify how the incidence of unemployment changes over time. Time-series data, on the other hand, is well able to track the changes in overall unemployment rates, but individuals and their characteristics then cease to be identifiable, and the groupings over which aggregated statistics are collected usually vary. It is then difficult to identify characteristics of individuals which contribute to the incidence of unemployment.

This paper sets out to explore one aspect of post redundancy careers in a more dynamic framework, using techniques which have been particularly developed for this purpose. The experience which is the focus is the duration of unemployment following after redundancy and the chances of reemployment. The paper also examines some of the other multivariate approaches to analysis of these experiences in order to compare their results. The study presented below sets out to demonstrate that whilst both cross-section and time series approaches have their virtues in extending our knowledge of unemployment following redundancy, the methodological problems that they face detract from their value. Here a longitudinal approach is adopted, which, while clearly illustrating how pure cross-section and pure time-series methods entail loss of information and can produce misleading results, more positively demonstrates the advantages of longitudinal methods in contributing to our understanding of unemployment-employment histories. Longitudinal data and the use of modern analytical tools can substantially add to our knowledge of the effects of individual attributes on the chances of unemployment and the duration of unemployment following redundancy.

The Michelin project database and the local labour market

In late 1984, the Michelin company announced large-scale redundancies at its UK tyre manufacturing headquarters in Stoke-on-Trent. These redundancies were put into effect in May 1985, with 2,137 individuals affected. This event has been used as a basis for a continuing study of some of the effects of a large-scale redundancy on the local economy and labour market.[1] As one part of this study, the labour market experiences of over two hundred ex-Michelin workers over an extended period were collated. These ex-Michelin employees were each interviewed at least three times and sometimes five times over the course of the two years plus two months following May 1985.[2] All the analyses that follow refer to a group of 227 for whom it proved possible to collect full information for the 110 weeks until August 1987.

The Michelin study was thus able to follow the day-to-day labour market experiences of what proved to be a group of mature, well-qualified, and 'employable' individuals for a two-year period following redundancy. The original sample could not be chosen in as formally random a manner as might have been wished from the entire redundant labour force, because the major participants (employer and union) felt unable on the grounds of confidentiality to supply the required information.[3] Our sample was therefore derived by more informal methods and sources, including 'factory-gate' approaches and appeals for volunteers. This is not a methodology generally recommended, but subsequent comparison with aggregate information about the whole redundant labour force with respect to age, gender and occupational classification was possible. Our conclusions from the comparisons were that the sample was adequately representative of the redundant population in most respects, but probably contained an under-representation of semi-skilled workers and, to a lesser extent, women. There are more than enough semi-skilled workers in the sample for this not to be a serious problem, but the numbers of women in the sample (only 18 in total, 7.8 per cent of the sample) and in the redundancies in aggregate (just 233 in total, 10.9 per cent of the redundant workers) were very small.[4]

The extent to which the final sample is representative of the entire redundant group is one important question, the extent to which the experiences of the group may be generalisable to the labour force as a whole is, of course, another. Although Stoke-on-Trent is certainly not untypical of English industrial cities, it is not a microcosm of the UK labour market. During the course of the 1980s, Stoke-on-Trent travel-to-work-area unemployment, for example, has moved from being below the national average, to being above the national average, and in the late 1980s is again below the national average. The comparison with national figures is shown in Table 1. During the course of the two-year period covered, Stoke-on-Trent was the site of the second National Garden Festival, which provided a boost to the local economy and a large number of temporary jobs during the spring and summer of 1986, including three for our sample.

Table 1

Stoke-on-Trent and national average (October) unemployment rates

Year	*UK* %	*Stoke* %
1984	11.7	12.5
1985	11.7	12.7
1986	11.5	12.0
1987	9.7	9.4
1988	7.5	6.6

Source: Department of Employment

The workers included in the study include both manual and non-manual occupational grades. Redundancy studies have previously mostly concentrated upon manual workers, but there seems little justification for this. In the Michelin case, the redundancies involved the closure of whole departments involving simultaneous loss of both manual and non-manual posts. As the redundancies at Michelin in 1985 were *compulsory* redundancies, the subsequent presence in the labour market of our sample of redundant workers was a fact for which the individuals themselves could not be held responsible. Their presence among the unemployed, at least in the short-term, need not therefore be taken by potential employers as reflecting individual 'lack of loyalty' or lack of productivity or work discipline or the like. Hence, it may be argued, potential employers considering the employment of one of this group could view them very differently from those who, for example, had been dismissed from their previous employment or even from those who had taken *voluntary* redundancy. Similarly, Michelin commonly had a reputation for being a high-paying but demanding employer, and other potential local employers might view past employment at Michelin as a desirable characteristic or 'positive' screening factor in job applicants.

In these ways, and in other particulars concerning personal and educational characteristics, it can be argued that the ex-Michelin sample could be favoured over the average unemployed in the search for new employment. Even so, evidence is available to advance arguments that the Michelin group was less favoured in the labour market. Especially important here might be arguments concerning the length of time that the group had spent at Michelin. As a loyal and long-serving work-force, it is possible that their skills had become too firm- and industry-specific to be of value to other potential employers. Similarly, the group may have other characteristics making it less desirable on average than the job-searcher in general. Certainly a high average age may be one such undesirable characteristic. During a period when much of the new employment available has been taken by (low-paid, part-time) women, the predominantly male character of the sample may also be disadvantageous.

Employment experiences over time

Among the questions asked of the individuals in the Michelin study were details of their employment status, hours worked, earnings, occupational status and dates for every employment that they took over the period of study. The data include, therefore, a complete post-redundancy work-diary/work-history for each individual in the sample. The unemployment rate, for example, for the group as a whole may therefore be determined for any date over the period,[5] and a time-series of such data may be derived for monthly, weekly or even daily data points.

It seems that, overall, these workers have (happily) progressed quite well since their redundancies, certainly better than the *a priori* expectations of the researchers engaged on the project and given the rather pessimistic results of other redundancy reports.[6] Of the 227 individuals, only 21 of those seeking employment had failed to find any gainful employment during the course of the first twelve months, and by the end of twenty-four months only 7 remained continuously unemployed.

More general results indicating how the ex-Michelin workers progressed in the labour market over the period are contained in the figures in Table 2, which show the redundant sample's employment status at twelve months and twenty-four months following the redundancy. As shown, by the first anniversary of their redundancy the unemployment rate had fallen to about 16 per cent, and after two years the unemployment rate was around 9 per cent.[7]

Table 2

Employment status at twelve and twenty-four months

	Twelve months		*Twenty-four months*	
	No.	*%*	*No.*	*%*
Unemployed	36	15.9	21	9.3
Employed	140	61.7	155	68.3
Self-employed	32	14.1	31	13.7
Retired	10	4.4	9	4.0
Other	9	4.0	11	4.8
	227	100	227	100

The raw figures for the situations at the end of twelve and twenty-four months are akin to the traditional 'one-shot' cross-sectional view of many redundancy studies and miss much of interest and importance. Detailed time-valued data are required to determine, for example, whether a dynamic equilibrium evolves, and to see the extent to which re-adjustment of employment status continues over time. Such time series effects are totally hidden to the purely cross-sectional approach to redundancy studies, but remain available to a longitudinal approach.

Time series of employment experiences

The basic time series of the return to employment of the group of workers is contained in Figure 1. This shows the percentage of the group unemployed, contractually employed and self-employed at the end of each week following the implementation of the announced redundancies at mid-May 1985. The figures do not include the individuals self-assessed as retired or otherwise out of the labour force, the total for which altered in aggregate only minimally over the period considered.

As may be seen, there were considerable changes in the proportions recorded as employed, unemployed and self-employed over the period as a whole, even if the month-to-month changes are far smaller. The major features to note on Figure 1 are the rapid and substantial fall in unemployment over the first few months, and the continuing trend decline in the unemployment proportion until well into the second year. The employment percentages rise by about two percentage points in each month up to about a year and one quarter after the redundancy. It is clear that full adjustment to a redundancy takes an extended period of time, certainly amounting to more than one year.

Also notable is the large proportion of individuals describing themselves as self-employed. To illustrate, the number in the

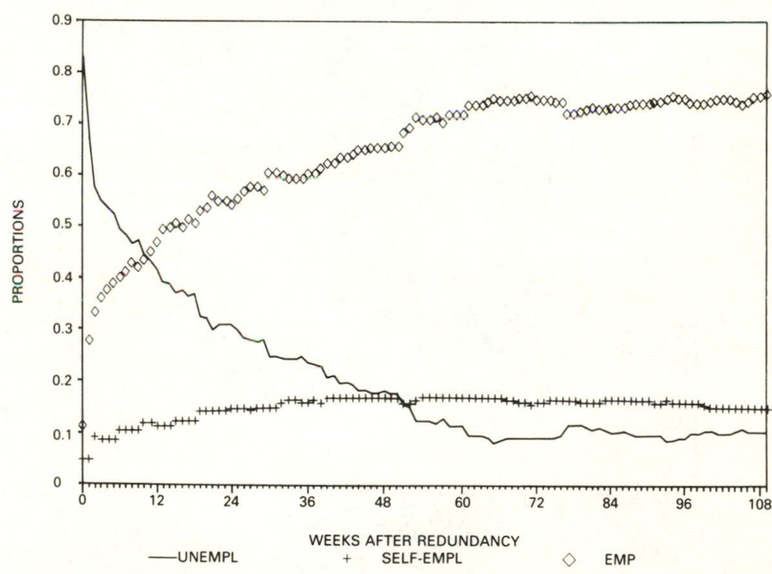

Figure 1
Employment rates over time – employed, self-employed and unemployed

sample who experienced any self-employment over the period amounts to no less than 47 persons, while the maximum number at any given date was 34.[8]

As is clear, the amount of movement between employment states taking place over the period is considerable. The number of individuals with changes of status from month to month is highest at the beginning of the period, and declines, if erratically, over time. This is illustrated in Figure 2, which shows the total of status changes from employment to unemployment and from unemployment to employment recorded during the month concerned. Here employment includes self-employment, and moves between employment and self-employment do not therefore count towards the total. The monthly totals of *all* changes of status recorded are somewhat higher.

Economists are traditionally interested in the notion of equilibrium or stability within a system. In the context of reaction to a redundancy, it may be argued that prior to the redundancy the group of workers at Michelin were in a stable equilibrium state. This stability was disturbed by the redundancies of May 1985, and some time was required before a new equilibrium could be

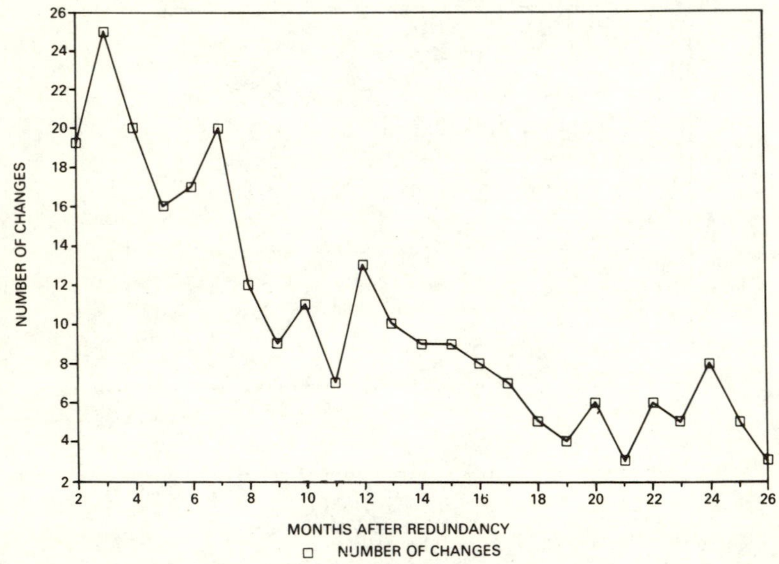

Figure 2
Number of individuals with status changes each month – monthly total

attained. Some individuals will find new employment quickly, some more slowly, and we would expect there to be some changing and switching between jobs by individuals in the group anyway. Changes over time in the employment state of individuals is to be expected in a normally and properly functioning labour market. Whilst individuals can swap and change their employment, *for the group as a whole* to regain an equilibrium requires stability in the way the group in aggregate behaves. The operational formalisation of a dynamic equilibrium in these circumstances is not an easy matter. As we expect individuals to be changing jobs over time as part of the proper workings of the system, even in equilibrium we would expect some positive unemployment to be seen within the group as individuals are observed between employments. Thus a zero unemployment rate is not an appropriate requirement for a new equilibrium. One workable necessary condition for the attainment of dynamic equilibrium or stability within the group is that the employment and unemployment *proportions* within the group become trendless over time (or at least vary only in line with regional and/or national indicators). This fits well with the common economic argument that equilibrium requires that the demand and supply sides of the system be in balance: stable proportions require that the inflows to and outflows from the unemployment pool be equal. If such notions are applied to the Michelin sample the new equilibrium does not come about before roughly sixteen months following redundancy.[9]

These straightforward descriptions of the data from the Michelin redundancy project demonstrate two early but very important conclusions. Firstly, it is clear that studies carried out on the basis of, say, a single, one-off, cross-sectional questionnaire survey administered at perhaps three- or six-months following a mass redundancy or other labour market shock can show very little of value to the understanding of how affected individuals adjust or how the affected group as a whole reacts to such shocks. This point is forcefully made in a theory context by Tuma Hannan and Groeneveld (1979). Secondly, the data show that, for the group as a whole, reactions to a major labour market shock such as a redundancy take a protracted time period to settle to some new equilibrium. The period over which a follow-up study would be required if it is to examine new equilibria is argued, on the basis of this study, to be longer than one year. This period is far longer than might be thought necessary if, for example, using the experiences of our survey average individual completed unemployment spell (13.96 weeks) or average duration of initial unemployment following the redundancy for those who found employment (13.52 weeks) were used as criteria for assessing the necessary duration of survey coverage. The reason for this is that considering the group as a whole over the period allows us to see individuals taking on what prove to be temporary or stop-gap employments with subsequent spells of unemployment before settling, perhaps, to an acceptable 'permanent' niche. Equilibrium for the group must await the stabilisation of employment status for the group overall. Only a longitudinal approach to the problem can provide the necessary information for such a view.

Employment experiences disaggregated by characteristics

When we consider the time-series of employment status of the group as a whole, we ignore the interesting and important question of how the unemployment rates for different sub-groups of the sample behave over time. As we have extensive information about the individual members of our sample, it is possible to disaggregate the sample by various characteristics. The two characteristics considered here are age and Michelin job manual/non-manual occupational classification. The extent of disaggregation possible is limited for the descriptive analysis of this section by the total number of observations in our sample. Given the limited sample size, examination of small sub-groups such as, say, women, or division into finer subsets such as older non-manual workers are not possible.

Figure 3 shows the unemployment percentage over time of the non-manual and manual worker sub-groups, as defined according to individuals' occupational grading at Michelin prior to redundancy. Figures are calculated for the end of each week indicated, and exclude all 'ceased to seek employment' categories. There are about 72 non-manual and about 135 manual workers (the total changing a little depending on the changing number 'seeking employment' over time). The figure illustrates that non-manual worker unemployment rates lie around 10 percentage points below the manual workers' rates over the bulk of the first year; that the time path of the non-manual workers' unemployment rate begins to flatten out, indicating new stability, earlier than does the manual workers' rate; and that the percentage figures are much closer together at the end of the period considered, with the manual worker figure dipping briefly below that for non-manual

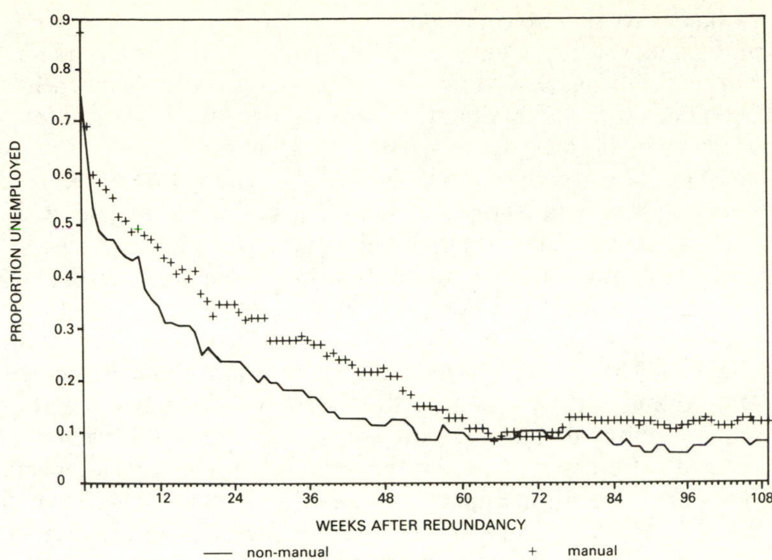

Figure 3

Unemployment rates over time – manual and non-manual groups

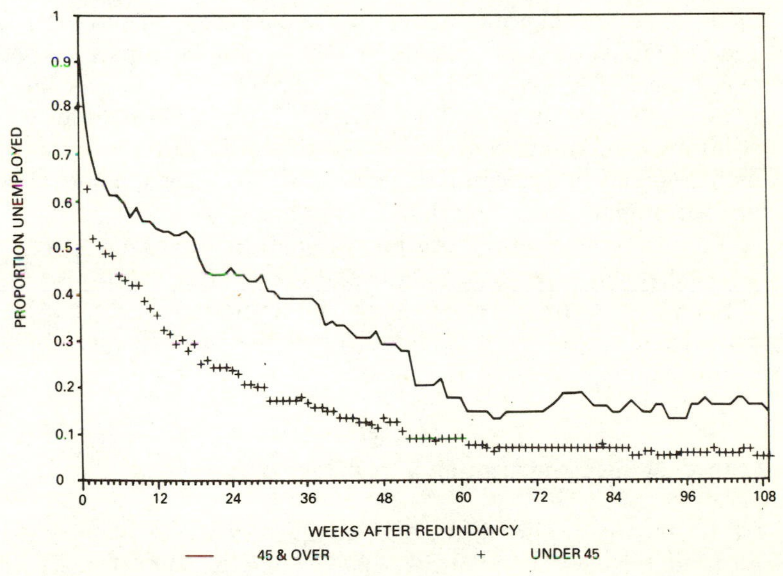

Figure 4

Unemployment rates over time – 45 and over and under 45 age groups

workers. We might conclude that, in terms of unemployment, non-manual workers tend to stabilise more quickly than manual workers. We might also note that a cross-sectional study carried out after six months would incorrectly overstate the degree to which manual workers unemployment would remain above that of non-manual workers in the long-run. The finding that differences in the employment statuses of sub-groups tend to diminish or die out over time is a finding that will recur in this paper.

Figure 4 shows the unemployment rates over time for the two different age groups considered. These are the under-45 and the 45 and over age groups, defined by an individual's age on leaving Michelin. There were about 70 45s and over and about 137 under-45s. Although it is clear that the older workers' unemployment remains above that of the younger workers, it is also clear that relative differences between the groups, though by no means eliminated, are substantially narrowed through the early course of the second year. Younger workers not only do better, they do better more quickly. Again it seems that the different sub-groups react and adjust at different speeds, a finding which would be hidden to anything but a longitudinal approach.

Although it is possible to derive and present the time-paths for numerous other subgroupings of the sample of redundant workers, general results of such procedures should now be apparent. The experiences of groups with different characteristics change over time, both absolutely and relatively. If the time-path for re-adjustment to labour market shocks differs for different groups, then observations taken at a single point in time may underestimate or overestimate long-run relative differences.

In the next section a more formal analysis is presented of the unemployment experiences of the ex-Michelin redundant workers in this survey using regression analysis to examine the relationship between unemployment and individual personal characteristics over time.

Individual unemployment after redundancy

One of the major aims of the Michelin project was to examine the post-redundancy employment and unemployment chances of *individuals*. However, as is obvious in a longitudinal context, the position of the individual will normally change over time, and a number of different ways of considering the position of the individual may be considered. Different conclusions are likely according to the different criteria chosen. One possibility is to consider a given specific date and to examine the determinants of whether individuals are employed or unemployed on that date. This would be equivalent to a single cross-sectional study investigating employment status at a given moment following a labour market displacement. As the choice of date is rather arbitrary given a longitudinal database, a number of dates might be considered. Otherwise, rather than a number of one-off snapshot cross-sectional examinations, better approximations to the overall employment situation of the individual following redundancy might be to take longitudinal measures, such as the proportion of time spent unemployed over the entire two-year period or the length of time until first re-employment following the redundancy for each individual. Alternative approaches may give different indications of how individual personal characteristics affect employment chances in the period following a redundancy. The work reported in this section and in the next concerns an examination of just these means and methods of looking at the employment history of the ex-Michelin sample.

Employment status and personal characteristics

In order to examine the determinants of the employment/unemployment status of individuals at different times, the work diaries of the respondents to the survey were examined at five different points following the original redundancies and covering the two-year period of study.

The Michelin survey provided indicators of all the factors commonly highlighted in the extensive literature as having an influence on the determinants of unemployment incidence; i.e. age, gender, level of occupational status and skill, past earnings and previous unemployment histories.[10] The variables are shown in Table 3. All are dummy variables.

The variables are mostly self-explanatory. Wage categories at Michelin, given occupational status, are taken as measures of human capital. A large number of other interesting and potentially important factors for the study had to be eliminated at an early stage because of high interdependence with included variables. For example, length of service at Michelin (important as an indicator, perhaps, for job-specific skills) and size of redundancy payment were highly correlated with age and could not therefore

Table 3
List of variables –, individual personal characteristics

Name	*Note*
APPREN	Takes value =1 if apprenticeship has been served, 0 if not
FEMALE	Takes value =1 if female, 0 if not
AG3544	Takes value =1 if aged between 35 and 44; 0 if not
AG4554	Takes value =1 if aged between 45 and 54, 0 if not
AG55PLUS	Takes value =1 if aged over 55, 0 if not
MIDWAGE	Takes value =1 if wage at Michelin between £120 and £160 per week, 0 if not
HIGHWAGE	Takes value =1 if wage at Michelin over £160 per week, 0 if not
OCC2	Takes value =1 if skilled manual worker at Michelin, 0 if not
OCC3	Takes value =1 if semi-skilled worker at Michelin, 0 if not
OCC4	Takes value =1 if unskilled worker at Michelin, 0 if not
UHIST	Takes value =1 if has unemployment spell of greater than 12 months prior to Michelin, 0 if not

be included separately. Similarly, a large number of educational achievement indicators had high associations with occupational status and were excluded. None of the independent variables included in the analysis was closely associated with any of the others.[11]

As all the variables are dummy variables, it is well to note that there are a number of excluded categories which form the 'base-case' against which the effect of the acquisition of the included personal attributes will be measured. The choice of the base-case is purely arbitrary, and of no special significance. The base-case is, in this case, a male, without a served apprenticeship, under 35 years of age, who was a low-waged non-manual worker at Michelin, without previous unemployment spells of more than 12 months.

The first dependent variable used in the analysis is whether or not the individual, at some date, given the person is willing and available for employment has in fact remunerative employment (including self-employment). Such a variable is also a binary variable taking the value unity (employed) or zero (unemployed). Individuals who were found to be unemployed on the date in question may have already had and left a job since redundancy;

similar transitions could also have occurred in the case of those found to be employed.

Ordinary multivariate linear regression is the usual technique of choice for disentangling the various influences of independent variables on a dependent variable, enabling the effects of, say, age, to be determined given the other characteristics remaining constant. However, multivariate linear regression has severe theoretical shortcomings where dependent variables are constrained in any way. It is usual to interpret the results of analyses on binary dependent variables as indicating the *probability* that an individual will be observed in one state (employment) rather than another at a given time. However, linear multivariate regression with binary dependent variables can give results which predict individuals to have probabilities of being in employment of greater than one or less than zero. Such probabilities outside the unit range have severe problems of interpretation.

In order to avoid this problem, as well as others, several alternatives to linear regression have been developed of which the most evident have been Logit and Probit Analysis (see, for example, Amemiya, 1981). These approaches both require Maximum Likelihood methods of estimation, and the structure of the estimates obtained are very similar, with identical signs, and, after simple conversion, very similar coefficient values (Maddala, 1983; Amemiya, 1981). Although both methods were initially applied, no substantive differences emerged from using one method rather than the other. As a result, only the logit regression results are presented, as Table 4.

Separate logit regressions were estimated for the sample at five cross-sections following the redundancy. As shown on the columns of the table, these cross-sections were at 3 months (end of week 13), 6 months (end of week 26), 12 months (end of week 52), 18 months (end of week 78), and 24 months (end of week 104). Similar sets of results were derived from identical analyses of a number of other dates for the sample, indicating that the conclusions presented are not special to this particular set of dates.

The logit coefficients in the table should be interpreted as the effect of the explanatory variable on the log of the odds of being in one state rather than the other. As all the variables used are dichotomous, such a coefficient measures the change in the log-odds resultant from the acquisition of the given characteristic, other characteristics remaining constant, compared to the base-case categories as noted above.

Table 4

Raw logit regression results – employment status

	Dependent variable is whether employed at given date post redundancy				
	3 Months	*6 Months*	*12 Months*	*18 Months*	*24 Months*
APPREN	0.312	−0.075	−0.252	0.016	0.020
	(0.38)	(0.19)	(0.42)	(0.03)	(0.33)
FEMALE	−0.788	0.470	−0.440	−0.927	−0.886
	(1.22)	(0.62)	(0.54)	(1.16)	(1.23)
AG3544	−0.815**	−0.297	−1.650	−0.378	−0.648
	(2.16)	(0.65)	(1.62)	(0.48)	(0.77)
AG4554	−0.605	−1.018**	−1.953*	−1.404*	−1.316*
	(1.41)	(2.08)	(1.87)	(1.81)	(1.70)
AG55PLUS	−2.296**	−2.156**	−2.038*	−2.520**	−1.595*
	(2.77)	(3.05)	(1.83)	(2.92)	(1.90)
MIDWAGE	0.171	−0.300	1.107	0.230	−0.044
	(0.44)	(0.67)	(1.20)	(0.35)	(0.07)

HIGHWAGE	−1.135**	−2.375**	0.262	0.822	−0.257
	(1.92)	(3.01)	(0.28)	(0.71)	(0.26)
OCC2	−0.135	−1.515*	0.649	−0.398	−0.667
	(0.23)	(1.92)	(0.50)	(0.37)	(0.74)
OCC3	−0.915*	−2.268**	0.012	−0.288	−0.273
	(1.90)	(3.07)	(0.01)	(0.34)	(0.35)
OCC4	−1.659**	−3.197**	−0.585	−1.777*	−0.891
	(2.27)	(3.49)	(0.64)	(1.73)	(0.97)
UHIST	0.018	−0.556	−0.134	−0.938	−0.423
	(0.03)	(0.93)	(0.15)	(1.20)	(0.53)
CONSTANT	1.450**	3.728**	4.301**	4.505**	5.933**
	(2.52)	(4.37)	(3.15)	(3.85)	(4.10)
Log-likelihood function:					
	−128.746	−105.692	−52.309	−55.143	−57.552
Number of observations:					
	208	209	208	208	207

Note: Individual observations indicating out of the labour market are excluded. Double and single asterisks indicate coefficients are significant at 5% and 10% levels respectively. t-statistics are shown in parentheses.

Hence, looking down the columns of Table 4, coefficients with negative signs indicate that possession of the characteristic concerned reduce the probability of employment at that date compared to the characteristics of the base-case; coefficients with positive signs indicate characteristics increasing the probability of being in employment. Thus, the characteristic of age above 35 reduces the probability of being in employment. In general, having an even greater age reduces the probability of employment by increasing amounts the higher the age band reached. Similarly, the less skilled the manual occupational category of the individual, the more likely it is that the individual is unemployed at that date.

There are several other features of this table worthy of attention. Some of the characteristics fail to show up as significant determinants of employment status at any of the times chosen for the analyses. Looking along the rows of the table indicates the changing effects of the possession of given characteristics over time, as distance from the redundancy increases. Clearly there are many more significant variables, and they are significant at higher levels, at the beginning of the period, after 3 months and 6 months, than later on. There are significant negative signs on the high-wage variable, but only at the beginning of the period. This is a finding that we shall re-examine later. Only the age group characteristics remain consistently and convincingly significant throughout the period. It is clear that the equations become increasingly unable to discriminate between individuals in different employment statuses as time progresses.[12] Given that the proportion of the group in employment rises over the period, with unchanging characteristics we would expect the constant to rise as observed.

These findings are not artifacts of the use of the particular variables chosen and presented above. Other sets of variables used in similar formulations with the data exhibited very similar results to those presented, with significant variables appearing in the equations at the beginning of the period, but, except for age variables, tending to become insignificant over time.

These results fit in well with what we saw in the previous section. Different subgroups with differing characteristics are seen to take different time-paths to equilibrium following the labour market shock, and the results here again reflect this argument. Variables like occupational status are significant distinguishing and discriminating factors for unemployment status only at the beginning of the period, and the increasing inconclusiveness of the equations of

Table 4 reflects the steadily diminishing explanatory power of the included independent variables over time. What these findings may be reflecting is the following argument. At the beginning of the post-redundancy period, before a new equilibrium is reached, those workers with certain attributes (skills, for example) quickly find their way out of unemployment, and variables indicating these desirable attributes show up as important discriminating factors between the employed and unemployed. However, although these attributes affect the speed at which individuals leave unemployment in the early period, once a new equilibrium situation is approached more random forces dominate. In a new equilibrium there is still turnover of employment status, with individuals entering and leaving jobs, but whether an individual is employed or unemployed is determined more by the chance of the market. In these circumstances, individual characteristics will tend to fail to discriminate so well.

'Summary' longitudinal work history measures

As individuals can be in and out of employment throughout the period, employment status on given days can only be a partial description of total post-redundancy work history experience. Although they cannot reflect the full work history information, there are many possible *summary* measures of work history experience available to a longitudinal approach which are rather richer than the measures employed above. Two important summary measures of how well or badly individuals have done in the labour market following a labour market displacement are the proportion of time available for employment that the individual in fact spent unemployed, and the length of time spent unemployed until the beginning of the first spell of employment after the redundancy. The results presented in this section are concerned with the analysis of these two summary measures.

Unemployment proportion

Given a work history diary, information on the proportion of time spent unemployed is straightforward to construct for each individual, and was calculated at the end of the period covered.[13] The dependent variable under these circumstances is a *continuous* rather than a binary or dichotomous variable, but again the value of the variable is constrained to lie between zero and one so that ordinary linear multivariate regression techniques are inappropriate, as they may lead to predicted values outside the unit range. Logit or Probit analysis or a similar method that constrains the predicted values as required is again the recommended analytic tool; and results using Logit analysis are presented here.

The independent variables, upon which it is hypothesised that the proportion of time spent unemployed depends, are the same personal characteristic variables presented in Table 3 and used in the results of Table 4. The results of the Logit regression procedure are presented in Table 5.

As can be seen, the variables used are more significant factors in explaining unemployed time as a proportion of labour market time since redundancy than they were in the section above as explanatory factors of employment status. All the variables, apart from two of the occupational status levels, are now significant at least at the 10 per cent confidence level. All the signs on the coefficients are in line with expectations. Compared to the base-

Table 5

Logit regression results – unemployment proportion. Dependent variable is proportion of time since redundancy spent unemployed, measured after 26 months

	Raw coefficient	*t-statistic*
APPREN	−1.026*	1.71
FEMALE	1.613**	2.05
AG3544	2.648**	3.22
AG4554	2.772**	3.16
AG55PLUS	7.419**	7.97
MIDWAGE	−1.759**	2.57
HIGHWAGE	−4.364**	4.16
OCC2	−0.310	0.31
OCC3	−0.714	0.88
OCC4	2.557**	2.64
UHIST	1.635**	2.64
CONSTANT	−5.675**	5.38
Log-Likelihood Function: −155.010		
Number of observations: 209		

Note: Individual observations showing less than 75 weeks within the labour market are excluded. Double and single asterisks indicate significance levels 5% and 10% respectively.

case categories, the coefficient signs indicate that being female, being in any of the over-35 years' age categories, being an unskilled manual worker at Michelin and having any unemployment of greater than 12 months before joining Michelin are all significantly associated with larger proportions of time spent unemployed. It will be noted that the size of the age category coefficients increase as age increases, showing that the older the individual the larger the proportion of time spent unemployed. Having served an apprenticeship, or being in the middle or higher wage bands at Michelin are significantly associated with smaller proportions of time spent unemployed.

There is, however, a discrepancy in the results obtained for the high-wage variable in the two analyses in Table 5 and Table 4. From Table 4, the high-wage category was associated (significantly), in the early period, with higher probabilities of being in unemployment. In Table 5 the high-wage category is associated (significantly) with lower proportions of time spent unemployed over the whole period of study. The discrepancy is due to the high-waged having rather long initial spells of unemployment immediately following the redundancy (as will be seen more clearly later), but having very stable (full) employment patterns thereafter. This long initial unemployment probably results from those with high wages at Michelin having high wage expectations for new employment, usually called high reservation wages. High reservation wages can result in long search times for those high in human capital. For the purposes of this paper, the change in implied sign on the same variable between the two tables perfectly illustrates the dangers inherent in single snap-shot views of dynamic processes such as adjustments in the labour market.

More generally, the contrast between the results of Tables 4 and 5 are quite striking. Variables have emerged here as significant factors explaining a longitudinally-based measure of work activity over time, which either emerged with different signs, or failed to emerge at all, or produced startlingly different levels of significance in explaining employment status on different dates over the same period of time. The summary longitudinally-based measure has enabled important factors underlying post-redundancy work-histories to be identified, which failed to emerge from the purely cross-sectional analyses.

Time to first employment: proportional hazard model

The second summary longitudinal work history description to be examined is the time taken after redundancy for first employment to be gained. This is an interesting and important measure. Time to initial employment may be argued to be related to the speed of readjustment to labour market conditions by an individual, but is also clearly only a partial description of post-redundancy employment experience because information relating to subsequent employment or unemployment spells is disregarded.

The usual starting point for the examination of the determinants of unemployment *duration*, such as time to initial employment, is the 'hazard function', which is concerned with the probability that an individual experiences an event (first employment) in some time period, given that the individual was subject to the risk that the event might occur (i.e. given continuing initial unemployment). As the hazard or risk of re-employment occurring is likely to change over time and over individual characteristics, it is necessary to decide the functional form by which the hazard may depend upon time and the explanatory variables. There may be little information upon which to base such choices. Cox's Proportional Hazard model (Cox, 1972) is a simple general approach to a class of such hazard models which is easily estimated. It is called 'proportional hazard' because for some formulations, as here, for any two individuals the ratio of their 'hazard' of finding employment is constant at all points in time. The method allows for individual observations to be 'censored' (where the event looked for has not occurred) or 'uncensored' (where the event looked for has occurred) in producing efficient estimates. Rather than spend an extensive amount of time reviewing the method here, the reader is referred to Allison (1984) and Kiefer (1988), and should view the process as a Maximum Likelihood regression model with a dependent variable related to first re-employment time in weeks following leaving Michelin.

The results from applying the Proportional Hazard model to the Michelin data-set are presented in Table 6. The coefficients marked with asterisks are significant at least at the 10 per cent confidence level. The signs of the coefficients indicate whether the possession of the personal attribute referred to adds to or subtracts from the chance of gaining first employment at any point in time following the redundancy. As may be seen, the results are much as expected given the discussion above. Being aged over 35 years

Table 6
Proportional hazard model – time until first employment. Dependent variable is initial unemployment duration following redundancy

	Coefficient	*t-statistic*
APPREN	0.043	0.25
FEMALE	−0.196	0.64
AG3544	−0.450**	2.46
AG4554	−0.665**	3.09
AG55PLUS	−1.292**	3.93
MIDWAGE	0.173	0.89
HIGHWAGE	−0.644**	2.21
OCC2	−0.380	1.42
OCC3	−0.660**	2.93
OCC4	−1.238**	3.34
UHIST	−0.482*	1.72
Log-likelihood function: −867.87		
Number of observations: 209		

Note: Individual observations showing less than 75 weeks within the labour market are excluded. Double and single asterisks indicate significance levels 5% and 10% respectively.

subtracts from initial re-employment probabilities, and by greater amounts the higher the age band. Having had semi-skilled or unskilled occupational status at Michelin reduces the initial re-employment probability compared to having had non-manual status. Any prior unemployment history of greater than 12 months similarly reduces the probability of first re-employment at any point. Neither the sex nor the apprenticeship variables show as significant here.

The table, however, also shows a significant negative coefficient attached to the high wage variable, indicating a lower chance ('hazard') of finding initial re-employment for those who had high wages at Michelin, other things constant. This is in contrast to the results of Table 5 which showed the high-waged spending lower proportions of time unemployed. These results are consistent with the argument put forward above that those with high wage expectations take longer to find first employment, but once in new employment tend to stay securely employed.

The results presented in this section underline the general findings of the paper. There are many ways of viewing and measuring the labour market experiences of workers. It would be convenient if analyses of single descriptions of work experience, for example employment status at some point in time, or proportion of time spent unemployed, all gave similar results. However, different approaches to describing work experience, taken singly, can tell different stories and can associate with different personal attributes. The researcher in longitudinal studies must take care that the conclusions resultant from empirical investigations are not an artifact of the particular work history description employed. The researcher in longitudinal studies, unlike other researchers, at least has the opportunity to check for such possibilities.

Conclusions

This paper has used a longitudinal database of individual work-histories to examine aspects of the post-redundancy work-history experiences over twenty-six months of 227 workers made redundant in 1985.

From a time-series point of view it was argued that the grouping of observations by major characteristics and the tracing of employment and unemployment rates over time showed that sub-groups with different characteristics differed in their paths back to employment stability. For example, the younger group not only tended to have a lower long-run unemployment rate, they approached this rate more quickly than the older group approached their long-run unemployment rate. From a cross-sectional point of view it was shown that the relationship between individual employment status and individual characteristics differed for the various dates examined over the two year period. Crucially, the effectiveness of individual characteristics in distinguishing between the employed and unemployed was shown to diminish sharply as time passed. Finally, two longitudinal measures, unemployment as a proportion of total labour time following redundancy, and time until first employment following redundancy, were shown to depend significantly upon the individual personal characteristics variables utilised, that is, on their age, occupational status, gender, apprenticeships and past unemployment history.

The results obtained concerning unemployment incidence and duration following redundancy are broadly consistent between the time-series, cross-sectional and longitudinal approaches adopted. However, the study has demonstrated the caution required when considering unemployment incidence and history. A snap-shot view can prove misleading, and different means of summarizing and viewing work histories are capable of telling different stories about the determinants of unemployment. This study clearly demonstrates the advantages of adopting a multi-dimensional longitudinally-based work history approach to the problem.

Notes

Helpful comments by Shirley Dex and Rosemary O'Kane greatly improved the presentation and emphasis of this paper, and their contributions are gratefully acknowledged. The database utilised was collected as part of two projects funded by the ESRC.

1 The Michelin Project was based at the University of Keele and was funded by ESRC grants F0023 2257 and F0023 2412.

2 Follow-up surveys of this kind are notorious for the difficulties involved in re-finding and re-interviewing a given group after any lapse of time. However, for the Michelin study, very few have in fact been lost, and 227 of the original 230 formed the final group interviewed. Of the three others, sadly one died during the period, and two proved untraceable. Although the data used in this paper covers only 26 months, we do have information on some sub-groups for much longer.

3 Given that this project has led to a series of papers which from Michelin's view permanently and uncomfortably commemorate the redundancies of 1985, the extent of Michelin's co-operation is gratefully acknowledged. Other local enterprises have proved totally unwilling to allow such investigations of the redundancy process.

4 For a more extensive discussion of the Michelin project, see Fishman *et al.* (1986) and Rosenthal *et al.* (1987).

5 Given the quantitative approach adopted by this paper, some clear and workable operationalisation of the concepts of employment and unemployment are required. Many writers would reject an easy binary division, arguing that a 'non-employment' (Walker *et al.*, 1985) 'grey area' (Davies and Esseveld, 1989) of temporary, informal and trial employment, withdrawal from the labour force and (forced or voluntary) early retirement lies between (permanent, desirable) employment and (absolute, unwanted) unemployment. Although evidence of such grey area non-employment may, arguably, be found within the Michelin sample, the numbers are *very* small, and so small that *no* alterations to the findings below occur on major redefinitions and/or inclusion or exclusion of such recorded statuses.

There are many possible working definitions of concepts such as employment, self-employment and unemployment. For the purposes of this paper, categories as self-assessed by the individuals themselves are the basic source used. The application of alternative criteria, such as the officially sanctioned definitions of unemployment would make only insubstantial changes to what follows. A similar caveat involves part-time working. Rather than present data made unnecessarily complex, part-time remunerative employment of more than 10 hours per week was deemed as employment, and less than 10 hours per week deemed as unemployment. Again, the reader may be reassured that both the numbers involved and the alterations required by alternative definitions are extremely marginal.

6 As examples of a large number of such studies see Carmichael and Cook (1981), Payne (1984) and Thames (1988). Harris *et al.* (1987: ch. 9) report 57.1 per cent

of their total sample never experiencing employment up to two and a half years after redundancy; and 32.4 per cent of those remaining in the labour market are reported as continuously unemployed up to that time.

7 The 'Other' category includes those individuals on educational or training courses, and it is the movement of individuals into and out of education and training that causes most of the fluctuation over the period in the number of individuals available for work. Walker *et al.* (1985) argue that, within their post-redundancy group, retirement increases with time and unemployment. In the much younger Michelin sample, the only change in the retired status comes from one individual who, ironically, reclassified himself from retired to unemployed after about one year.

8 Much lower proportions of redundant workers are reported as entering self-employment by Carmichael and Cook (1981) and Payne (1984). More information and detail on the self-employed among the Michelin sample is contained in Leece (1988).

9 For a more formal analysis of these and other time-series of adjustments after the Michelin redundancy, see Rosenthal (1990).

10 Among the vast literature on unemployment incidence and duration in the UK, see Nickell (1978), White (1983) and Bosworth (1987).

11 None of the independent variables were associated with each other with a correlation coefficient of greater than 0.1, except for mutually exclusive categories of the same factor: for example, being semi-skilled is quite highly correlated with the absence of being skilled.

12 Direct comparisons of the values of the likelihood function are problematical because of the changes in the dependent variable used in each equation, the changing number of observations and the changing sample over the period. Linear Discriminant Analysis was also applied to the dataset, and gives similar conclusions.

13 All individuals in the sample who had retired, withdrawn from the labour market entirely, or had otherwise spent less than 75 weeks in the labour market were removed (although really quite similar results emerge even if they are not removed). As before, periods of self-employment and part-time employment of more than 10 hours per week are treated as employment.

References

Andersen, S., (1989), *Unemployment among Laid-off Shipyard Workers*, Institut for Informationsbehandling: Aarhus School of Business.

Allison, P.D., (1984), *Event History Analysis: Regression for Longitudinal Event Data*, Sage University Papers series on Quantitative Applications in the Social Sciences, 07-046, Beverly Hills and London.

Amemiya, T., (1981), 'Qualitative response models – a survey', *Journal of Economic Literature*, (December): 483–536.

Bosworth, D.L., (1987), 'Characteristics of the long-term unemployed; an analysis of the labour force survey', Research Report, Institute for Employment Research, University of Warwick, Coventry.

Carmichael, C.L. and Cook, L.M., (1981), *Redundancy, Re-Employment and the Tyre Industry*, London: Manpower Services Commission.

Cox, D.R., (1972), 'Regression models and life tables', *Journal of the Royal Statistical Society*, Series B, 34: 187–202.

Davies, K. and Esseveld, J., (1989), 'Factory women, redundancy and the search for work: toward a reconceptualisation of employment and unemployment', *The Sociological Review*, 37 (May): 219–52.

Department of Employment, *Employment Gazette*, various issues, London: HMSO.

Edlin, P.-A., (1988), *Individual Consequences of Plant Closures*, Uppsala University: Department of Economics.

Fishman, L., Leece, D., Proops, J.L.R., and Rosenthal, L., (1986), *Re-Employment Experiences of Redundant Michelin Workers*, University of Keele: Department of Economics and Management Science.

Harris, C.C., and the Redundancy and Unemployment Group, (1987), *Redundancy and Recession*, Oxford: Basil Blackwell.

Kiefer, N.M., (1988), 'Economic duration data and hazard functions', *Journal of Economic Literature*, 26: 646–79.

Leece, D., (1988), *The Self-Employment of Redundant Michelin Workers*, Working Paper 88–33, University of Keele: Department of Economics and Management Science.

MacKay, D.I. and Reid, G.L., (1972) 'Redundancy, unemployment and manpower policy', *Economic Journal*, 82: 1256–72.

Maddala, G.S., (1983), *Limited Dependent and Qualitative Variables in Econometrics*, Cambridge: Cambridge University Press.

Nickell, S., (1978), 'Unemployment duration and re-employment probability', *Economic Journal*, 88; 693–706.

Payne, D., (1984), *Closure at Linwood: A Follow-up Survey of Redundant Workers*, Edinburgh: Manpower Services Commission.

Rosenthal, L., Proops, J.L.R., Leece, D. and Fishman, L., (1987), *Labour Market Experiences of Redundant Michelin Workers: Two Years On*, University of Keele: Department of Economics and Management Science.

Rosenthal, L., (1990), 'Time to re-establishment of equilibrium for a group of redundant workers', *Applied Economics*, 22(1), 93–5.

Thames, (1988), *Shutdown*, London: Thames TV PLC.

Tuma, N.B., Hannan, M.T. and Groeneveld, L.P., (1979), 'Dynamic analysis of event histories', *American Journal of Sociology*, 84(1): 820–54.

Walker, A., Noble, I. and Westergaard J., (1985), 'From secure employment to labour market insecurity: the impact of redundancy on older workers in the steel industry', *New Approaches to Economic Life*, B. Roberts, R. Finnegan and D. Gallie (eds), Manchester: Manchester University Press, pp. 319–37.

White, M., (1983), 'Long-term unemployment – labour market aspects', *Employment Gazette*, (October): 437–43.

Wood, S., (1984), 'Redundancy and female employment', in *The Sociological Review*, 29(4): 649–83.

Youth unemployment and work histories

Meredith Baker and Peter Elias

Introduction

This article examines the role of work history information in terms of its ability to assist with an understanding of the relationships between youth unemployment, labour turnover, and the occupations and earnings of young people. The paper focuses upon the issues which arise when one attempts to unravel the *causal* processes which yield the observed relationships, rather than using such information in a descriptive fashion. This issue is central to the argument that work history information provides a better understanding of the labour process. If some form of economic interdependence can be shown to exist between previous events in an individual's working life and their later economic position, knowledge of the previous economic status of an individual will generate a better understanding of their current or future economic position. For this reason, particular attention is paid to the issue of 'state dependence', the notion that a person's future labour market status may be influenced in some way by their current and previous experience. If some form of state dependence exists, for example, where a record of unemployment in an individual's work history *causes* them to experience future unemployment, policies to reduce this future risk might focus more on employer recruitment practices than upon the 'employability' of the individual. Thus, knowledge of the nature and existence of state dependence could influence labour market policy.

After outlining the concept of 'state dependence' in the analysis of work history information, we survey recent studies of the work histories of young people in the UK and the USA which are concerned with this issue, drawing together the evidence revealed by these studies. At times, we resort to a mathematical notation for ease of exposition. Those who are unfamiliar with such notation will find that the accompanying text gives sufficient information to convey the essential ideas.

The paper concludes with an assessment of the insights that have been gained in the study of youth unemployment by incorporating information about a young person's work history, together with an agenda for further research on the complex issues raised by these studies.

Heterogeneity, state dependence and work histories

Work history information is usually investigated to examine for a relationship between the previous socio-economic circumstances of an individual, or group of individuals, and their later socio-economic status. For example, economists are interested in the relationship between the early labour market experience of minimum age school leavers and their earnings at some later date, usually the date of a survey. A question under investigation might be: does the experience of unemployment lead to reduced labour earnings later on in the economic life of the individual? Alternatively, does frequent turnover improve or worsen one's later job prospects? Does a spell of unemployment increase the probability of experiencing a further spell of unemployment? Does a person's chance of regaining employment deteriorate the longer the spell of unemployment they experience? In asking such questions however, it is necessary to discriminate between the impact of the event in question as a separate factor contributing towards an individual's later employment experience, and the characteristics of the individual; their motivation, preferences and abilities as factors which will predispose them towards a particular pattern of events. The former links the relationships which may exist between events in an individual's work history with their economic status at some later stage and is referred to as *state dependence*. These relationships are common to all individuals who experience a particular pattern of events. The latter emphasises the relationship between the individual's specific characteristics and their later economic status and is referred to as *heterogeneity*, a term which emphasises the differences between individuals.

The problem for the quantitative social scientist relates to the unravelling of these sets of influences. To what extent does state dependence exist after taking account of individual differences?

This again poses a problem, for differences between individuals may derive from unobserved factors.

The term 'unobserved factors' is used, for it is generally assumed that factors which are observed by the investigator will be controlled for in some fashion. The unobserved factors may be an individual's motivation, their preferences for work and so on. If these are likely to give rise to a particular pattern of events in an individual's work history and if they are also correlated with later economic status, the apparent state dependence is deceiving. The observed relationship in this case is derived from the so-called *heterogeneity*, the unobserved pattern of differences between individuals.

Different types of state dependence have been described in the literature, such as *incidence dependence*, where the experience of a particular economic state, no matter how short, influences later events. *Duration dependence* is defined as the link between the length of time a person stays in a particular state and the subsequent sequence of later events. The common feature they all share is that it is the experience of an event itself which has some impact upon one's subsequent status, and that this is extrinsic to the individual.

For the reasons outlined above, many of the recent studies, particularly those relating to US data, are concerned with the separation of 'state dependence' from 'heterogeneity'. That this is an important distinction to make is unquestionable. If, for example, the experience of unemployment increases the probability of experiencing a further spell of unemployment, *ceteris paribus*, then it could be argued that unemployment itself has an effect upon the individual in terms of his or her future employability (i.e. through loss of work experience, disillusionment, etc. or upon an employer's perception of the 'productivity' of the individual). Alternatively, if there exists a group of individuals with certain characteristics who are likely to display a particular pattern of repeated spells of unemployment, one could not argue that the experience of unemployment itself had such a debilitating effect. An important benefit of panel or work history data is that it enables the investigator to control for individual-specific effects (possibly unobserved) which are correlated with other variables in the specification and thus tease out the effects of heterogeneity from state dependence.

This paper examines a particular set of issues which have been addressed using longitudinal labour force information for individuals: the relationship between youth unemployment and subsequent labour force status. Before doing so, the next section presents a stylised view of the youth labour market; a set of commonly-held propositions which often appear in the literature pertaining to youth unemployment and the behaviour of young people. We shall refer to some of these propositions throughout the remainder of this article, returning to re-evaluate them after a review of recent research based upon the analysis of work history information from young people.

Youth unemployment: a stylised view

Listed below are six propositions which yield a stylised view of the youth labour market. They are referred to as 'stylised' because they are frequently mentioned without question in the analysis of youth labour markets. Some will be regarded as contentious, others will be regarded as intuitively obvious. The purpose in presenting them is to provide a background against which recent research on these issues can be evaluated. They are listed below, not necessarily in any order of importance.

1. Young people are relatively unattached to the labour market and have lower financial, family and social commitments. They are more likely to 'shop-around' in such circumstances, displaying higher turnover. They may become voluntarily unemployed to engage in job search activities. Consequently, young people are likely to experience more, but shorter, spells of unemployment than their older counterparts.
2. Young people are more likely to engage in further education and general training than older workers. Transitions between employment and unemployment may be further complicated by movement into and out of the education sector.
3. Unemployment is disproportionately high among young people and has a high, pro-cyclical component, primarily due to the operation of 'last-in, first-out' hiring policies of employers or the exclusion of new labour market entrants in times of falling labour demand.
4. The rise in 'credentialism', or 'new vocationalism' has led to an increasing demand for young people with qualifications. This has, in turn led to an increase in the proportion of unqualified persons among the young and unemployed.

5. Young people in the UK receive higher pay relative to their older counterparts than in most other Western democracies. These costs, together with the possibility of 'substituting' other categories of labour (women working part-time, for example), has caused employers to reduce their demand for young workers, thereby contributing to higher levels of youth unemployment.
6. Youth unemployment is a transitory phenomenon, reflecting the demographic changes in the population. The peak in the birth-rate in the 1960s led to a demographic population 'bulge' which the labour market could not absorb.

Clearly, each of the propositions listed above is open to question or reinterpretation. Indeed, research is continuing on many of these issues. Nevertheless, the list serves well to contextualise the theoretical debate about young people and unemployment.

Search-theoretic models of unemployment have often been employed by economists to account for the early labour market experience of young people (e.g. Lippman and McCall, 1976). There is plenty of evidence (for a summary see Elias and Blanchflower, 1989) to show that this early labour market experience is quite different from that of older workers in one respect; young people are likely to display higher turnover, experience more unemployment and to have had more jobs within a given period of time than older workers. The theoretical issue this raises is whether or not such behaviour should be viewed as voluntary or involuntary. While young workers may lose their jobs through no action of their own, the 'search-theoretic' approach assumes that the duration of their subsequent spell of unemployment will depend upon prior and post-redundancy search activity and upon the probability of job offers being received. In turn, these are postulated to depend on individual characteristics and the state of the market. The intensity of their search activities will depend upon the anticipated gains from further searching versus the probability of gaining a 'better' job from such a search. For young people, theory predicts longer than average search behaviour if the distribution of job offers varies through the year. For example, a young college leaver may decide to spend a year 'unemployed', anticipating an active job search at the start of the annual recruitment drive by employers in the following year. While search theories of unemployment may yield a rationalisation of the observed higher levels of joblessness among certain qualified age groups of young people, they do not assist with our understanding of the generally higher levels of turnover in youth labour markets.

Human capital theory (Becker, 1964) has also been employed by economists to account for various phenomena in the youth labour market. Human capital theory predicts a relationship between qualifications, labour market experience and turnover. Those with fewer qualifications and less work experience are assumed to be less productive in the labour market, will not command high wage rates and are more likely to be made redundant in times of falling labour demand. These predictions appear to accord well with the facts; the more highly qualified a young person, the higher their pay and the less likely they are to become unemployed. It is, however, essentially a 'supply-side' theory, emphasising the relationships between education, knowledge, work experience and labour productivity.

Yet another theory, claiming to explain youth labour market behaviour, labour segmentation theory is, in contrast, orientated towards the perspective of the employer and the signalling process through which potential workers gain jobs. According to segmentation theory, an individual's history of unemployment or high labour turnover may be taken by an employer as indicative of the poor worker quality or weak labour force attachment, assigning that person to a particular segment of the labour market in which high turnover and low pay are the norm. The outcome of this process can be viewed as 'a vicious cycle of unemployment' (Ellwood, 1982: 350). State dependency in unemployment is thus a central part of segmented labour market theory. Moreover, it is contended that teenagers face a limited number of entry level jobs which lead to better jobs; those who miss the good jobs are permanently 'tracked' onto inferior career structures. It is important to note though that the existence of state dependence in the unemployment history of a young person does not prove or disprove a particular theoretical approach to the analysis of youth labour markets. Human capital theorists would invoke the notion of 'capital depreciation' in times of unemployment, making the individual less productive and less likely, therefore, to regain employment.

An extension of segmentation theory as applied to women in the labour market is the 'crowding' hypothesis of Bergmann (1980). According to the 'crowding' school, unemployment amongst female teenagers may lead to further spells of unemployment as employers (perhaps erroneously) discriminate on the basis of gender and crowd women into short-tenure, high turnover jobs. Early unemployment may also assign women to these types of jobs with ultimate consequences for lifetime earnings.

Thus, a search theory model where the job offer probability does not depend on an individual's past experience of unemployment, suggests that teenage unemployment and high turnover are a necessary consequence of the process, early in the labour market career, of young people attempting to match their skills to appropriate jobs. Due to inexperience, or lack of information, this process is more 'noisy' for young people than for older, more experienced workers. For this particular search theory model, early unemployment has no significant long term effects on employment status. Human capital theory, on the other hand, suggests that there may well be a relationship between early unemployment and later economic status, though the precise nature of this process is open to interpretation. Adopting such a theoretical stance, one could argue that unemployment may lead to a diminution of work experience, a reduction in skill development or reduced opportunities for training, lowering the individual's capacity to compete for and perform well in more 'productive' jobs. On the other hand, as segmentation theorists would argue, unemployment can be taken as a signal by employers of the productive capacity of the individual, thereby assigning them to lower status jobs and reduced training opportunities.

In contrast with the search theories, both human capital and segmented labour market theories of unemployment place much emphasis on a process which is, by definition, one of *state dependence*. On the demand side, firms may use unemployment records in their hiring decisions, given workers are heterogeneous in some unobserved components of ability. Firms are hypothesized to use this unemployment record as a signal of worker quality; with a record of unemployment in an individual's work history being used as an indicator of worker productivity. On the supply side, unemployment experience may not only alter work experience and therefore future prospects of employment but also may actually change the individual by fostering poor work attitudes and behaviour.

> In both cases, prior unemployment experience has a genuine behavioural effect in the sense than an otherwise identical individual who did not experience unemployment would behave

> differently in the future than an individual who experienced unemployment. Structural relationships of this sort give rise to true state dependence (Heckman and Borjas, 1980: 247).

The counter-argument, of course, suggests that individuals are not influenced by the experience of unemployment but differ in certain unmeasured variables that influence the probability of experiencing unemployment. Then, in the case that these unmeasured variables are correlated over time and are not subject to statistical control, a spurious relationship between previous unemployment and future unemployment is observed. The process which gives rise to the high level of turnover in youth labour markets and the observed frequent spells of unemployment among particular groups of young people would then be essentially a consequence of individual *heterogeneity*.

Analytical techniques for measuring state dependence

In the above discussion we have simplified matters by referring to unemployment experience in a very general manner. However, as we come closer to examining the issues at hand we need to be more specific about the nature of such experience and the associated state dependence. In seeking to examine whether state dependence exists we can distinguish between the effect of;

(i) the number of spells of unemployment (incidence or occurrence dependence) on later economic status;
(ii) the length of the current spell (duration or experience dependence) on later economic status; and
(iii) the lengths of previous spells of unemployment (lagged duration dependence) on later economic status.

Within the literature, investigators have also distinguished a fourth type of state dependence; Markovian dependence or Markov-persistence (Heckman and Borjas, 1980). The key notion of Markov persistence is based on the concept, within a continuous time model, that for a short enough time period, then for a given spell of employment the probability of remaining in that state is always greater than the probability of entering it from another state.

> Virtually all persons who work one minute will work the next, regardless of their underlying propensity to work over a month, year or decade (Ellwood, 1982: 363).

Thus each individual, conditional on being in a particular state whether it be employment or unemployment, has a certain 'escape' probability over a period of time, independent of their past history of spells or states. This inertia has traditionally been captured by a Markov model.

Broadly speaking, within the literature there are three different strands of econometric and sociometric techniques used by investigators which consider, to varying degrees, the problems of distinguishing between state dependency and heterogeneity in unobserved factors in the analysis of panel data. One technique is based upon extensions and variations of the Markov model (e.g. Tuma, Hannon and Groeneveld, 1979; Chamberlain, 1985; and Heckman and Borjas, 1980). Another includes techniques used within the standard ordinary least squares (OLS) regression model (e.g. Chamberlain and Griliches, 1975 and Hausman and Taylor, 1981). The third technique involves the estimation of 'mixture' models in which the unobserved individual effects are incorporated within the estimation procedure (Ezzet and Davies, 1988). We outline these below.

Tuma, Hannan and Groeneveld (1979) extend a continuous-time Markov model to deal with heterogeneity and time-dependence. They outline a maximum-likelihood procedure for estimating the model for event-history data. The Markov model generates transition rates (r_{jk}) between states j and k, with the length of time between transitions having an exponential distribution, and a survival function which suggests that as the length of time increases then the probability that a person will remain in a given state (e.g. employed, unemployed) will decline exponentially. Heterogeneity is introduced into this model by incorporating a log-linear relationship between each transition rate and a set of observable variables, X;

$$\ln r_{jk} = \theta_{jk} X \qquad \forall\ j,k,\ j \neq k$$

where θ represents a vector of parameters to be estimated.

Naturally, the ability of this form to account for observed heterogeneity is only as good as the included variables in X and moreover does not account for unobserved heterogeneity. Tuma *et al.* (1979) incorporate time-dependence by accommodating different parametric forms of the exit rate out of a particular state and also allow the rates to vary from one time period to another.

An auto-regressive logistic model, based on the Markov model, has been developed by Chamberlain (1985). Work history information for each individual is coded sequentially as a set of zeros and ones, depending on which of two states an individual is in at each point in time. If an individual's history of previous states does not help to predict his or her future state given the current state, this represents a Markov process. If there is no duration dependence then the sequence of zeros and ones will be what is known as a first-order Markov chain. Departures from this model provide evidence of 'duration dependence' at the individual level. Chamberlain (1985) also provides an outline of models which are appropriate to use when there are observations of the duration of time spent in the states and develops models for measuring duration dependence which attempt to eliminate bias due to unmeasured heterogeneity.

Using the continuous-time discrete-state Markov process as a starting point, Heckman and Borjas (1980) undertake extensions which allow for an examination of state dependence effects of unemployment, enabling one to distinguish between occurrence, duration and lagged duration dependence. Previous occurrences of unemployment or employment are allowed to have an impact upon transition rates by indexing the rate according to the number of these spells. Thus r_{jk}^{mn} is the transition rate from the jth to the kth state and it depends on m (the number of previous spells of unemployment) and n (the number of previous spells of employment). If the marginal exit time distributions are identical for successive spells of employment and successive spells of unemployment, then there is no occurrence dependence in being employed or unemployed at a particular point in time (Heckman and Borjas, 1980: 258).

Incorporating the idea of duration dependence into the model requires introducing what is known as the hazard function. The hazard function is defined as the probability that an individual will leave the unemployed state during a small time period conditional on being unemployed. We can express the hazard or probability of leaving unemployment (h) as:

$$h(t)dt = g(t)dt/(1 - G_T(t))$$

where g is the probability density function of accepting a job offer between t and t + dt and G(t) is the distribution of the duration of unemployment T. The denominator of this expression, $(1-G_T(t))$ is known as the survivor function and is the probability of staying in the unemployed state. Duration dependence is said to exist if the hazard function depends on the length of time elapsed in the state in the current spell. From the above expression we can derive an expression for the likelihood that a particular duration of unemployment will be observed. This likelihood function can then be used to estimate the parameters of the hazard function. To generate a likelihood function, it is necessary to make an assumption about the nature of the underlying probability distribution (G). One such distribution is the Weibull (others include the log-logistic and Gompertz distributions). Thus, assuming the hazard can be decomposed in the following manner (Cox, 1972);

$$h(t) = \psi_1 (X)\, \psi_2(t)$$

it can be shown that the hazard function for the Weibull distribution may be written as (Lancaster 1979; Heckman and Borjas 1980):

$$h(t) = \exp(X' \beta)\, \lambda\, t^{\lambda - 1}$$

where $X'$is a vector of appropriate explanatory variables (see e.g. Lynch 1985, 1989 and Lancaster and Nickell 1980). The size of λ relative to 1 will tell us whether the re-employment probability changes with the length of spell. For $\lambda = 1$, the hazard is constant, implying that only the explanatory variables will determine differences in the lengths of spells (i.e. heterogeneity accounts for different re-employment probabilities). If $\lambda < 1$ the hazard is decreasing, then *ceteris paribus*, the probability of becoming re-employed falls as the spell length increases. Conversely, for $\lambda > 1$, (positive duration dependence) the probability of re-employment rises as spell length increases. Depending upon the assumptions made, job search theory makes no strict *a priori* predictions on the size of λ. For example, as the spell of unemployment continues, the individual's reservation wage falls, thereby increasing the probability of accepting job offers at lower wages than at an earlier time in the unemployment spell *ceteris paribus*. Therefore the prediction will be $\lambda > 1$ (positive duration dependence). On the other hand, if employers use the length of spell of unemployment as a signal of potential productivity or if longer spells lead to some form of discouragement, then the prediction will be $\lambda < 1$ (negative duration dependence) (Lynch, 1989: 38–9).

An important point to note here is that if no account is taken of unobserved heterogeneity, then it is quite possible that size of λ will depend critically upon the nature of these unobserved factors. The parameter estimates will be biased due to the omission of unobserved variables which in turn will lead to spurious estimates of negative duration dependence.

Heckman and Borjas (1980) extend these models to allow for heterogeneity, distinguishing between what they call pure heterogeneity and state dependent heterogeneity. Pure heterogeneity they suggest are those components of individuals which are completely exogenous to the employment/unemployment process, but nevertheless may vary over time. In other words, pure heterogeneity causes but is not caused by the outcomes of the unemployment and employment processes. State dependent heterogeneity, on the other hand, are those unobserved individual differences which are endogenous to the process of employment and unemployment. This definition of heterogeneity appears somewhat confusing at first sight given our earlier detailed discussion on the differences between state dependency and heterogeneity in the second section. One way to think of the Heckman and Borjas (1980) definition of state-dependent heterogeneity is that it captures the notion that the sign of the effect of the variables on the r_{jk} parameters may be different in the employed state than in the unemployed state; for example the effect of ability on the transition probability will be different if one is in the state of employment than if one is in the state of unemployment. The procedure for allowing this more flexible form of heterogeneity in the Weibull and log-normal models is outlined in their paper.

The main result derived from the seminal work of Heckman and Borjas (1980) is:

> without strong distributional assumptions about the nature of heterogenity, and the nature of admissible true duration dependence, it is impossible to use longitudinal data to separate true duration dependence from spurious duration dependence. (Heckman and Borjas 1980: 259)

The conditions required to identify occurrence dependence are less formidable. Nevertheless, they require that some arbitrary assumptions be made about the dynamic nature of the economic environment in which the young people are observed.

The econometric techniques for handling state-dependency and heterogeneity described above have involved extensions and variations based on what is termed the 'Markov-persistence' model. Within the standard ordinary least squares (OLS) regression model commonly used in empirical work, various techniques for controlling unobservable individual effects in panel data sets have been developed. Consider the following model:

$$Y_{it} = X'_{it}\,\beta + Z'_i\,\gamma + \alpha_i + \epsilon_{it} \qquad i = 1, \ldots, N \quad t = 1, \ldots, T$$

where β and γ are vectors of coefficients associated with time-varying (X) and time-invariant (Z) observable variables respectively. The error term ϵ_{it} is assumed uncorrelated with X, Z and α. The problem with the specification above is that in the presence of unobserved heterogeneity (captured by α_i) which is correlated with the variables in X and Z then OLS estimation procedures will provide biased and inconsistent estimates of β and γ.

There are a number of techniques which have been employed to overcome the formidable problems of estimating the parameters of such a model. The first technique for overcoming this problem is to transform the data into deviations from individual means. The coefficients from such a model, known as 'within-group' or 'fixed-effects' estimators, have two defects however:

(i) all time-invariant variables (for example, social background, schooling) which affect the process are cancelled out thus cannot be estimated; and
(ii) since the estimators ignore variations across individuals in the sample, they may be 'inefficient'. That is to say, by taking account of such variation it may be possible to estimate the βs with more precision.

A second method, is to use instruments for those variables in X and Z which are potentially correlated with α_i. Investigators invariably encounter difficulties in finding such instruments. Moreover this procedure ignores the time-invariant characteristic of the latent individual effect α_i.

Another possible approach is the factor analytic model which relies upon an orthogonality assumption imposed on the observable and unobservable components of α_i for identification (see Chamberlain and Griliches 1975).

Hausman and Taylor (1981) present a two-stage method which enables consistent and efficient estimation of all the βs and the γs. The first stage involves partitioning the X and Z matrices into those which are correlated with the αs (X_1 and Z_1) and those that are not (X_2 and Z_2). (In practice it is difficult to make this partition.) Taking deviations from individual means in the columns of X_2 enables unbiased estimation of the βs. The second stage uses the individual means of the columns of X_2 as valid instruments for Z_I, allowing consistent and efficient estimation of the γs.

Finally, based upon the theoretical work of Kiefer and Wolfowitz (1956) as developed by Lindsay (1983a, b), recent work by Ezzet and Davies (1988) has led to the development of non-parametric mixing models, in which the individual-specific residual heterogeneity is assumed to have a particular distribution which can be characterised by a finite number of mass points. The technique 'integrates' or sums up the effects of residual heterogeneity on the observed variables to eliminate the 'nuisance' of residual heterogeneity through each individual's work history.

Having discussed the importance of distinguishing between state-dependency and heterogeneity in the light of assessing the consequences of youth unemployment, we briefly reviewed the theoretical models outlining the hypothesized processes at work and outlined some appropriate econometric techniques. We turn now to a review of the evidence provided by empirical work undertaken in the US and the UK. In particular we focus on those studies of youth unemployment which have paid more than just lip service to the issues of state dependency and heterogeneity.

Youth unemployment and work histories: empirical evidence

(1) Evidence for the US

Until recently, the US literature appeared to suggest that there was relatively little state dependence arising from the experience of youth unemployment, having controlled for individual differences (Heckman and Borjas, 1980; Ellwood, 1982). However, youth unemployment (or non-employment in the case of women) does appear to have some impact on future earnings (Ellwood, 1982; Corcoran, 1982; Becker and Hill, 1980, 1983, etc.). In this section we look at the narrow issue of the effect of early unemployment on subsequent economic status, defined here to include the probability of future employment. We compare the findings separately for males and females. In the next section we review the findings of studies dealing with the effect of early unemployment on subsequent earnings, again separately by gender.

(a) *The effect of early unemployment on future employment*
Surprisingly enough, given the concern in the literature over the consequences of youth unemployment on subsequent employment

behaviour and patterns in the US (Kalachek, 1969; Freeman, 1976) there has been relatively little empirical research using work history or panel data, such as those data available from the National Longitudinal Surveys (NLS). Much of the earlier work (e.g. Stevenson, 1978a and 1978b; Becker and Hill, 1980) does discuss the necessity of obtaining accurate estimates of the potential impact of early unemployment on future employment patterns. In practice, however, the empirical work falls short of the desired objective. Both Stevenson (1978b) and Becker and Hill (1980) examine the wages of persons beyond their teens; they regressed wages on the duration and/or spells of teenage unemployment several years earlier, together with several 'background' variables to control for heterogeneity. They did not adjust for unobserved heterogeneity. While the studies document lower wages as a result of early unemployment, they fail to answer one of the main issues on their agenda: whether unemployment causes later unemployment. Moreover, where Stevenson (1978a) does estimate the probability of unemployment for both males and females, aged 16–19, conditional on being in the labour force, he does not include previous unemployment experience as one of the explanatory variables.

There are three major US studies which present convincing evidence of state dependency in male youth unemployment (Heckman and Borjas, 1980; Ellwood, 1982; Lynch, 1989). For females, the evidence on state dependency in unemployment is limited to two studies (Corcoran 1982 and Lynch 1989). Heckman and Borjas (1980) use monthly work histories available in the NLS data set of young men during 1969–71. The sample is restricted to white males who have a high school diploma, were interviewed in the 1969, 1970 and 1971 surveys, who completed their education in the autumn of 1969 and for whom a continuous work history up to the end of 1971 could be compiled. These requirements gave rise to a sample of work histories for only 122 males. Using the regression techniques and tests developed in that paper based on the Markov model together with both Weibull and log-normal distributions and with length of the spell of unemployment as the dependent variable they conclude:

(1) that there is no evidence of lagged duration dependence in the exit times for employment and unemployment states after corrections are made for heterogeneity;
(2) that there is no evidence of occurrence dependence in the

> exit times from employment and unemployment states once corrections are made for sample selection bias;
> (3) imposing strong and intrinsically arbitrary assumptions, there is weak evidence of positive duration dependence in the exit times for employment and unemployment states.
> (Heckman and Borjas 1980: 275)

However in view of the weak evidence of duration dependence estimates, Heckman and Borjas stress that the final conclusion should be interpreted with some care. Moreover the small sample sizes together with the fact that their results are based on a short period at the beginning of the young men's careers in the late sixties and early seventies, present important caveats to their work.

Ellwood's (1982) analysis is based on a slightly larger sample of young males than studied by Heckman and Borjas (1980). The sample of 364 young men comprised those who left school 'permanently' in 1965, 1966 and 1967 with less than fourteen years education and includes only those who have work history information available in the first four years after leaving school. Ellwood's initial analysis of the data indicates that the patterns of employment and unemployment are more stable than would be predicted by a first order Markov process and he goes on to investigate whether the observed persistence is a reflection of individual differences (heterogeneity) or whether it is causally related to past experience (state dependency). Ellwood transforms the traditional specification from a dichotomous dependent variable to a continuous variable using Heckman's (1978a and 1978b) model, together with a transformation which distinguishes the Markov escape probabilities and a measure of experience dependence. Accounting for heterogeneity, either by differencing the data or using instrumental variables, eliminates all evidence of state dependency. After making other corrections to the data they conclude that a small amount of experience dependence is present in the short-run but does *not* represent a serious permanent effect:

> For this group of youngsters there is no evidence of a long term cycle of recurring periods without employment induced by an early episode out of work. (Ellwood, 1982: 374)

By contrast, Ellwood's results with weeks worked as the dependent variable, with corrections for heterogeneity, while reducing by two-thirds the parameter, suggest some duration dependence remains.

Three *caveats* apply to Ellwood's findings. First, the fact that these teenagers entered the labour market in favourable times may affect his estimates, which are based on only four years of experience. Secondly, the sample is not random. The long-term unemployed are under-represented and the Vietnam War imposes a potential sample selection bias, because work history information was not available for draftees. Finally, the sample was too small to isolate separate effects by race or low income groups.

The recent work of Lynch (1989) overcomes many of these deficiencies by utilising data from the more recent samples of the NLS youth cohort. This large cohort of young people consists of over twelve and a half thousand persons aged between 14 and 21 years at the end of 1978. Those who were not employed at the date of the 1982 interview, but who had left school and had some work experience, formed the basis of her sample. This group, consisting of 761 males and 892 females, was used to estimate the parameters of the hazard or re-employment probability function. There is strong evidence of a decreasing re-employment probability as the duration of unemployment increases (i.e. $\lambda < 1$ in the Weibull specification), after controlling for ethnicity, schooling, local unemployment rates, health and various other factors. Moreover, Lynch undertakes a number of controls in order to account for unobserved heterogeneity. Her results appear to be quite robust when the unobserved heterogeneity problem is accounted for.

Lynch's findings of strong evidence of state dependency contrast with the previous findings of Heckman and Borjas (1980) and Ellwood (1982), which are indicative of small amounts of state dependency in youth unemployment. However, the previous results have been based on relatively small sample sizes and have been analysed at a time when the labour market was relatively tight. Lynch's results are based on a period covering a recession and on much larger sample sizes. The *causes* of this strong negative duration dependence remain an open question. Whether it is a result of employers using the length of spell of unemployment as a signal of some undesirable and unobservable features of the young worker versus the negative impact of a long spell of unemployment on the attitudes of youth to work is an issue to which we return in the next section.

The evidence on state dependency versus heterogeneity in the early labour market experience of young women is just as sparse as for their male counterparts. The issue is further complicated by the fact that family formation makes the distinction between unemployment and periods spent 'out of the labour force' less clear for women. Corcoran (1982) in her analysis of the National Longitudinal Survey of Young Women, presents fairly convincing evidence of slightly higher state dependency in employment experience than observed for young males in Ellwood's findings. She finds that past (non) employment raises the probability of current (non) employment. Moreover, her analysis does not separate unemployment from periods classified as 'out of the labour force'. Corcoran uses Chamberlain's auto-regressive logistic model to investigate the extent to which a woman's past history influences her current work behaviour. The model eliminates the effects of unobserved individual specific factors by comparing the likelihood of a woman working given she has worked in the previous year, with the likelihood that the same woman works given she did not work in the previous year. Given controls for heterogeneity (each woman is allowed her own employment probability), the results suggest that the odds that the *same* woman works given she worked in the previous year are 7.8 times higher than if she did not work in the last year.

Lynch (1989) estimates the re-employment probability functions described above separately for males and females. For young women, she finds evidence that the probability of becoming re-employed as the length of spell continues, falls faster for females than for males (Lynch, 1989: 42).

In summary then, the early US studies reviewed here suggest that there exists some short-term state dependency in unemployment experience, somewhat larger for females than for males and therefore much of the observed pattern in employment and unemployment is accounted for by individual differences. More recent evidence (Lynch, 1989), however, provides strong evidence of state dependency in youth unemployment. With the exception of Lynch (1989), the majority of studies were based upon small sample sizes. Moreover, the earlier studies relied upon relatively short observation periods. Further work on the long term consequences of early unemployment on later employment patterns would be beneficial in this area.

(b) *The effect of early unemployment on earnings*

Turning now to the effects of early unemployment or non-employment on wages, the US literature is almost unanimous in its findings of lower wages following early unemployment, while controlling for heterogeneity. The effect for males has generally been found to be greater for women than for men (see Ellwood, 1982 and Corcoran, 1982).

Ellwood (1982) examines the effect of work experience on wages on the second, third and fourth years out of school from his sample of young men from the early NLS. Controlling for individual effects, the data suggested that early work experience had a sizeable impact on wages (between 10 per cent and 20 per cent higher per year). By implication therefore early non-employment matters for later wages. The data, however, did not allow for the possibility of a later 'catch-up' effect, nor for testing how long the wage differentials persisted.

Using a longer period over which to estimate the consequences of early unemployment amongst young men, Becker and Hill (1983) undertake standard regression techniques in their examination of both spells and duration of unemployment together with a measure of turnover, therefore extending their earlier work (Becker and Hill, 1980). In contrast to the findings of Ellwood (1982) and Stevenson (1978a, b), Becker and Hill (1980) conclude that teenage unemployment does not always have a deleterious influence on subsequent wages and, in fact, brief periods of unemployment were positively associated with wages nearly eight years later. Becker and Hill (1983) confirm their earlier findings but with some significant differences in the race effects. Their results suggest that for blacks, 1–5 weeks of unemployment meant higher pay while those blacks with no unemployment and infrequent job changes had the lowest wages. By contrast, whites with the highest wages were those with no teenage unemployment and frequent job changes. Employment 'instability' is consistent, on average, with upward mobility (consistent with the findings of Latack and D'Amico, 1986). While white youths consistently have a more favourable experience, in neither case do modest levels of early unemployment contribute to a lower wage than does consistent employment. Moreover, the results in terms of the size of the coefficients suggest that initial labour market experience matters more for blacks than whites. Becker and Hill's (1980, 1983) techniques, however, make no adjustment for unobserved heterogeneity.

With regard to the evidence for females, Corcoran (1982) finds that the wage effects from early non-employment are smaller than found in Ellwood's study. Corcoran adjusts her estimates for selection bias and includes only modest controls for heterogeneity and makes no attempt to adjust for unobserved heterogeneity.

Thus the wage effects from non-employment are likely to be overstated. The results suggest that both black and white women's wages increase with experience. Moreover, having not worked for prolonged periods early in the work history lowered white women's wages by about 0.7 per cent for each of the non-working years, in addition to lowering wages indirectly by reducing total experience. This additional affect was not observed for black women.

(2) Evidence for the UK

(a) *The effect of early employment on future employment*

Turning now to the UK evidence on the effect of the unemployment of young people on their later economic status, the evidence is much more thin on the ground. Lynch (1985) uses work history information from a sample of 68 youths selected from an initial study of 1,922 young people in London who had planned to enter the labour market at the minimum school leaving age of 16 years in the summer of 1979. The selected youths were those who had entered the labour market and were unemployed one year after leaving school. These individuals were reinterviewed six months later to determine their work status during the intervening period. Using a similar model to that developed by Lancaster (1979), she estimates that the re-employment probability is a strongly decreasing function of the duration of unemployment.

There are three major birth cohort studies which have been conducted in the UK; the National Survey of Health and Development (NSHD), a study of a group of persons born in March 1946; the National Child Development Study (NCDS), a census of eighteen thousand persons born in one week during March 1958 and the Child Health and Education Study concerned with persons born in 1970. The former two of these studies reveal interesting information about the work histories of young people and their later economic status. These studies differ from the work of Lynch in that they allow a longer time perspective to be investigated. They also allow us to examine the relationships between particular types of work history that an individual has followed and their occupations and earnings. There is the same need to distinguish between state dependence and heterogeneity in this work, yet there has, as yet, been no systematic attempt to unravel the dynamic sequence of events recorded in these elaborate longitudinal data sources.

(b) *The effect of early unemployment on earnings*

A significant issue which has been studied in some detail in the UK birth cohort studies is the relationship between the high level of job turnover recorded by some individuals and their later economic status. A variety of local studies of young people entering the labour market conducted over the past twenty-five years reveal that between 5 and 10 per cent of minimum age school leavers will experience four or more jobs in the two years following the date upon which they complete school (Carter, 1962; Maizels, 1970; Sawdon, Pelican and Tucker, 1981; and Roberts, Dench and Richardson, 1986). Using the work history information contained in the NSHD birth cohort, Cherry (1976) examines the occupations and earnings of persons at the age of 26 years who had displayed high levels of job turnover in the preceding 10 or 11 year period. She found little evidence of any economic disadvantage experienced by the high turnover group relative to other members of the birth cohort study. However, the decade spanned by these work histories covered the period from the early 1960s to the early 1970s. Only a few members of the birth cohort experienced any significant spells of unemployment in their work histories. The high levels of turnover related to frequent movement between jobs without intervening spells of unemployment.

By the late 1970s, the economic situation in the UK had deteriorated markedly, such that a significant proportion of the later NCDS birth cohort, who attained the minimum school leaving age in 1974, were to experience spells of unemployment in their subsequent work histories. Elias and Blanchflower (1989) investigated the work histories of this group, distinguishing between those who displayed some turnover or job changing, but no intervening spells of unemployment, and those who had one, or multiple spells of unemployment in their work history. Their findings indicated that, in general terms, job changing did have a negative impact upon the earnings potential of the individual, and that job changing interspersed with spells of unemployment had an even more marked negative impact upon earnings potential. However, these findings raise the issue of the extent to which the observed relationship between work histories, unemployment and later economic status depicts some direct process (state dependency). These direct processes may work through a variety of channels: through general discouragement or disillusionment with work on the part of the individual and caused by joblessness; a loss of access to internal labour markets which could otherwise have provided opportunities for promotion; or a rationing/screening mechanism used by employers in the recruitment/training process and biased against job applicants or employees with a record of unemployment in their work histories. Alternatively, the observed relationship might derive from the differences between individuals in an indirect fashion (heterogeneity), in that those who are more likely to experience spells of unemployment are also those most likely to be observed lower down the distribution earnings at some later point in their lives.

The study by Elias and Blanchflower (1989) provides an opportunity to investigate further the issue of state dependence versus heterogeneity of early unemployment on subsequent earnings using British data. Out of the original sample of over 18 thousand individuals who comprised the NCDS birth cohort, twelve and a half thousand were recontacted at age 23 years in 1981. Detailed information on their employment history from the time they first completed their full-time education to the date of the interview was collected. Earlier contact with the birth cohort, at ages 7, 11 and 16 had established a wealth of information about their social background, health and education. For 11,515 members of the birth cohort, a binary variable was constructed representing their occupational earnings at age 23 years. Elias and Blanchflower argued that a better indicator of an individual's position in the distribution of earnings was the median earnings associated with the occupational category in which they were employed. The practical way in which this procedure was handled was to adopt a binary dependent variable, taking the value of unity if the person was observed to be in an occupation in the upper half of the earnings distribution and zero otherwise. In total, 44 per cent of the sample were in 'above average earnings' occupations at the age of 23 years. Full details of the construction of this binary indicator of occupational earnings, together with the rationale behind the selection and definition of the full set of variables shown in Table 1, are given in Elias and Blanchflower (1989).

Table 1 presents a series of regressions which relate the work histories of these individuals to their occupational earnings at age 23 years, successively controlling for various 'personal' attributes of each individual. We can thus see how the estimates of coefficients change as more individual characteristics and work history information are added. For ease of interpretation, ordinary least squares regression estimates are given. Although it is not particularly efficient (see Maddala, 1988: 15–16), this technique

Table 1

The relationships between social background, father's education, mathematical and reading abilities at age 11 years, school leaving age, work history and occupational earnings at age 23 years

	Dependent variable is occupational earnings at age 23 years (1 if occupation in upper half of occupational distribution of earnings, 0 otherwise)				
	1	2	3	4	5
Travel-to work area unemployment rate, 1981	−.006(−6.1)	−.006(6.1)	−.002(−1.8)	−.001(−1.5)	−.0001(−.9)
Work history (from leaving school to 1981):					
Continuously employed, one employer	. .	—	—	—	—
Continuously employed, more than one employer	. .	−.100(−7.6)	−.066(−5.1)	−.058(−4.6)	−.057(−4.6)
Educational returner	. .	.009(0.5)	−.033(−1.7)	−.046(−2.5)	−.054(−2.9)
One spell of unemployment	. .	−.229(−14.1)	−.195(−12.4)	−.175(−11.2)	−.173(−11.1)
One spell out of the labour force	. .	−.241(−12.7)	−.189(−10.2)	−.172(−9.4)	−.169(−9.3)
Between two and six spells of unemployment or periods out of the labour force	. .	−.326(−24.2)	−.275(−20.8)	−.249(−19.0)	−.247(−18.9)
Six or more spells of unemployment or periods out of the labour force	. .	−.383(−18.7)	−.298(−14.8)	−.271(−13.6)	−.270(−13.6)

Left school at age ⩽ 16 years	. .	. .	−.255(−27.6)	−.184(−18.6)	−.172(−16.9)
Reading comprehension below average	. .	. .	. .	−.106(−9.8)	−.102(−9.4)
Maths comprehension below average	. .	. .	. .	−.090(−8.4)	−.086(−8.0)
Father's social class:					
I	. .	. .	. .	. .	—
II	. .	. .	. .	. .	.012(0.6)
III non-manual	. .	. .	. .	. .	.017(0.7)
III manual	. .	. .	. .	. .	−.009(−0.4)
IV	. .	. .	. .	. .	−.035(−1.6)
V	. .	. .	. .	. .	−.025(−1.1)
Father left school at age ⩽ 15 years	. .	. .	. .	. .	−.038(−3.5)
R^2	.003	.077	.135	.158	.161
F	37.2	139.1	225.0	218.4	138.7
n	11,515	11,515	11,515	11,515	11,515

Note: A dash indicates that the variable is the omitted category, two dots indicate that the variable was not included in the equation. The terms in brackets are 't' statistics.
Source: National Child Development Study

performs satisfactorily given the large sample and the fact that the mean of the binary dependent variable (occupational earnings at age 23 years) is close to a value of one half.

The first regression, shown in column 1 of Table 1, indicates the relationship between the state of the local labour market in which the respondent was living at the age of 23 years and their occupational earnings. The unemployment rate prevailing in mid-1981 in the respondent's travel-to-work area is used to represent the local labour supply/demand imbalance. A clear negative relationship exists between the local unemployment rate and the measure of occupation, indicating that in travel-to-work areas in which the unemployment rate was 10 percentage points higher than average, the probability that a survey respondent would be in a better than average paying job would be reduced by about 6 percentage points.

The additional columns of Table 1 show the impact of introducing, successively, a set of mutually exclusive dummy variables indicating the type of work history that the respondent had experienced between leaving school and being interviewed at the age of 23 years, the respondent's school leaving age, the results of standard tests of reading and mathematical abilities, father's social class and father's education. A seven-fold typology of work histories is used to categorise work experience, relating to the continuity of employment experience, unemployment and labour turnover. These are:

1. Continuous employment with one employer.
2. Continuous employment with more than one employer.
3. Educational returner (a respondent who left full-time education for more than six months but who returned for more than three months).
4. One spell of unemployment. This category excludes persons who had only one spell of unemployment of three months or less immediately upon completion of their full-time education. Such people are classified to categories one or two as appropriate.
5. One spell 'out of the labour force'. Again, a spell of duration less than 3 months immediately upon completion of full-time education is disregarded.
6. More than one but less than six separate spells of unemployment or periods 'out of the labour force'.
7. Six or more spells of unemployment or periods 'out of the labour force'.

Further discussion of the choice of these categories to classify the work histories of the young people in this study is given in Elias and Blanchflower (1989).

From the second column of Table 1, there is clear evidence of a relationship between the work history of the individual and their later position in the occupational distribution of earnings. Relative to continuous employment, any turnover is associated with lower occupational earnings. Spells of unemployment have a significant negative relationship with later earnings. Multiple spells of unemployment have a most pronounced negative effect.

The possibility exists, however, that the observed relationship between unemployment and turnover in the work histories and later occupational earnings is derived for the omitted variables in this regression. Further information about each individual is added to the model shown in column 2 in an attempt to control for such observed heterogeneity. The NCDS is particularly rich in this respect allowing us to add information on schooling, childhood mathematical and reading abilities, and parental social background. It is interesting to note that the sizes of the coefficients associated with the work history variables are reduced as more information on each individual is entered into the model, but that the scale of the reduction is almost insignificant once information on the number of years of schooling (age at which left school) is included. In other words, detailed information on observed heterogeneity does little to affect the apparent state dependence between unemployment in an individual's work history and their later position in the occupational distribution of earnings. While this result does not imply that there is no unobserved heterogeneity affecting the results, it is strongly suggestive that longer term state dependence between unemployment and earnings in the youth labour market exists in Britain.

Summary and conclusions

We have examined in some detail the ways in which work history information of young people can be used to unravel the causal processes which underlie the observed relationship between youth unemployment and later economic status. Theories about the workings of the youth labour market make varying predictions about these relationships so that an investigation of the relationship enables us to choose between theories to some extent.

There are a number of economic theories which may be used to predict the consequences of teenage unemployment. Search theory suggests that teenage unemployment and high turnover are necessary consequences of the early job search process and thus early unemployment has no significant long term impacts. By implication therefore much of the observed relationship is related to individual differences (heterogeneity). On the other hand, for human capital and segmented labour market theories, early unemployment does have long term impacts either via the diminution of work experience and skills or via unemployment acting as a signal to employers of the productive capacity of the individual. This process is by definition one of state dependence. In examining these various hypotheses relating to the consequences of youth unemployment, work history information is invaluable since it enables the investigator to distinguish between individual characteristics and the event of unemployment itself as two separate factors contributing to later employment experiences. That is, work history information enables the important distinction to be made between state dependency and heterogeneity in analysing the consequences of early unemployment.

Having reviewed current econometric and sociometric techniques which consider to varying degrees the problems of distinguishing between state dependency and heterogeneity in the analysis of panel or work history data, we reviewed the empirical evidence provided in the literature from the US and the UK. In our review we concentrated exclusively on those studies which tackled the problem of accounting for observed and unobserved heterogeneity in their estimates of the impact of unemployment on subsequent economic status. In particular, we confined our focus to the findings of those studies concerned with the effect of early unemployment on subsequent employment prospects and the effect on subsequent earnings.

Until recently, the US literature appeared to suggest that the impact from the experience of youth unemployment on the probability of future employment was negligible, having controlled for individual differences (Heckman and Borjas, 1980; Ellwood, 1982; Corcoran, 1982), and much of the observed pattern in employment and unemployment was accounted for by heterogeneity. More recent evidence from the US, based upon a larger sample and importantly during a period covering a severe recession, may be found in Lynch (1989). Contrasting with the previous results, she found strong evidence of state dependency in youth unemployment for both males and females after controlling for unobserved heterogeneity.

The predominant lesson from the US literature is that lower wages follow early unemployment, after controlling for heterogeneity. The effect of early unemployment on males has generally been found to be greater for women than for men (Ellwood, 1982; Corcoran, 1982). Unfortunately, however, the relatively short observation periods inhibit an assessment of any 'catch-up' effects which tend to reduce the long-term consequences of early unemployment on wages. Becker and Hill (1983), using a longer time period, and contrasting with the findings of Ellwood (1982) and Corcoran (1982), provide evidence suggestive of job turnover being consistent with upward mobility.

The evidence for the UK of the impact of early unemployment on later economic status is relatively sparse compared to that for the US. Lynch (1985) provides the only UK estimates of re-employment probabilities from completed and uncompleted spells of unemployment for young people in Britain. Her findings are indicative of state dependency in youth unemployment. Her results however are based on a small sample and are conducted over a relatively short space of time (one year).

Elias and Blanchflower (1989) provide estimates of the effect of early unemployment on occupational earnings at the age of 23 based on the much larger NCDS sample. After accounting for observed individual differences, they find that the experience of early unemployment significantly reduces the probability of an individual being in an occupation in the upper half of the occupational distribution at age 23 years. This contrasts somewhat with the findings of Cherry (1976) who found little evidence of any economic disadvantage experienced by high turnover early in individual's work histories. Similar to the US evidence, the contrasting evidence of Elias and Blanchflower (1989) and Cherry (1976) appear to be related to the state of the labour markets during their respective sample periods. Cherry's findings are based on the NSHD cohort during the low unemployment decade from the early 1960s to the early 1970s, while Elias and Blanchflower's evidence is based on the later NCDS cohort during a period of marked deterioration in the UK economy.

Thus in summary, it would appear that the empirical evidence using panel data in the US and the UK points towards there being evidence of short-term state dependency in youth unemployment, controlling for heterogeneity. However the size of the effect of early unemployment experience depends to some extent on the state of the labour market, with relatively tight labour markets tending to reduce the size of any state dependency effect on subsequent employment probabilities. It is clear, however, that longer term impacts of youth unemployment on re-employment probabilities and wages need to be assessed. In the US and the UK this will occur naturally as more samples are added to the panels of the NLS and NCDS data sets respectively.

This finding of short-term state dependency enables us to make an assessment of the stylised views of youth labour markets outlined earlier. In particular, the proposition that young people's unemployment experience is largely voluntary in nature due to 'shopping around' for various jobs in the market is seriously questioned. The view that youth unemployment is a transitory phenomenon with no serious consequences for future employment experience therefore appears to be refuted by the findings of the US and the UK literature. After controlling for individual differences, the existence of spells of unemployment in the early labour market experience of young people does appear to have a deleterious effect upon their employability and earnings. Further, this effect appears to be related to the state of the labour market.

One of the important issues arising from this finding of short-term state dependency relates to the factors *causing* this result. Is it that unemployment experience itself has a deleterious effect on the individual in terms of his or her future employability through loss of work experience and skills, disillusionment or the instilling of poor work habits? Or is it that firms use unemployment records as a signal of worker quality? Are there differences by race and gender? These we see as the critical issues for further research on this important problem.

Note

The authors would like to thank Wiji Narendranathan and Shirley Dex for their helpful comments and suggestions. The diligent and patient wordprocessing of this paper by Moyra Butterworth, Barbara Wilson and Janet Burnell is acknowledged with thanks.

References

Becker, G., (1964), *Human Capital*, New York: NBER Columbia University Press.

Becker, B.E. and Hill, S.M., (1980), 'Teenage unemployment: some evidence of the long run effect on wages', *Journal of Human Resources*, 15(3): 354–72.

Becker, B.E. and Hill, S.M., (1983) 'The long run effects of job changes and unemployment among male teenagers', *Journal of Human Resources*, 18: 197–212.

Bergmann, B.R., (1980), 'Occupational segregation, wages and profits when employers discriminate by race or sex', in A.H. Amsden, (ed.), *The Economics of Women and Work*, Harmondsworth: Penguin Books, pp. 277–82.

Carter, M.P., (1962), *Home, School and Work. A Study of the Education and Employment of Young People in Britain*, New York: Macmillan.

Chamberlain, G., (1985), 'Heterogeneity, omitted variable bias, and duration dependence', in J.J. Heckman and B. Singer (eds), *The Longitudinal Analysis of Labour Market Data*, Cambridge: Cambridge University Press.

Chamberlain, G. and Griliches, Z., (1975), 'Unobservables with a variance components structure: ability, schooling and the economic success of brothers', *International Economic Review*, 16: 422–49.

Cherry, N., (1976), 'Persistent job changing, is it a problem?', *Journal of Occupational Psychology*, 203–21.

Chiplin, B. and Sloane, P.J., (1980), 'Sexual discrimination in the labour market', in A.H. Amsden, (ed.), *The Economics of Women and Work*, Harmondsworth: Penguin Books, pp. 283–321.

Corcoran, M., (1982), 'The employment and wage consequences of teenage women's non-employment', in R.B. Freeman and D.A. Wise (eds), *The Youth Labor Market Problem: Its Nature, Causes and Consequences*, Chicago: University of Chicago Press.

Cox, D.R., (1972), 'Regression models and life tables', *Journal of the Royal Statistical Society*, 34 (Series B): 187–220.

Elias, P. and Blanchflower, D., (1989), *The Occupation, Earnings and Work Histories of Young Adults: Who Gets the Good Jobs?* Department of Employment Research Paper 68, London: HMSO.

Ellwood, D.T., (1982), 'Teenage unemployment: permanent scars or temporary blemishes?', in R.B. Freeman and D.A. Wise (eds), *The Youth Labor Market: Its Nature, Causes and Consequences*, Chicago: University of Chicago Press.

Ezzet, F.L. and Davies, R.B., (1988), 'A manual for mixture', Centre for Applied Statistics, Lancaster: University of Lancaster.

Freeman, R.B., (1976), *The Overeducated American*, New York: Academic Press.

Hausman, J.A. and Taylor, W.E. (1981), 'Panel data and unobservable individual effects', *Econometrica*, 49(6): 931–59.

Heckman, J., (1978a), 'Dummy endogenous variables in a simultaneous equation system', *Econometrica*, 46(4): 931–59.

Heckman, J., (1978b), 'Simple stochastic models for discrete panel data developed and applied to test the hypothesis of true state dependence against the hypothesis of spurious state dependence', *Annales de l'INSEE* (30–1): 227–70.

Heckman, J.B. and Borjas, G.J., (1980), 'Does unemployment cause future unemployment? Definitions, questions and answers from a continuous time model of heterogeneity and state dependence', *Econometrica* 47: 247–83.

Kalacheck, E., (1969), *The Youth Labor Market*, Policy Papers in Human Resources and Industrial Relations 12, Institute of Labor and Industrial Relations and National Manpower Policy Task Force: Ann Arbor Michigan.

Kiefer, J. and Wolfowitz, J., (1956), 'Consistency of the maximum likelihood estimates in the presence of infinitely many incidental parameters', *Annals of Mathematical Statistics*, 27: 887–906.

Lancaster, T., (1979), 'Econometric methods for the duration of unemployment', *Econometrica*, 47(4): 939–56.

Lancaster, T. and Nickell, S., (1980), 'The analysis of re-employment probabilities for the unemployed', *Journal of the Royal Statistical Society*, Series A, 143(2): 141–65.

Latack, J.C. and D'Amico, R.J., (1986), 'Career mobility among young men: a search for patterns', in S.M. Hills (ed.), *The Changing Labor Market: A Longitudinal Study of Young Men*, Massachusetts: Lexington Books.

Lindsay, B.G., (1983a), 'The geometry of mixture likelihoods: a general theory', *The Annals of Statistics*, 11: 86–94.

Lindsay, B.G., (1983b), 'The geometry of mixture likelihoods, part II: the exponential family', *The Annals of Statistics*, 11: 783–92.

Lippman, S. and McCall, J., (1976), 'The economics of job search: a survey', *Economic Inquiry* 14: 155–89.

Lynch, L.M. (1985), 'State dependency in youth unemployment: a lost generation?', *Journal of Econometrics*, 28: 71–84.

Lynch, L.M., (1989), 'The youth labor market in the eighties: determinants of re-employment probabilities for young men and women', *Review of Economics and Statistics*, 71(1): 37–45.

Maddala, G.S., (1988), *Limited Dependent and Qualitative Variables in Economics*, Econometric Society Monograph, New York: Cambridge.

Maizels, J., (1970), *Adolescent Needs and the Transition from School to Work*, London: University of London, Athlone Press.

Roberts, K., Dench, S. and Richardson, D., (1986), *The Changing Structure of Youth Labour Markets*, Department of Employment Research Paper 59, London: HMSO.

Sawdon, A., Pelican, J., and Tucker, S., (1981), *Study of the Transition from School to Working Life*, III, London: Youthaid.

Stevenson, W., (1978a), 'The transition from school to work' in Adams, A.V., and Mangum, G.L. (eds), *The Lingering Crisis of Youth Unemployment*. Kalamazoo, Michigan: W.E. Upjohn Institute for Employment Research, pp. 65–92.

Stevenson, W., (1978b), 'The relationship between early work experience and future employability', in Adams, A.V. and Mangum, G.L. (eds), *The Lingering Crisis of Youth Unemployment*, Kalamazoo, Michigan: W.E. Upjohn Institute for Employment Research, pp. 93–124.

Tuma, N.B., Hannan, M.T. and Groeneveld, L.P., (1979), 'Dynamic analysis of event histories', *American Journal of Sociology*, 84(1): 820–54.